The Random Factor

The publisher and the University of California Press Foundation gratefully acknowledge the generous support of the Richard and Harriett Gold Endowment Fund in Arts and Humanities.

The Random Factor

HOW CHANCE AND LUCK PROFOUNDLY SHAPE OUR LIVES AND THE WORLD AROUND US

Mark Robert Rank

 UNIVERSITY OF CALIFORNIA PRESS

University of California Press
Oakland, California

© 2024 by Mark Robert Rank

Cataloging-in-Publication data is on file at the Library of Congress.

ISBN 978-0-520-39096-6 (cloth : alk. paper)
ISBN 978-0-520-39097-3 (ebook)

Manufactured in the United States of America

33 32 31 30 29 28 27 26 25 24
10 9 8 7 6 5 4 3 2 1

Contents

1   *The Wheel of Fortune*

Sometimes the slightest things change the directions of our lives, the merest breath of a circumstance, a random moment that connects like a meteorite striking the earth. Lives have swiveled and changed direction on the strength of a chance remark.

—BRYCE COURTENAY, 1996

Have you ever stopped to wonder how you arrived at where you are? Sit back for a moment and think about it. Ask yourself, "How did I end up at my current job, in this city or state or country, with these particular friends and family?" If you are like most people, you will probably think back to some of the major decisions you made throughout your life. You might consider the skills, interests, and talents you have acquired across the years. Perhaps you will recall the hard work and effort you have exerted in order to get to where you are. Undoubtedly, these are all important factors in helping to explain the specific twists and turns that have occurred in our lives.

But there is another factor that may be just as important. Yet it is the one element that we often forget when explaining our journey. It is the random factor.

This book will argue that randomness exerts a profound influence in shaping the course of our lives and the world around us. It has both large and small effects on the manner and direction that our lives take. It may not always be obvious at first, but across time, it is frequently profound.

I began to appreciate this while working on an earlier book, *Chasing the American Dream: Understanding What Shapes Our Fortunes*.[1] In that book, my co-author Kirk Foster and I interviewed 75 people from all walks of life. They ranged from an older man who was homeless and sleeping on the streets to an entrepreneur whose wealth was valued at well over a billion dollars. During the span of a year I wanted to learn more about the particulars of how these lives turned out, as well as listening to their thoughts and ideas about the American Dream. I was also interested in the commonalities and differences that defined their lives.

Yet over the course of interviewing, something very interesting came to light. As we explored the twists and turns in people's lives, the role of luck and chance in shaping the directions of those twists and turns became increasingly apparent. A fortuitous meeting, a missed appointment, a forgotten telephone call, a serendipitous discovery—all of these and more were mentioned as having a profound influence on how people's lives unfolded. At the time, they may have appeared inconsequential, but in hindsight they took on immense importance.

During our interviews, I listened as individuals repeatedly mentioned these twists of fate and the importance they had in shaping their lives. Sometimes for the good, sometimes for the bad, and sometimes in ways that were just different. Interviewees talked about chance encounters, accidents that occurred, happenstance conversations that changed lives, being in the wrong place at the wrong time, being in the right place at the right time, and on and on.

Such randomness can be unsettling because it represents that which we basically have no control over. In America, we like to believe that we have agency over our destiny—that the future is predicated on our current actions and behaviors. We are very much steeped in the notion of rugged individualism, where we are expected to chart our own futures and break our own frontiers through ability and hard work.[2]

Yet much of life also revolves around luck and chance. Truth be told, there is considerable randomness to life. Philosophers, playwrights, and novelists have long recognized and written about the elements of life that we can neither control nor predict, and yet can have profound ripple effects upon our well-being.

Despite the importance of such randomness, social scientists and sociologists such as myself have generally shied away from studying the role of luck and chance in affecting our lives. Part of the reason may be that today's heavy emphasis upon statistics and prediction does not lend itself to modeling randomness. By definition, chance events are unpredictable, and are therefore difficult to fit into an equation. However, that does not mean that they are unimportant. Quite the contrary.

Perhaps another reason we downplay the role of randomness in our lives is that we tend to be governed by daily routines. Many of us get up in the morning, eat breakfast, go to work or work from home, have dinner, watch TV or surf the internet, go to bed, only to repeat the same routine the next day. The world can often appear as a continuous cycle of routine. Yet as will be abundantly clear, within such routines there are endless ripples of randomness that can affect and bend the wider currents that push our lives forward.

And as mentioned, another factor for ignoring randomness may be our strong belief as Americans in the importance of agency. America has long been steeped in the ethos of rugged individualism and the Protestant work ethic, both of which place little weight on the importance of luck and chance in influencing life outcomes.

Background

"On Friday noon, July the twentieth, 1714, the finest bridge in all Peru broke and precipitated five travelers into the gulf below."[3] So begins

Thornton Wilder's Pulitzer Prize–winning novel, *The Bridge of San Luis Rey*. As chance would have it, a Franciscan monk named Brother Juniper has witnessed the tragedy. Wilder's book and Brother Juniper grapple with questions: Why were these five travelers the ones to unfortunately find themselves in such an unlucky position, resulting in their deaths? Was there something that connected these five lives together? What sense or meaning can be found in such a random event?

Brother Juniper spends the next six years gathering information about each of the five individuals in order to attempt to understand the tragedy. He asks himself, "Why did this happen to *those* five?" Wilder goes on to write,

> If there were any plan in the universe at all, if there were any pattern in a human life, surely it could be discovered mysteriously latent in those lives so suddenly cut off. Either we live by accident and die by accident, or we live by plan and die by plan. And on that instant Brother Juniper made the resolve to inquire into the secret lives of those five persons.[4]

Unfortunately, neither Wilder nor Brother Juniper is able to answer this question. Brother Juniper compiles an enormous volume of pages detailing the lives of the fallen, but in the end comes to no firm conclusion. However, his blasphemous attempt at understanding such a tragedy beyond divine intention has fallen upon the eyes of the town's judges steeped in the Spanish Inquisition, and he and his book are ordered to be burned at the stake.

For centuries, writers and philosophers have tried to answer the questions that Brother Juniper grappled with in *The Bridge of San Luis Rey*. Why are we put on this earth and for what purpose? Why do some of us experience tragedies while others do not? How might things have turned out differently if only . . . ?

Certainly these must have been some of the questions that weighed heavily upon the relatives and friends of those killed in the 9/11 tragedy of the Twin Towers in New York City, the Pentagon in Washington, DC, and the open fields in Shanksville, Pennsylvania. If only a subway connection wasn't early (or late) that day. If only a meeting hadn't been cancelled the night before. If only . . . Surely these random occurrences exerted monumental effects upon the lives of these individuals and their families. Like the bridge of San Luis Rey, nearly 3,000 individuals were in the wrong place at the wrong time.

In his book *The Only Plane in the Sky*, Garrett Graff spent three years gathering the personal stories of those who were directly touched by the tragedy of 9/11.[5] Over and over he was struck by the role that luck and chance played with respect to who lived and who died.[6] As he writes in *The Atlantic*,

> In all those published accounts and audio clips, and in the interviews I conducted, one theme never ceases to amaze me: the sheer randomness of how the day unfolded, who lived, who died, who was touched, and who escaped. One thousand times a day, we all make arbitrary decisions—which flight to book, which elevator to board, whether to run an errand or stop for coffee before work—never realizing the possibilities that an alternate choice might have meant. In the 18 years since 9/11, each of us must have made literally 1 million such decisions, creating a multitude of alternate outcomes we'll never know.[7]

Randomness is thus a constant companion as we live out our lives. It exerts its influence in ways that are obvious and not so obvious. In this book we explore the manner in which this companion walks beside us.

The topics of chance, luck, and randomness have been considered since antiquity. Written discourse regarding unexpected and chance events had its beginnings in ancient Greece. Indeed, the Greek gods of Zeus, Poseidon, and Hades were thought to have drawn lots to determine which realm of the world they would rule over, with Zeus drawing the sky, Poseidon the seas, and Hades the underworld.[8] Epicurus, Aristotle, Euripides, and other Greek philosophers grappled with whether there was such a thing as chance and/or whether the world operated by a knowable and constant set of laws.

The discussion continued into the Roman Empire, where fortune and luck were represented by the goddess Fortuna. One of the tools she relied on to deliver her decisions was the wheel of fortune. The Roman poet Ovid describes how Fortuna would blindly spin her wheel, bringing good fortune to some and ill luck to others. She was considered the deity that affected all walks of life. The philosopher Pliny wrote,

> For all over the world, in all places, and at all times, Fortune is the only god whom everyone invokes . . . To her are referred all our losses and all our gains, and in casting up the accounts of mortals she alone balances the two pages of our sheet. We are so much in the power of chance, that chance itself is considered as a God and the existence of God becomes doubtful.[9]

There is an image of Fortuna taken from a manuscript in the Hohenburg Abbey in Alsace, France. Here we find Fortuna spinning her wheel with a handheld crank. Riding the wheel on the left is an aspiring monarch whose future is upward. At the top is the crowned monarch. On the right a falling monarch who will soon be losing his crown, and at the bottom a failed monarch being crushed and thrown off the wheel. In this manner Fortune has her say over the future outcomes of us all.

The idea of luck and chance being depicted as a wheel of fortune was carried into the Middle Ages through a seminal work written by the Roman statesman Boethius in 523. His writing took place over the course of a year during which he was imprisoned and ultimately executed. This work, *The Consolation of Philosophy,* has been described as the single most important text in the West influencing Medieval and early Renaissance Christianity. Following Plato's lead in the *Dialogues,* the book centers around a dialogue that occurs between Boethius and a woman representing the spirit of philosophy. Chance and fortune feature extensively in the work.

Philosophy tells Boethius that Fortune by her very nature is fickle and constantly changing. In fact, if she stays still, she would no longer be Fortune. As she turns her wheel, she relishes in the fact that those on the bottom of the wheel are brought to the top, while those on the top of the wheel are brought to the bottom. In this way, an individual's good luck and fortune may sour, just as one with bad luck may unexpectedly experience good fortune. As she proclaims,

> This is my art, this is the game I never cease to play. I turn the wheel that spins. I delight to see the high come down and the low ascent. Mount up, if you wish, but on the condition you will not think it a hardship to come down when the rules of my game require it.[10]

Yet how much of life is ruled by such chance and luck? Boethius does not provide an answer to this question, but others throughout history have ventured a guess.[11]

In *The Prince,* Niccolo Machiavelli gives advice and instructions for the would-be prince. The phrase "Machiavellian" has come into usage to convey the techniques that he espouses for the prince to strengthen his power and authority. But Machiavelli also discusses the role of fortune affecting the chances of success or failure. And here he ascribes the odds at approximately 50/50. He notes that at the time of his writing, great changes have taken place across Europe, and that some might argue these are beyond our control:

"Sometimes pondering over this, I am in some degree inclined to their opinion. Nevertheless, not to extinguish our free will, I hold it be true that Fortune is the arbiter of one-half of our actions, but that she still leaves us to direct the other half, or perhaps a little less."[12]

Machiavelli goes on to compare fortune to a raging river that has the power to move all within its path. And yet, when the weather is fair, an individual can prepare for the flood by building "defences and barriers, in such a manner that, rising again, the waters may pass away by canal, and their force be neither so unrestrained nor so dangerous. So it happens with fortune, who shows her power where valour has not prepared to resist her, and thither she turns her forces where she knows that barriers and defences have not been raised to constrain her."[13]

In another attempt to place a percentage upon how much of life is governed by chance, Frederick the Great in the eighteenth century was accustomed to saying, "The older one gets the more convinced one becomes that his Majesty King Chance does three-quarters of the business of this miserable universe."[14]

Yet for much of the sixteenth, seventeenth, and eighteenth centuries, randomness and chance fell out of favor. This was the result of both the power of the church to proclaim all things preordained, and the rise of the scientific method in which the prevailing view was that all of nature is governed by universal laws.

With respect to the teachings of the church, because God is viewed as omniscient and all knowing, there can be no room for chance or randomness. Everything must have a purpose and design according to God's plans. The existence of randomness is simply unfathomable within such a worldview. As John Calvin announced in 1561, "There is no such thing as fortune or chance."[15]

With regard to the scientific method, there grew a strong belief among scientists and philosophers that the world operated by a set of laws, and that with enough investigation, these laws were both knowable and essential for prediction purposes. Such a perspective was epitomized by Sir Isaac Newton's laws of motion and universal gravitation. His is a world devoid of randomness, where there is cause and effect, and where the regularities of the physical and natural world rule. As Voltaire writes, "All have acknowledged that chance is a word without meaning. What we call chance can be no other than the unknown cause of a known effect."[16] Or as Albert Einstein famously remarked, God does not play with dice.[17]

Much of the above arguments fall under the broad rubric of determinism. This school of thought negates the possibility of chance and randomness. Rather, the world is viewed as one in which every event has a cause and a trajectory that lead to that event's occurrence. As a result, any event can theoretically be perfectly predicted. The fact that events cannot be perfectly predicted is only the consequence of our not having total or complete knowledge of the manner in which those causes play themselves out. As the MIT cosmologist Max Tegmark states, "There is no true randomness in the cosmos, but things can appear random in the eye of the beholder. The randomness reflects your inability to self-locate."[18] Therefore, the logical conclusion is that all events are completely determined by their antecedent conditions. This line of thinking can be traced back to the ancient Greek philosophers, and continues in various forms to the present day.[19]

It was only during the middle of the nineteenth century that chance and randomness came back onto the scene, most notably with Charles Darwin's theory of evolution by natural selection. I discuss Darwin in more detail in chapter 3, but suffice it to say that a major component of his revolutionary theory was based upon the notion of chance and randomness. Likewise, the rise of quantum mechanics and chaos theory in the twentieth also reintroduced the importance of randomness in helping to explain the way the world operates.

In their overview of the history of chance and randomness, Christoph Luthy and Carla Palmerino conclude that the question of randomness remains a lively and open subject:

> We have not been able to detect any dialectical progress from the ancient Greeks up to today's physicists in the way in which scientists and philosophers resolved the perennial tension between the predictable and the unpredictable; between the necessary and the contingent; between necessity and chance; or to dismiss fate, fortune, the accidental and the random. Given the developments in evolutionary biology and quantum physics of the past 150 years, it seems rather as if "chance," "randomness," and "coincidence" had been restored to a place of respectability that they had previously lost. Indeed, whether our personal surprise at a given event is merely a sign of personal ignorance or is instead a necessary feature of this universe has once again been elevated to the status of unresolved question.[20]

What about chance and randomness in the social sciences? To what extent have social scientists and specifically sociologists explored the role of randomness in the social world? The answer is very little. This is surprising given that randomness appears all around us. After losing a huge sum of money in a South Sea bubble in 1720, Sir Isaac Newton remarked, "I can calculate the movement of the stars, but not the madness of crowds."

The social sciences, and sociology in particular, would appear to be fertile grounds for studying how chance and luck influence the course of our lives. Yet as sociologist Michael Sauder writes in his review, "Sociology . . . has been almost completely silent about luck, essentially ignoring the concept as well as its influence on social processes and outcomes."[21] He goes on to point out, "There is no literature on luck, there are very few articles that mention the word *luck* in their title or abstract, and only a handful of articles discuss luck at all."[22]

While there have been a few cases of sociologists incorporating luck and chance into their analysis, they are far and few between. Robert K. Merton analyzed the role of serendipity in leading to scientific discoveries (discussed in chapter 3), while Mark Granovetter looked at the influence of luck in finding a job (discussed in chapter 6).

One area of research where social scientists have entertained the role of chance has been in the field of decision theory. The attempt here has been to guide the decisions an individual might make given the different probabilities surrounding the various choices available and the positive or negative values associated with those choices. By combining these two, one arrives at an overall expected value behind each choice. This then allows the individual to make the best decision available given the underlying circumstances. In this manner decision theory seeks to take into account the random factor. Game theory also attempts to incorporate probability and chance into its modeling.[23] But beyond these specific areas, the analysis of chance, luck, or randomness has been notably absent from the field of sociology and the social sciences.

There are several potential reasons behind this absence. First, as noted earlier, chance and randomness can be difficult to measure and model. Second, as in the natural sciences, the social sciences are generally interested in explanation and prediction. By its very nature, chance does not lend itself to such objectives. And third, the role of chance runs counter to the sociological emphasis upon structural forces impacting life chances. Sociologists often focus on the influence of factors such as class, race, and gender upon life outcomes. Luck and chance might be viewed as contradictory to this largely deterministic take on the world.

The Argument and Evidence

My argument throughout this book is that chance and randomness are fundamental elements to understanding the world and the manner in which our lives unfold. Rather than undermining social science knowledge, randomness adds a much needed ingredient into the mix.

A major theme across the chapters will be that chance interacts dynamically with the larger forces that influence our world and our lives. We might think of the random factor as a constant but unpredictable dance partner. It plays a key role in shaping the direction of our lives and the world around us. This interplay occurs in a variety of ways, many of which we will explore.

For example, in the next chapter we examine some of the means by which the trajectory of history has been shaped and bent through chance and luck. History is pushed forward through forces such as technological change, but randomness exerts its influence upon the types of technological innovations that are invented and discovered. Or take the manner in which our individual lives play out. Factors such as gender, race, and social class exert a direct impact upon life outcomes. But within these larger currents are the many ripples of randomness. Outcomes such as specific careers chosen, who and if we marry, where we live—all are partially the result of a dynamic mix between the deterministic and the random.

Likewise, the process of serendipity with respect to scientific discoveries and inventions is another illustration of how chance interacts with larger forces such as cognition. From the discovery of X-rays to penicillin to DNA to Velcro, a random event was responsible for sparking a scientist's ultimate understanding of these phenomena.

Of course it is extremely difficult to place an exact value on how much of life is the result of agency and how much is due to chance.

As the eminent philosopher Nicholas Rescher notes, it is "next to impossible to specify the relative proportion of what happens to people through fate and fortune, through actual effort, and through simple luck . . . For this proportion is variable and alters with the shifting sands of conditions and circumstance."[24] Throughout these pages we will explore the influence of chance across these shifting sands.

A second theme is that the specific timing of chance events can be crucial for understanding their impact upon life outcomes. For example, a fortuitous event that happens early in one's career can have positive repercussions across the rest of one's life. Similarly, a negative chance event early in one's life may set in motion a cascading downward spiral. I turn to my research on cumulative advantage and disadvantage in the middle chapters in order to further illustrate this process.

The specific timing of random events is also critical for understanding social change within the wider context. The point at which a particular chance event occurs can be as important as if it occurs in the first place. We will see this with respect to history and the natural world.

A third major theme asserts that the economic context matters regarding the types and responses to chance events that one is exposed to. Those from an affluent background are more likely to take advantage and / or to shield themselves from specific twists of fate than their impoverished counterparts. In this manner, social class differences may be amplified through chance and luck.

The idea that chance and randomness can amplify inequality is a unique insight with important implications. Here I turn to much of my research on poverty to illustrate that a detrimental chance occurrence, which may be an inconvenience to the affluent, can be disastrous for the poor.

A fourth theme found throughout the book is that individuals are often unaware of the role that chance plays in their lives and the world around them because they have but one history to consider. As a result, it appears that A led to B which led to C. However, when A was occurring, there were alternative paths that could have been taken. Consequently, A might have led to D. Michael Sauder states this well:

> We are able to ignore the influence of luck in our day-to-day lives in part because we are often not even aware of having experienced good or bad luck. We stop to tie our shoe before turning a corner, oblivious to the fact that the large chunk of ice falling from the building's eaves would have landed on us if we had not. We did not get the job we applied for because our application was misplaced by the hiring committee, but we assume we reached too far and attribute the outcome to our lack of worthiness.[25]

Similarly, world history appears as a fait accompli since there is only one timeline to consider. Yet we will discover that given a different role of the dice, history might have easily bent in another direction.

A final theme will be that individual agency becomes an important part of this story with respect to how we react to chance events. While we may lack control over the occurrence of randomness, we can exert some leverage in terms of how we respond to such events. Thus, chance and agency are brought together to provide a more complete narrative. The patterns of our lives are certainly influenced by structural forces such as class, race, and gender, but also by chance and randomness, along with individual agency. In this way, a fuller picture of life as it is actually lived is hopefully provided.

A wide array of evidence is utilized to build my case to support these points. These include an eclectic mix of source materials, from data gathered by social scientists to historical events to offerings found in popular culture. In addition, I turn to much of my life course research to demonstrate how randomness exerts itself in our daily lives. I also use my policy research to describe some of the lessons that can be learned through a greater appreciation and understanding of the random factor.

Finally, a brief disclaimer. This book covers a vast array of topics. Many of these subjects I am quite familiar with and have conducted research on. But others are relatively new to me. In these cases I have sought out works by some of the leading thinkers and experts in such areas. While I certainly do not claim expertise in these latter subjects, I will argue that the bringing together of the pieces of the puzzle I am calling the random factor is unique. In this regard, I hope to offer an enlightening experience for my readers.

Organization

The Random Factor is organized into three broad parts. We begin by exploring some of the ways that randomness has impacted and changed the world around us. An excellent place to start is with the trajectory and path that history has taken. History is filled with countless examples of monumental events and decisions that have often hinged on chance, luck, and randomness. We explore three of these in chapter 2. They include the Cuban Missile Crisis in October of 1962, the defeat of the Equal Rights Amendment in the early 1970s, and random events that have sparked social movements.

In chapter 3 we examine the role that randomness plays in shaping our natural world. Most striking is the very reason we are here. Some 66 million years ago an asteroid hit the Earth at precisely the right angle and location to annihilate the dinosaurs, paving the path for our ascendency. Had there been as little as a 10-mile difference in its path of entry, we would not be here today and the dinosaurs might still be roaming the land. We will also explore the role of randomness with respect to natural selection and meteorology. Randomness can also be quite useful in particular situations. For example, the fields of statistics and political polling are based on the ability to acquire what is known as a random sample. In addition, scientific discoveries are often the result of serendipity, as we will learn.

In chapter 4 we will examine some of the ways that randomness exerts itself in everyday life. From the stock market to your favorite sports team, randomness and luck are sure to play a role. To take but one example, the fact that some actors and musicians are able to achieve fortune and fame often has as much to do with luck as it does with talent.

The middle third of the book explores the manner in which luck and chance impact upon the course and patterns of our individual lives. Social science research has demonstrated that there are powerful currents that push our lives in particular directions. The most important of these are class, race, and gender. Yet within these powerful currents, there are ripples of randomness that help shape the specifics within those trajectories. It is here that we see much of the impact that chance has upon individuals and their families.

In chapter 5 we begin with the biggest lottery of all—the lottery of birth. We obviously do not control who our parents are, our country of origin, our innate abilities, and many other attributes. Yet have we really stopped to consider what the implications of this may be, given that our start in life is completely random? We also will explore the impact that the time period and cohort size in which we are born can have upon life outcomes.

In chapter 6 we look at the role of luck in shaping specific key events and milestones in our personal and professional lives. Who we form relationships with, what careers we go into, where we reside—these and many more are often influenced by chance.

Chapter 7 examines the dynamics in which the random factor exerts itself with respect to the course of our lives. These include the timing of when randomness strikes in our lives, the role of wider social forces in helping shape the types of randomness we are exposed to, and the cumulative impact of random events. In exploring these dynamics we begin to gain a firmer understanding of how chance plays itself out with respect to the life course.

The final section of the book turns to several broad implications for living and thriving in a world of randomness. Given that we occupy an environment where chance and luck are ever present, how best to appreciate and make use of this situation? Chapter 8 examines the manner in which our social policies might be restructured in light of the random factor. I argue that we should consider new ways of thinking in designing policies that allow individuals to thrive in this uncertain world. Much as the natural sciences have recognized and incorporated randomness into their understanding, so too should public policy.

Chapter 9 takes up some of the personal lessons to be learned. These insights can help us in navigating the seas of uncertainty and change. They include both positive and cautionary lessons into how the random factor can shape our understanding of who we are.

Chapter 10 draws the book to a close by recapping what we have learned over the course of the chapters and provides some final thoughts. It is a journey filled with unexpected twists and turns, surprising conclusions, and hopefully a new understanding of our unpredictable world.

Defining Our Terms

One point of clarification before we get started. The words random, chance, and luck are used throughout this book. In many ways, these terms hold much in common. They all refer to the idea that events are unpredictable and beyond individual control.

However, there is also a slight difference in how I am using the terms. Luck and chance are generally terms that are applied to the individual. In other words, we refer to a person facing uncertain chances, or that they have had a streak of good luck. To make a further distinction, luck is typically viewed through the lens of good or bad fortune, whereas chance is a more neutral concept. Nicholas Rescher defines luck as "a matter of having something good or bad happen that lies outside the horizon of effective foreseeability."[26]

With respect to how I am referring to chance events, there are several points to be made. First, a chance event is something that lies outside the individual's control. They have no say or influence in whether or not the event occurs. Second, a chance event is random with respect to the specific individual affected. In other words, the individual encountering the event could just as easily have been someone else. For example, in the earlier-mentioned case of a falling chunk of ice, assuming that many people were walking underneath the building's eaves at a specific time, that chunk of ice could have just as easily have fallen upon Person A rather than Person B. And third, the process by which a chance event occurs is often the result of a happenstance coming-together of separate factors. As psychologist Albert Bandura notes, "In a chance encounter the separate chains of events have their own causal determinants, but their intersection occurs fortuitously rather than through deliberate plan."[27]

On the other hand, the words random and randomness are generally used when referring to the wider social order. Consequently, the society or the economy is characterized as having considerable randomness within it. Likewise, scientists refer to the natural world as containing elements of randomness. Michael Mauboussin, in *The Success Equation*, defines these terms in a similar fashion: "Randomness and luck are related, but there is a useful distinction between the two. You can think of randomness as operating at the level of a system and luck operating at the level of the individual."[28]

Randomness, as with luck and chance, is defined by its unpredictability and lack of pattern. By its very nature, the random factor cannot be predicted nor can it be anticipated. It comes, as they say, "out of the blue."

Several other terms are used throughout the chapters. These include serendipity, contingency, fortune, coincidence, and stochastic. Serendipity generally refers to an important discovery that is triggered by a chance or accidental event. Contingency can be thought of as another word for chance, while fortune is often used in the context of luck. For example we might say that one's life was marked by good or bad fortune. The word fortunate, therefore, implies that of having good luck or fortune. Coincidence refers to a seemingly random coming-together of two or more events. Finally, stochastic often pertains to a process involving a randomly determined sequence of observations, and is generally used within the scientific literature.

In reflecting on his life, the author Kristopher Jansma writes, "What I still dwell on is the coincidence of it all." In a *New York Times* essay he discusses the various twists of fate that have shaped his life. Concluding the piece, he notes, "It fills me with a kind of wonder at life—at the ways in which tiny coincidences and their consequences shape it, and how we adjust our own narratives to absorb this randomness. Being able to see that has been a gift."[29]

Having set the stage, let us begin our exploration into the unpredictable world that we live in.

I *The World Around Us*

2   *The Arc of History*

To all appearances, the hand of luck rests heavy on the shoulders of human history.

—NICHOLAS RESCHER, 1995

We begin our exploration of randomness by looking at some of the ways that chance has impacted the manner in which our world has unfolded. An excellent place to start is with the trajectory and path that history has taken. History is replete with countless examples of monumental events and decisions that have often hinged on luck and randomness. Certainly there are powerful forces that push history in particular directions, but so too do elements of chance and luck.

Take the rise of Adolf Hitler and Nazi Germany. It is not an exaggeration to call this one of the most destructive and far-reaching events of the twentieth century. The ascent of Hitler to power in Germany during the 1920s and 1930s led to both World War II and the Holocaust. Yet Hitler's rise to power might have been averted by a simple administrative decision—the acceptance of his application to art school.

It turns out that Hitler's grand ambition as a youth was to gain admittance to the Academy of Fine Arts in Vienna and become an artist. He had made it past the first round of entrance exams, but failed to get through the final round that would have begun his career as an artist. According to the admissions committee, his talents were felt to lie in architecture rather than art. And yet, the judging of art can be quite subjective. Had the admissions committee been composed of a slightly different makeup or met on a different day, the decision might well have been positive.

The 19-year-old Hitler had been expecting to pass the examination with flying colors, and the fact that he did not was "an abrupt blow from nowhere," as he writes in *Mein Kampf.* In an argument one night, not long after his rejection, his roommate recalled,

> "This academy!" Hitler yelled. "Nothing but a pack of cramped, old, outmoded servants of the state, clueless bureaucrats, stupid creations of the civil service! The whole academy should be dynamited!" His face was pale, his lips were pressed so tightly together that they went white. His eyes were glowing. How uncanny his eyes were! As if all the hatred of which he was capable were burning in those eyes.[1]

One month later a friend of a friend of Hitler's asked a highly regarded professor at the academy to intervene on Hitler's behalf. The professor wrote back, "Young Hitler should come see me and bring samples of his work so that I can see what they're like."[2] Perhaps having been rejected once and fearing a second rejection, Hitler failed to follow up.

Had he done so, or had his initial rejection to art school been an acceptance, his path and that of the world might have been quite different. As Volker Ullrich writes in his two-volume definitive history of Hitler, "People have perennially speculated about how history might have turned out had Hitler passed that admissions test. Most likely not only his life story, but Germany's and the world's would have taken a different course."[3]

One postscript to this story. Hitler assumed power in 1933, and on September 1, 1939, he began WWII with the invasion of Poland. Yet the destruction that lay ahead might have been largely averted but for another twist of fate.

Each year Hitler gave a speech in Munich on the anniversary of the Beer Hall Putsch, which was a failed attempt by the Nazi party in 1923 to overthrow the German government. For several months prior to Hitler's November 8, 1939 speech at the Bürgerbräukeller, Georg Eler had worked secretly each night to conceal a powerful bomb inside a column next to where Hitler would be speaking.

Hitler's normal anniversary speeches ran close to two hours, but on this day he decided to reduce it to one hour and to start a half hour early in order to board his train and arrive back in Berlin sooner. William Shirer, a wartime correspondent and author of *The Rise and Fall of the Third Reich,* wrote in his diary the next day what happened:

> Twelve minutes after Hitler and all the big party leaders left the Burgerbrau Keller in Munich last night, at nine minutes after nine o'clock, a bomb explosion wrecked the hall, killed seven, wounded sixty-three. The bomb had been placed in a pillar directly behind the rostrum from which Hitler had been speaking. Had he remained twelve minutes and one second longer he surely would have been killed. The spot on which he stood was covered with six feet of debris.[4]

When Hitler was informed of the bombing later that night by Joseph Goebbels at his train stop in Nuremberg, he remarked, "A man has to be lucky." Certainly this was a monumental stroke of luck for Adolf Hitler, and just as unlucky for the rest of the world.

This is but one of thousands of examples that could be given to illustrate how luck and chance profoundly shape the direction that history takes. We have but one history to reflect on and yet there are endless possibilities of alternative scenarios were it not for chance or luck. Historians refer to these alternatives as counterfactuals. We generally cannot fathom these possibilities because we are not privy to all of the randomness that occurs on a daily basis. Nevertheless, there are times when this randomness comes to the fore in a particularly monumental way. Let us look at three such points in our recent history. The first pertains to the Cuban Missile Crisis of 1962. The second deals with the defeat of the Equal Rights Amendment in the 1970s. And the third is found in the sparks that random events can deliver in igniting social movements.

The Cuban Missile Crisis

Historian and Pulitzer Prize–winning author Martin Sherwin writes in *Gambling with Armageddon* that chance

[has] altered the course of history in much the same way as genetic mutations have transformed species. But unlike biologists, historians tend to overlook those deviations caused by inexplicable luck, both good and bad: They are too hard to discern, even harder to contextualize, and—most problematic—they resist rational explanation.

Such oversights notwithstanding, good luck and bad are immutable parts of the human experience. They are often the fulcrums around which major events pivot. In no area of historical research is this truer than in the study of nuclear weapons in general, and the Cuban missile crisis in particular.[5]

Indeed, the start of the nuclear age had a strong element of luck running through it. After the atomic bombing of Hiroshima on August 6, 1945, the second Japanese city targeted by the United States for destruction was Kokura, not Nagasaki. On August 9, the flight crew aboard the B-29 aircraft code named Bockscar took off from the island of Tinian. Flying time to Japan was approximately six hours and weather reports indicated clear skies over Kokura. However, several unanticipated delays had caused the B-29 to arrive much later than scheduled. The skies above Kokura were now 70 percent obscured by clouds and drifting smoke, making it difficult for the bombardier to drop the bomb visually as he was ordered to do.[6] After three attempted bomb runs and fuel running short, Bockscar flew to its secondary target, the city of Nagasaki. The weather over Nagasaki was also partially obscured, but at 11:01 a.m. Japanese time there was a break in the clouds, allowing the bombardier to visually sight the target and release the bomb named Fat Boy. The mushroom-cloud explosion led to the immediate deaths of at least 40,000 men, women, and children.

The temporary cloudy weather on August 9, 1945, had been an exceptionally lucky break for the city of Kokura and an exceptionally unlucky one for the city of Nagasaki. Since the dropping of the first atomic bombs, humanity has escaped several close calls of nuclear annihilation. The closest of those calls was during the Cuban missile crisis of 1962. As President Kennedy's secretary of state Dean Acheson put it, nuclear war in 1962 was averted by just "plain dumb luck."

To set the stage, hostilities between the United States and Cuba had dramatically escalated following the failed 1961 U.S. attempt to overthrow Fidel Castro and the communist ruling party. Known as the Bay of Pigs invasion, it had proved to be a major embarrassment for the Kennedy administration and a warning to the Castro regime. In May of 1962, Fidel Castro and Soviet first secretary Nikita Khrushchev agreed to secretly deploy strategic nuclear missiles in Cuba, with the intention of providing a strong deterrent to any potential U.S. invasion in the future. The Russian missiles and equipment would be disassembled and shipped aboard freighters bound for Havana, to be reassembled on site.

On October 14, a high flying U-2 spy plane photographed a missile construction site in western Cuba. This marked the beginning of the 13 days in October known as the Cuban Missile Crisis. After heated deliberations with his Cabinet and advisors, President Kennedy decided on a naval blockade surrounding Cuba to prevent further Soviet ships from passing through. In addition, the removal of all missiles and equipment already in Cuba was demanded.

This began a standoff between the United States and Russia, with the final outcome being the disassembly and removal of the Cuban missiles as well as the U.S. removing its Jupiter missiles in Turkey and Italy. But what was not known until fairly recently was the following.

During the crisis, the Soviet Union had sent four of its Foxtrot-class submarines to the crisis area. Each submarine carried 36 mines and 22 two-ton torpedoes, but unbeknownst to the United States, one of those 22 torpedoes was nuclear-tipped with a warhead yielding 15 kilotons, or a force equivalent to the Hiroshima bomb. In a briefing before the four submarine commanders set sail, Vice Admiral Rassokha of the Soviet Northern Fleet gave instructions that if attacked by the American fleet, "I suggest to you commanders that you use the nuclear weapons first, and then you will figure out what to do after that."[7]

His advice came incredibly close to being carried out. In approaching the blockade area on October 27, Captain Valentin Grigorievich Savitsky's submarine U-59 had been under prolonged harassment from U.S. Navy warships on the water. Needing to surface to recharge the boat's electrical system, he thought he had emerged into a full-scale conflict. Surrounded by naval ships and planes, Captain Savitsky gave the order to immediately dive and prepare the nuclear torpedo for firing. And here was where pure luck intervened. Staff Captain Vaily Alexandrovich Arkhipov, his authority equal to Captain Savitsky's, and a signaling officer aboard U-59 likely prevented World War III. Martin Sherwin continues the story:

In 1997 Arkhipov provided his own version of what happened when B-59 was forced to surface. Surrounded by an aircraft carrier, nine destroyers, four P2Vs, three Tracker airplanes, and coast guard forces, the officers on the conning tower were overwhelmed. "Overflights by planes just 20–30 meters above the submarines conning tower, use of powerful searchlights that blinded Savitsky, fire from automatic cannons (over 300 shells), dropping depth charges, cutting in front of submarines by destroyers at dangerously [small] distance, targeting guns at the submarine, yelling from loudspeakers to stop engines, etc."

Convinced that he was under attack, Savitsky ordered an "urgent dive" and "arm torpedo in the front section" [the nuclear torpedo]. But when he tried to descend he was [luckily] blocked by the signaling officer who had somehow in his excitement become stuck near the top of the conning tower ladder. During that short delay Arkhipov realized that the planes were firing "past and along the boat." It was not an attack. "Cancel dive, they are signaling," he countered.[8]

World War III was very likely averted as a result of a brief delay in time caused by a signaling officer who happened to be stuck in the right place at the right time, along with a second in command who, after being given a few extra seconds, perceptively realized that the boat was not under attack. Had this not happened, Captain Savitsky would have dived and in all likelihood within five minutes fired his nuclear-tipped torpedo, causing a cataclysmic reaction. As Sherwin writes, "The extraordinary (and surely disconcerting) conclusion has to be that on October 27, 1962, a nuclear war was averted not because President Kennedy and Premier Khrushchev were doing their best to avoid war (they were), but because Capt. Vasily Arklipov had been randomly assigned to submarine B-59."

As chance would have it, a few hours earlier on the island of Okinawa, the 873rd Tactical Missile Squadron had received mistaken instructions to fire its cruise missiles at their targets in the

Soviet Union and China. Each missile was capped with a 1.1 megaton warhead. Similar to the plot played out in the 1964 movie *Fail Safe*, the commander had received an alert code indicating he should open a top-secret black pouch. If the codes in the pouch matched the alert codes, he was to follow the enclosed targeting instructions and use his launch keys to fire the missiles. The codes matched. The proper procedure was to launch the missiles.

However, the senior launch officer, Air Force Captain William Bassett, felt that something was not right. The Strategic Air Command Defense Condition was at level 2 rather than level 1. A launching of the missiles would be out of the ordinary unless they were at level 1. Yet they had received their orders and they had been confirmed. Regardless, Bassett felt that he needed further confirmation. At the same time, a junior launch officer, "a lieutenant whose missiles were targeted for the Soviet Union, announced that he was going to fire them. Captain Bassett, he said, did not have the authority to override a confirmed order from a major."[9]

Again, World War III hung in the balance. Bassett quickly ordered two airmen with sidearms to run down the underground tunnel after the lieutenant and, if necessary, shoot him if he tried to launch. Several minutes later Bassett received confirmation that the launch orders had been a mistake.

As a postscript to this story, what was unknown until 30 years after the crisis was that the Soviets already had in place nearly 100 short-range tactical nuclear weapons in Cuba, and that "nine nuclear-tipped Luna coastal defense missiles had been armed and ready to be launched against any U.S. invasion force." Furthermore, "the Soviet commanders on the island did not need permission or launch codes from Moscow to fire these weapons."[10] Had the United States decided to militarily strike Cuba during that October, some of these missiles may very well have been fired on the U.S., potentially leading to an all-out nuclear exchange.

An Unexpected Telephone Call That Changed History

History is sometimes changed as a result of a monumental collision being averted by chance and luck. Othertimes, history can be changed by something as simple as an unexpected telephone call out of the blue. This was the case for Phyllis Schlafly, who I interviewed in St. Louis when she was 86.

Partially in response to the Cuban Missile Crisis, Schlafly had had a longtime interest in the Soviet missile threat and the strategic balance of arms when I interviewed her. She was raised in the Midwest and grew up during the hard times of the Great Depression, attending the local university in spite of her family's economic struggles. In order to pay for her college expenses, Schlafly worked in a munitions plant making bullets and ammunition for the American soldiers fighting in WWII.

After graduating from college at the end of the war, she worked briefly at the newly formed conservative think tank, the American Enterprise Institute in Washington, DC, before returning home to the St. Louis area. She married and started a family, but remained keenly interested in politics. In 1952 the Republican Party asked her to run for a congressional seat in her district, which she agreed to do. Although she lost the race, Schlafly became increasingly involved in shaping the direction of both the state and national Republican Party. Her influence reached a zenith when she played a pivotal role in helping Barry Goldwater receive the Republican nomination for president in 1964. After Goldwater's defeat, she turned her attention in the later 1960s and early 1970s to the Soviet missile threat and the strategic balance of arms.

And then in late 1971 there would be a twist of fate that would change both Schlafly's life as well as the direction of the country. It was a phone call she received completely out of the blue from a friend of hers in Connecticut. As she recounts:

Then in, I think probably November '71, some friend in Connecticut wanted me to come and speak for some group, some series they had at the local public library. And I said, "Okay, I'll talk on the strategic balance." "No, no," she said, "I don't want to hear about that. We want to hear about the Equal Rights Amendment," which was then plowing through. "Well," I said, "I haven't looked at it. I don't know whether I'm for it or against it." She said, "I'll send you a packet of material, and I know which side you will be on" [chuckle]. I am very predictable [laugh]. So anyway, she sent it to me, and I gave the speech.

The Equal Rights Amendment was originally debated in Congress in 1923. Since then it had been introduced into every congressional session from 1923 to 1970, but routinely failed to reach the floor for a vote. That changed in 1972, when it was voted on and approved by both houses of Congress. It was then sent to the states for ratification, needing 38 states to ratify before becoming law. The amendment stated, "Equality of rights under the law shall not be denied or abridged by the United States or by any State on account of sex."

Schlafly objected to the ERA primarily on the belief that women would stand to lose a number of benefits and traditional privileges with its passage. After her initial speech at the public library, she became increasingly opposed to its ratification and increasingly active in stopping it. Although it had been ratified by nearly 30 states at the time she became fully engaged in the fight, Schlafly was able to mobilize opposition to the amendment, causing it to eventually fall short of final ratification by three states. Her ability to raise a number of fears and concerns regarding the ERA, and to get those concerns heard in a wider context, was seen by many as critical in turning the tide against the amendment. Through her sustained effort and political skill, Schlafly was able to significantly alter the American social landscape.

Well, I guess I lived the American Dream. I mean I don't know, somebody else could've done what I did. I don't know that I had any special genes or qualifications for what I did, but I just did it. I wasn't born a leader. I've given speeches on this. I grew up very shy. I had to learn all these things. Anybody could've learned it. For example, taking on the Equal Rights Amendment fight, all those people were out there, all they needed was somebody to raise the flag and say let's march and keep the faith.

So what might have happened if Schlafly had not received a call from her friend asking her to speak about the ERA at a small public library in Connecticut? I asked her this question, and she said that in all likelihood she would not have gotten involved in the issue, or if she had, it would have been later in time and too late to stop the ratification process. One could argue that someone else might have stepped in and been as effective as Schlafly in halting the ERA. While possible, such a scenario is unlikely. A random factor had placed her at the heart of the controversy, and it shaped both her life as well as the direction of the country.

It is not an exaggeration to view the defeat of the ERA as marking a first step in the country's move toward a more conservative direction that has continued over the last 50 years, and that Phyllis Schlafly played an important part in bending history in such a direction. Had that telephone call not been made by a friend in small-town Connecticut, American history might very well look different than it does today. It certainly would look different with respect to the Equal Rights Amendment becoming a part of the Constitution.

One other point should be noted. The Connecticut phone call by itself did not cause these changes. Schlafly had to be willing to take advantage of the opportunity that came her way. When her friend telephoned about the speaking engagement, Schlafly could have simply declined the invitation and continued to work on the issue of strategic arms balance. Yet she did not. She choose to take the opportunity to learn more about the topic, and to actively engage with it.

> It's American to believe that we are the land of opportunity. I think one of the reasons I could beat these feminists and the ERA is they really didn't believe I could do what I was doing. They really didn't. So they conjured up these conspiracy theories that I was financed by the insurance companies and various other conspiracy theories. They really didn't believe it.

In the end, history was changed because of a pure random event coupled with a woman who had the motivation to take on the challenge that came her way.

> I've gotten to enjoy the fight. Politics is a fight. My husband really was Irish . . . and the Irish do enjoy the fight, and he taught me to enjoy that. You know, Bill Bennett [former education secretary in the Reagan administration] tells a story about the Irishman who's walking down the street, and he saw a street brawl going on. And he went up to one of the guys and tapped him on the shoulder and said, "Is this a private fight or can anybody get in?" [laughter]. So I learned to enjoy the fight and not let it bother me.

One of Phyllis Schlafly's last public appearances was in support of Donald Trump's successful run for the presidency in 2016. At a rally in St. Louis on March 11, 2016, the 91-year-old Schlafly gave her ringing support, saying,

> We've been following the losers for so long—now we've got a guy who's going to lead us to victory . . . He does look like he's the last hope. We don't hear anybody saying what he's saying.[11]

A single telephone call from 45 years prior was in all likelihood the reason that Schlafly was asked to give her final conservative endorsement and share the stage with the future president of the United States.

Sparks Igniting Social Movements

One of the ways to observe how randomness interacts with social and historical forces is through seemingly random events that ignite social movements. These occurrences were neither planned nor intended to spur on a widespread protest and yet they did.

Many examples of this dynamic exist, but here I point to three. The first was the killing of Michael Brown in Ferguson, Missouri, which helped ignite the Black Lives Matter movement. The second was the horrific death of Mohamed Bouazizi in Tunisia that spurred the Arab Spring. And the third is that of Rosa Parks not giving up her bus seat, which in turn rallied those around her in Montgomery, Alabama, and across the civil rights movement.

In each case, the injustices that fueled these social movements had been simmering for years. The social and economic conditions that fostered each movement were building over many decades. But it was a specific random spark that ignited these injustices into the uprisings and collective action that followed. These sparks helped determine the where and when each social movement caught fire.

Less than 10 miles from my home lies the community of Ferguson, Missouri. On August 9, 2014, a young man named Michael Brown was shot and killed by a policeman on the streets of Ferguson. Unfortunately, this was nothing out of the ordinary for the St. Louis region.[12] Street violence has been a part of life for too many, particularly young African American men. But what was different about this death was that the body of Michael Brown lay in the street for four hours before being removed. This seemed to epitomize in a very graphic way the little regard that those in authority had for young Black men, even in death.

Michael Brown's killing, and the subsequent decision not to indict police officer Darren Wilson, became a flash point for the Black Lives Matter movement. The phrase "Black Lives Matter" had actually appeared in July of 2013 after the acquittal of George Zimmerman in the shooting death of Trayvon Martin in Florida. The hashtag, #BlackLivesMatter, was first seen on social media at that time. But it was the death of Brown on August 9 that fueled the movement from that point forward.

Protestors began appearing the next day to show their solidarity with Michael Brown and his family. As more protestors joined, the local police escalated their show of force. I can recall watching protestors being met by military-grade equipment. This again seemed to epitomize the lack of understanding by authorities of the sense of injustice felt in the community. Eventually the protests spread to over 170 cities across the U.S.

When Michael Brown began his day on August 9, 2014, he had no idea that it would be his last, or that his death would ignite a social movement that continues to this day. Many had wrongfully died at the hands of the police, and many more would die. But somehow, his death created an impetus for change. Similarly, the sickening murder of George Floyd that took place in Minneapolis over a nine-minute span on May 25, 2020, created an outpouring of rage and support.[13] Had it not been recorded and posted on social media by several pedestrians randomly passing by, the nation and the world might never have known about this atrocity.

The Arab Spring represents a second instance of how a seemingly isolated event triggered a widespread political uprising. Mohamed Bouazizi was a young street vendor living in the town of Sidi Bouzid in Tunisia. His life had been one of poverty and struggle. Each day he would borrow enough money to buy fruits and vegetables to sell in the market, and then try and earn enough to pay off his debt with a small profit the following day. Early in the morning he would gather his produce in a wheelbarrow along with his weighing scales and walk to the center of town. For months he had been harassed by the police, who were constantly demanding bribe money.

On December 17, 2010, he began his morning at 8:00 a.m., needing to sell approximately $200 of produce to earn back his loan for the day. At 10:30 that morning the local police began harassing him about not having a vendor's permit. On this day, Bouazizi could not come up with the bribe money. The police confiscated his scales and cart, struck him, and insulted his father, who had recently passed away.

Angered and outraged by this, he rushed over to the town office to complain to the local governor and demand his scales back. The governor had no time to hear his complaint. He was ordered out. This was the proverbial stick that broke the camel's back. Bouazizi returned an hour later in the front of the governor's office and shouted, "How do you expect me to make a living?" In the middle of traffic he doused himself with gasoline and set himself on fire. As Philip Tetlock and Dan Gardner continue,

Only the conclusion of this story is unusual. There are countless poor street vendors in Tunisia and across the Arab world. Police corruption is rife, and humiliations like those inflicted on this man are a daily occurrence. They matter to no one aside from the police and their victims.

But this particular humiliation, on December 17, 2010, caused Mohamed Bouazizi, age twenty-six, to set himself on fire, and Bouazizi's self-immolation sparked protests. The police responded with typical brutality. The protests spread. Bouazizi died on January 4, 2011. The unrest grew.

The Arab world watched, stunned. Then protest erupted in Egypt, Libya, Syria, Jordan, Kuwait, and Bahrain. After three decades in power, the Egyptian dictator Hosni Mubarak was driven from office. Elsewhere, protests swelled into rebellions, rebellions into civil wars. This was the Arab Spring—and it started with one poor man, no different from countless others, being harassed by police, as so many have been, before and since, with no apparent ripple effects.[14]

Like Michael Brown, when Mohamed Bouazizi began his day on December 17 he certainly had no idea that it would be his last. And he surely would not have thought that his final act of desperation would ignite a social and political movement across the Arab world. There had been unrest and protest over the years in these countries, but they had always been put down through ruthless state violence and repression. Yet this turned out to be something different.

One man's desperation and outrage would spread from a small town in Tunisia to protests and political change across the Arab world. Protests occurred across northern Africa and the Middle East, with leadership changes occurring in Tunisia, Libya, Egypt, and Yemen as a result. Longtime dictators such as Mubarak and Colonel Muammar Gaddafi of Libya would fall. Who could have imagined that one poor man's frustration at the injustice he experienced on a December morning would lead to a widespread movement? It was the random factor that ignited the long-simmering injustices into a dramatic political force.

On Thursday, December 1, 1955, Rosa Parks boarded a bus at 6 p.m. in Montgomery, Alabama, for her ride home after a day at work. Since 1900 Montgomery had enforced an ordinance that segregated Whites and Blacks on city buses. The seats in the front of a bus were reserved for Whites. If those seats were filled, then the seats in the middle of the bus would also be available to Whites only. On that Thursday evening, Parks took a seat in the middle of the bus, which was open to Blacks at the time of her boarding. However, after several stops, the all-White front seats became filled, causing the bus driver to tell those in the middle of the bus to give up their seats for the two or three White bus riders now standing and move to the back. Three of the four Black riders got up and moved to the back of the bus. Rosa Parks did not. As she explained in her autobiography,

> People always say that I didn't give up my seat because I was tired, but that isn't true. I was not tired physically, or no more tired than I usually was at the end of a working day. I was not old, although some people have an image of me as being old then. I was forty-two. No, the only tired I was, was tired of giving in.[15]

After years of humiliation and discrimination in riding the buses of Montgomery, she had had enough. As she explains, "When that white driver stepped back toward us, when he waved his hand and ordered us up and out of our seats, I felt a determination cover my body like a quilt on a winter night."[16]

Parks was ordered off the bus and arrested by a police officer. She was charged with disorderly conduct and violating a city ordinance. Her arrest triggered what became known as the Montgomery bus boycott. That Sunday, Black churches across Montgomery announced plans to boycott the city buses. The Black community was asked to forgo any bus services and to make other arrangements for getting to work. A young minister at the Dexter Avenue Baptist Church was elected to spearhead the boycott. His name was Martin Luther King Jr. The boycott would last 381 days, and ended with the U.S. Supreme Court ruling that segregation on public buses was unconstitutional.

The Montgomery bus boycott was a key victory for the civil rights movement. King and others would go on to organize and fight for African Americans who were being denied their constitutional rights. The conditions of Jim Crow, intimidation, violence, and segregation had existed since the latter nineteenth century, with many attempts over the years to resist and change this system of exploitation and humiliation.[17] But it was the brave actions of one woman on a city bus that helped to ignite and coalesce thousands to mobilize their anger and bring down the segregation of buses. This was only one step along the pathway to equal rights and protections under the law. But it was a very influential step. The day began for Rosa Parks like any other ordinary day, but it ended with a spark that helped ignite a racial awakening in the United States.[18]

In each of these three cases—Michael Brown, Mohamed Bouazizi, and Rosa Parks—there was no intention or thought that their actions would ignite a social movement. And yet in each case, they did. The underlying conditions of social injustice had prevailed for decades, yet a spark was needed to ignite a coalescing around a cause. Many similar events had occurred in the past but failed to produce any reaction. Those potential sparks came and went without much notice. Rather, it was the random factor that played its hand in the where and when each social movement would ignite.[19]

Understanding the Role of Chance in History

Is history simply a collection of chance events occurring randomly? Of course not. Has the arc of history been profoundly shaped by the random factor? Most definitely.

As I argue throughout the book, there is a dynamic interplay between social processes and the random factor. We might think of this interplay as a tango between these two partners. There are certainly powerful forces that push history in particular directions, but randomness also exerts its influence upon the direction and speed of these dance partners.

Take the example of Adolf Hitler given at the start of this chapter. Germany emerged out of WWI badly damaged. The Treaty of Versailles and its stipulation of sizeable reparations created widespread resentment among the German people. Hyperinflation and the Great Depression made the economic situation that much worse. Against this backdrop of economic destitution, a growing rise of antisemitism provided a convenient target to blame Germany's woes upon, while the ascendency of fascism led by Benito Mussolini in Italy served as a political model.

The conditions were therefore ripe for a fascist and antisemite such as Hitler to rise to power in Germany. Nevertheless, many historians argue that Hitler was unique in terms of his ability to mobilize and channel the hatred and resentment in Germany following their defeat in WWI. Through his skill as an orator and a ruthless political operative, he turned Germany into a dictatorship and a military juggernaut. Without Adolf Hitler, history would have undoubtedly played out much differently.

William Shirer was able to observe Hitler firsthand from 1934 to the end of 1940. As a foreign correspondent he attended dozens of Hitler's speeches and events. During this time he kept a diary about the daily happenings in Germany and Europe. In one of his last entries on December 1, 1940, he reflects on the tendency in German society to emphasize domination and the acquisition of territory: "The urge to expansion, the hunger for land and space, for what the Germans call *Lebensraum,* has lain long in the soul of the people."[20]

But he goes on to observe that it was Hitler in particular who was able to channel those sentiments into words and actions. Shirer writes, "It is the evil genius of Adolf Hitler that has aroused this basic feeling and given it tangible expression. It is due to this remarkable and terrifying man alone that the German dream now stands a fair chance of coming true."[21] Had Hitler not come to power, Shirer concludes that history would be much different.

The random factor thus interacts with the various social and economic forces in history to produce a unique historical thread. As I will argue in upcoming chapters, understanding this interaction is key to comprehending the world around us. It is an intricate dance between partners as they move across the dance floor.

In 1955 Pulitzer Prize–winning historian Oscar Handlin published *Chance or Destiny: Turning Points in American History*. Every chapter was devoted to a particularly important turning point in U.S. history. Handlin argued that each of these turning points were heavily influenced by the element of chance. As he writes,

> But at any given point there is no inevitability to the direction of the turning. The way taken is determined by the momentary convergence of a myriad of factors, personal and social; and the fact of their convergence is itself often the result of some contingency, unpredictable in its occurrence. Therein is concealed much of the drama of the past.[22]

One reason we often do not see this dynamic is because we have but one history to reflect on. As a result, it appears that event A led to event B which then led to event C. Yet at the moment history is unfolding, it could travel in many different directions. Event A might not at all lead to event B. It is only with hindsight that we piece together a narrative of what has happened. That narrative is merely one among a multitude of possibilities. It is the random factor that often influences which thread of history we are left with.

The popular historian David McCullough writes in the introduction to his *Brave Companions*:

> In writing history, to catch the feeling as well as the "truth" of other times, it is of utmost importance, I believe, to convey the sense that things need not have happened as they did. Life in other times past was never on a track, any more than it is now or ever will be. The past after all is only another name for someone else's present. How would things turn out? They knew not better than we know how things will

turn out for us. The problem, as Thornton Wilder said, "lies in the effort to employ the past tense in such a way that it does not rob those events of their character of having occurred in freedom."[23]

In his fascinating *Undelivered: The Never-Heard Speeches That Would Have Rewritten History,* Jeff Nussbaum uncovers many monumental addresses that would have been delivered had a twist of fate not intervened. These included General Eisenhower's apology for the failure of the D-Day Invasion of June 1944 and President Kennedy's planned speech of a military strike against Cuba during the Cuban Missile Crisis. As Nussbaum writes,

> When we look back at historic events, we do so with a sense of certainty: Events happened because they had to happen that way. In retrospect, the outcome seems preordained. What we fail to realize is that there could just have easily been a very different path, and the following speeches give us a peek down that path.[24]

History is clearly replete with chance and luck. The direction it takes is influenced as much by contingency as it is by intention. The dance of these two partners results in a past filled with what-ifs and a future filled with possibilities.

3   *The Natural World*

It's tough to make predictions, especially about the future.

—Attributed to YOGI BERRA (among others), derived from a Danish proverb

Sixty-six million years ago an asteroid was hurtling through space on a collision course with the earth. In all likelihood that asteroid and its trajectory are the reasons why you and I are here today and the dinosaurs are not. Over seven and a half miles wide and traveling at 40,000 miles per hour, it struck the earth with the force of 10 billion Hiroshimas. Known as the Chicxulub impactor, it created a crater 93 miles wide and 20 miles deep off the Yucatan Peninsula in Mexico. Rock was turned to liquid and spewed into the atmosphere. Heat from the fireball reached 10,000 degrees Fahrenheit, vaporizing everything within 600 miles of impact.

Approximately 10 minutes after impact, the skies began to darken around the world, radiating searing heat and smoke. This led to much of the world burning. Soon after, the earth would have entered into a prolonged winter with freezing temperatures and little sunlight reaching the ground, causing photosynthesis to stop and water to become acidic. A mass extinction took place, affecting up to 75 percent of the world's plant and animal species, including the dinosaurs. The Chicxulub impactor ended their reign and jump-started the rise of the mammals, including ourselves.

Yet what recent research has shown is that where the asteroid hit was particularly critical in leading to this cataclysmic event. If the asteroid had struck a minute or two earlier or later, the story might have been very different given the earth's rotational spin. The fact that its entrance lined up with the Yucatan Peninsula rather than the Atlantic or Pacific Ocean made all the difference in the world. The reason is that where the asteroid impacted "burned enough oil-rich sedimentary rocks to inject around 1.5 billion tons of fine-particle black carbon into the atmosphere."[1] Only 13 percent of the earth's surface contained rocks that could have burned off that much soot. The result was the extreme global winter that finished off the dinosaurs. As Paul Chodas, manager of the Center for Near Earth Object Studies at NASA's Jet Propulsion Laboratory, observed, "We have often remarked on how unlucky this massive impact was for the dinosaurs, and how lucky it was for us, as the top of the mammal family, but now we have a measure of just how unlucky the dinosaurs were and how lucky we were!"[2]

One might argue that the asteroid was predestined to strike the earth when and where it did. Yet as I will discuss with the rotation of the planets, in all likelihood considerable randomness influenced its path and trajectory across the millions of years. Chance gravitational forces and impacts could have easily resulted in altering its path such that the result was a near miss rather than a direct hit.[3]

In this chapter we explore several of the ways in which randomness affects our natural world. As noted, the very fact that we are here today as a species is the result of a completely random and very lucky (for us) collision upon the planet.

Chance and Natural Selection

In the history of science there are a handful of ideas that are truly monumental—Nicolaus Copernicus's formulation that the sun rather than the earth lies at the center of our solar system; Sir Isaac Newton's laws of motion and universal gravitation; Albert Einstein's theory of relativity. And certainly one must add to this list Charles Darwin's theory of evolution by natural selection. This was an idea that truly changed the way that scientists and the public viewed the world. And at its heart lies the element of chance.

Darwin began formulating his revolutionary ideas during an around-the-globe expedition aboard the HMS *Beagle*. The captain of the *Beagle*, Robert FitzRoy, had told the Admiralty that "he would like a well-educated gentleman" to accompany him on the voyage.[4] FitzRoy wanted someone he could share his meals with and discuss ideas and scientific matters during the two- year trip (which eventually wound up taking five). But Charles Darwin was not the first to be asked. Two others had turned down the Admiralty's offer, and it was to Darwin's good fortune that they did. The 22-year-old jumped at the opportunity, and in 1831 the *Beagle* departed.[5]

During the voyage, Darwin was able to observe and gather a vast multitude of plant and animal species, along with a wide collection of fossils. These became the foundation from which he built his theory of evolution and natural selection. After returning to England, he began to piece together the puzzle that would eventually become his tour de force. That of course was *On the Origin of the Species,* first published in 1859. The book had an immediate impact on our understanding of the world. As biologist Hanne Strager writes, "One aspect of the book's success was without a doubt its accessibility to non-specialists. It rarely happens that one person, with one stroke, changes our understanding of how the world is put together but even more rarely does he express himself in such a way that any educated person can follow his reasoning."[6]

In its simplest form, the theory is based upon several key observations. First, all creatures that reproduce will sire offspring slightly different than themselves. Occasionally these differences may be the result of mutations that occur within the DNA. Most are inconsequential and have no effect on the offspring's survival. Some, however, may be negative, causing harm to the offspring, while a few may be positive, providing an advantage for survival.

Nature itself is ruled by what Herbert Spencer labeled "the survival of the fittest." Those more likely to survive and pass their gene pool on to the next generation do so because they are better adapted to their environment than others in their species. And it is here where natural selection and the random factor come into play. A chance mutation providing a particular individual with an advantage will give that individual a greater probability of surviving and reproducing. As a result, such an advantage is passed on to the next generation. Nature thereby helps select the winners and losers in this game of survival. Through this process, species change and evolve over time such that they become better adapted to their physical environment. In this way randomness and the forces of natural selection interact to produce change. A poetic phrasing comes from Sean Carroll, who writes, "So chance invents, and natural selection propagates the invention."[7] Or as Ed Smith notes,

> Chance and selection . . . interact to produce something quite new. Success, to use a metaphor from chemistry rather than biology, is not a mixture. It is a compound. Luck is a crucial ingredient that goes into making an end-product that may be unrecognizable from its constituent parts.[8]

Darwin, however, was walking a dangerous line. By delegating chance a major role in his theory, he appeared to be discounting the importance of a Divine presence in creating the world. Just as Galileo and other scientists before him had experienced, Darwin was quite aware and concerned about this potential land mine throughout his writings and career. After the 1859 publication of *Origin of the Species*, Darwin continued to modify and revise his language in later editions of the book. As Darwin scholar Curtis Johnson points out, "Most of the changes center on decisions he was making about how to disguise or render innocuous the role of 'chance' without really removing it from its central position in his theory."[9]

Moving the story forward, recent research in evolutionary biology has repeatedly confirmed the process of chance and natural selection. The earliest example of natural selection within a fairly short time period was the peppered moth of nineteenth-century England. The moth itself was rather nondescript, having grayish-white wings that were speckled with black. This matched the bark on the trees where the moths spent much of their time, providing a natural camouflage to the local birds waiting to devour them. As the level of pollution in England increased, the trees soon became covered with a black soot from nearby factories. The natural coloring of the moths no longer provided the protective camouflage important for their survival, and they became easy targets for the birds. However, a few of the moths had a mutation that caused them to be dark colored, and thus they blended into the blackened tree coloring. As a result, they were more likely to survive and pass on their advantage to the next generation. By the end of the century, nearly all of the moths in the polluted communities were dark colored.

To bring the story to a close, from the 1950s onward, pollution has been dramatically reduced in England, causing the tree bark to return to its original coloration. This, in turn, has resulted in the peppered moth reverting back to their original color markings, once again through the process of natural selection.

More recent laboratory and field experiments demonstrating natural selection at work can be readily found. One of the world's premier evolutionary biologists, Jonathan Losos, documents many of these in *Improbable Destinies: Fate, Chance, and the Future of Evolution*. From guppies to lizards to finches, the process of chance and natural selection have been shown to play themselves out in a variety of ways.

An interesting idea that Losos puts forth is that there are a potpourri of adaptation possibilities and solutions open to a species. A mutation may start a species down one particular road. Yet a different mutation could have led to an alternative but equally successful adaptation. For example, fast propulsion through the water can be accomplished by vertebrate animals in a variety of ways through a variety of adaptations. A particular mutation may open the door to one approach while closing the door on another. According to Nobel Prize recipient Francois Jacob, natural selection should be thought of "not like an engineer, constructing the optimal solution to the problem at hand . . . Rather . . . think about a tinkerer, a handyman who makes use of whatever materials are available to fashion whatever solution is feasible—not the best solution possible, but the best attainable under the circumstances."[10]

Here again we see the interplay of the random factor with the larger forces in nature to push forward the process of evolution. That process certainly applies to us a species. Losos notes: "If any of countless number of events had occurred differently in the past, *Homo sapiens* wouldn't have evolved. We were far from inevitable and are lucky to be here, fortunate that events happened just as they did."[11] He concludes his book with a final thought:

From the vantage point of the origin of life several billion years ago, any particular evolutionary outcome would have seemed improbable. But history happened as it happened and here we are today, the result of billions of years of natural selection and the flukes of history that sent life down one path and not others. Lucky? Yes. Destined, no. We should make the most of our evolutionary good fortune.[12]

Cloudy Skies Ahead

Is there any subject more discussed on a daily basis than the weather? And is there any complaint more often raised than that the forecast was wrong? Predicting the weather has been the bane of forecasters since time immemorial. To be sure, recent decades have seen advances in accuracy with tools such as Doppler radar and computer simulation programs, but forecasting still remains an art as well as a science.

This is particularly the case when trying to predict the weather more than five or six days into the future. There is a saying in my part of the country that if you don't like the weather, wait a few minutes. In areas where the weather can change on a dime, it becomes especially difficult to predict.

This can have dire consequences. In the Midwest, tornadoes are a frequent occurrence, particularly during the spring. My hometown of St. Louis has had its share of twisters. In fact, the first and second costliest tornados in the history of the United States have happened here, and more fatalities have occurred in St. Louis due to tornados than in any other city in the United States.[13]

St. Louisians such as myself experience frequent tornado watches when the conditions are ripe for one to occur, while a tornado warning is sounded when a twister has been sighted. Yet it is virtually impossible to predict exactly where a tornado might strike. In the aftermath of a tornado you might find buildings on one side of a street torn up and destroyed, while those on the other side remain untouched. The path of a tornado can be as narrow as 100 feet or as wide as several miles, and it may travel along the ground for a mile or two, or perhaps 60 or 70.

Similarly, other weather events can be extremely difficult to predict. These include hailstorms, where hurricanes make landfall, and the amount of snowfall from a storm. In each case, forecasters have struggled to get their predictions right. And trying to predict the weather more than a week or two into the future is generally futile.

On a related topic, a substantial amount of research has gone into attempting to predict when and where the next major earthquake will strike. This is particularly the case along the San Andreas Fault in California. The economic and human damage from a large earthquake in heavily populated southern or northern California could be catastrophic. Yet as Susan Hough concludes in *Predicting the Unpredictable*:

> Whether reliable earthquake prediction will ever be possible, we can't say. But the point bears repeating: for all of the optimism, for all of the past promise, for all of the past hopes generated by apparently promising prediction research, none of it has borne fruit. And as scientists continue to pursue prediction methods, unpredicted quakes continue to strike.[14]

However, Hough goes on to note: "We can't predict any one earthquake, but, standing back to look at earthquakes as a system, we can say a lot about how the system behaves."[15] In other words, we may never be able to predict precisely when and where the next earthquake in California or elsewhere will occur. The random factor is such that this may simply not be feasible. Nevertheless, we can narrow the scope of likelihood to specific areas that display considerable seismic activity as a result of plate tectonics. And we can roughly estimate a time frame in which another large earthquake is likely to strike given previous earthquake activity. In this manner science can help steer us in the right direction, but it is simply unable to completely rein in the random factor.

Returning to the weather, why is it so hard to predict? Part of the answer has to do with what is known as chaos theory. The origins of this theory can be traced to an MIT professor named Edward Lorenz. As so often happens in science, an unintended (might we say chance) occurrence lead to a major discovery.

Lorenz had long been interested in weather prediction. In 1961 he was working in his MIT lab with a very early computer. On this particular project he had been using 12 weather-related variables such as temperature, air pressure, and wind speed to simulate weather patterns, analyzing how changes in one or more of these variables would affect future weather conditions. After running one of his simulations, he wanted to look at the data again, but in order to save time, he started the simulation in the middle of its course by imputing the numbers from the earlier computer printout. Much to his surprise, the weather now being predicted was radically different from the first simulation, even though the numbers were the same.

At first Lorenz thought there was something wrong with the computer. But finally he hit upon why there were such differences. In the printout he was using, the numbers had been rounded out to three decimal places. However, the computer itself was using numbers carried out to six decimal places. In other words, he was using a number such as 4.235 when the computer was actually using 4.235116. This nearly indistinguishable difference was causing major changes in predicting the weather into the future.

There were two implications of this finding. The first was that even minute changes in the starting conditions of a weather system can result in major changes in outcomes. This pattern became known as the "butterfly effect." When Lorenz presented his work at a 1972 conference in Washington, DC, he had not yet titled his paper, so the organizer of the conference suggested one—"Predictability: Does the Flap of a Butterfly's Wings in Brazil Set off a Tornado in Texas?" The butterfly analogy stuck. The idea was that a tornado in Texas (or

St. Louis) might be influenced by something as small as a butterfly's flapping of its wings in Brazil several weeks earlier.

The idea of the butterfly effect was first written about in a 1952 science fiction story by Ray Bradbury entitled "A Sound of Thunder." The crux of the story is that time travel has become possible in the year 2055 by a company named Time Safari, Inc. Three men go back in time 66 million years ago, but unbeknownst to them, one has accidently stepped on and killed a butterfly. When they return to 2055, the present has been subtlety changed. Words are spelled a bit differently, the air has a slightly different smell, and the results of a presidential election from the day before have reversed. The killing of a single butterfly has rippled through time, creating a world that has been altered 66 million years later.

The second implication from Lorenz's work is also germane to our interests. And that is, because of uncertainty and chaos, we can only predict the weather up to a certain point. Even with the most precise measurements, our predictions are only useful for a limited period of time, and after that, we might as well use randomness as our guide. In other words, a system such as atmospheric weather has a finite prediction horizon. As he wrote in his 1972 paper, "Although we cannot claim to have proven that the atmosphere is unstable, the evidence that it is so is overwhelming."[16]

This represented a major challenge to what is known as Cartesian thinking. The Cartesian premise is that there are knowable laws of nature which allow us to understand and predict various phenomena. What Lorenz was proposing was clearly thinking outside of this box—some phenomena and events cannot be predicted because of what we might call chaos or randomness. Long-term weather predictions are one such example.

Even for short-term weather predictions, randomness comes into play. For example, in forecasting whether it might rain tomorrow, you will see on the local newscast or your smartphone a probability. This reflects the reality that the forecaster cannot be certain whether or not it will rain tomorrow, only that the odds are more or less favorable. In addition, forecasters will provide multiple predictions (based on simulations) for trying to determine certain weather events such as the path and landfall of a hurricane. This again is the result of uncertainty and instability in the system.

Even something as regular as the orbits of the planets in our solar system, over time, are subject to randomness. MIT scientists using a supercomputer simulated the solar system for the next 100 million years. What they found was that after 12 million years, the orbits of the planets could not be predicted reliably. Beyond that point, the solar system begins to behave chaotically, showing deviations from Newtonian laws of physics.[17] Certainly 12 million years is nothing to sneeze at. But in terms of the 4.5 billion years that the earth has been around, it is but a small slice of time. The moral of the story is that even something as constant as the rotation and orbits of the planets may eventually depart from their routines due to the random factor.

The instability of the weather and atmosphere is particularly relevant with respect to global warming. Over the past 200 years, increasing amounts of carbon dioxide have been released into the atmosphere through the burning of fossil fuels. This has resulted in the earth heating up as measured by temperatures around the world.[18] The mechanism behind these rising temperatures is the well-known greenhouse effect. Similar to the glass walls and ceiling of a greenhouse, sunlight is allowed in, but carbon in the atmosphere helps to retain more of the warmth as the sunlight is refracted back into space.

The industrial age has injected this dangerous by-product into the atmosphere, which as we are learning, has both known and unknown effects. It is the unknown effects that may be particularly worrisome. Atmospheric scientists have spent years modeling the effects of rising CO_2 and methane levels upon the earth's future climate. The latest report from the Intergovernmental Panel on Climate Change finds that since the nineteenth century, humans have heated the planet by approximately 2 degrees Fahrenheit.[19] This global warming has accelerated particularly in the last 30 years. But because of the random factor, we cannot be sure of what all of these effects might be. Some have argued that we will reach a tipping point, where the climate is fundamentally changed in ways that we cannot predict. Others have argued that we are on a downward trajectory, with little or no hope of returning to a more stable prior state.

In either case, the results may be cataclysmic. Rising sea levels, changes in the jet stream, the melting of the permafrost releasing large amounts of methane into the atmosphere, increasing numbers of extreme weather events—all of these and more may be waiting for us in the future. It is not an exaggeration to call this the most serious challenge facing humankind and the world itself. Perhaps we will have luck on our side and avert the worst of these predictions. Then again, perhaps we will not. But one thing is for sure—the random factor will undoubtedly play an important role in this story.

Random Sampling

The disciplines of sociology, political science, economics, and anthropology began in the mid-to-late nineteenth century as ways of understanding the social world around us. The premise was that just as there are knowable patterns and dynamics in the natural world, so too for society. The term "social science" encapsulates this idea.

One of the ways such information has been gathered is through asking people questions. The social survey is a technique for doing so. The researcher constructs an array of questions designed to elicit information regarding a topic of interest. For example, if I was interested in understanding what is meant by the concept of the American Dream, I might develop a series of questions asking individuals to rate how important various components of life and success are to their notion of the Dream (which I have done).

From the 1950s onward, the social survey became the dominant methodological approach in the social sciences, particularly within sociology, demography, and political science. Much of the knowledge in these fields has been acquired through survey data. For instance, the information gathered by the U.S. Census Bureau and the Bureau of Labor Statistics is acquired almost entirely through social surveys.

But beyond constructing a questionnaire, there is another critical component to social surveys. And that is, who do we select to answer these questions and how representative are they of the larger population? This gets at the methodological issue of sampling. And it is here that the random factor becomes the researcher's best friend.

Social scientists are rarely able to contact everyone in the population they are interested in studying. The logistics and expense of doing so makes this infeasible. Rather, they draw a sample of individuals or households with the hope that what they find within their sample will be similar to what they would find in the total population. For example, the Current Population Survey is conducted by the Census Bureau each March with a national sample of approximately 60,000 households across the United States. From this survey, the bureau calculates the average annual income in the United States. This is derived by asking the head of household a series of questions regarding the various sources of income that the family has received during the year. The Census Bureau is confident that the results they acquire in their sample mirrors the total U.S. population, and that their estimate of annual income in the sample is nearly identical to what it is in the total population.

How can they be so sure? The answer is random sampling. If a sample is drawn randomly from the population, if the response rate is high, and if the sample size is large enough, then we can be certain that the results will be an accurate reflection of the overall population. Randomization ensures that everyone in the larger population has an equivalent chance of being selected for the sample. The result is that the sample should mirror the wider population.

What you will often see in the reporting of surveys, such as political polling, is a margin of error and a confidence interval. These are statistically calculated and indicate how certain we can be that the results from our polling data are a true reflection of the total population. For example, during a presidential election year, many national and statewide polls are conducted to gauge the sentiment of the voting public. You might see a result that reports 55 percent of the voting-age population indicated they would vote for candidate A, with a 95 percent confidence interval of plus or minus 2 percent. What this means is that in 95 out of 100 times of drawing our sample, we can be sure that between 53 to 57 percent of the total population would say they intend to vote for candidate A (whether they actually do so is another story). It is always a possibility that the true total population voting preference percentage for candidate A could fall outside this confidence interval, but quite unlikely (a less than 5 percent chance).

Randomization thus allows the researcher to generalize their results to the wider population. And this is key. Social scientists typically want to assert that what they have found in their sample is reflective of the larger population they are interested in. By drawing enough individuals randomly, one is able to do so. And that is why randomization is the researcher's best friend.

On the other hand, when a sample is not drawn randomly, the researcher often runs into serious trouble. Many examples can be found of polling results being wrong. Perhaps the most famous was the 1936 *Literary Digest* poll. The *Literary Digest* was a weekly magazine that since 1924 had correctly predicted the outcome of the prior presidential elections. A few days before the 1936 contest between Democratic incumbent Franklin Delano Roosevelt and Republican

Alf Landon, the magazine published the findings of its 1936 presidential poll.

The poll itself was based on a very large sample of 2.4 million individuals. The headline story from the *Digest* on October 31, 1936, proclaimed their polling results. Their prediction was that Landon would receive 55 percent of the total popular vote to 41 percent for Roosevelt. The actual election percentages were 61 percent for Roosevelt and 37 percent for Landon (William Lemke, a third-party candidate, received 2 percent of the vote). How could they have gotten it so wrong?

The standard explanation goes as follows. In order to gather their sample, the *Digest* mailed out 10 million postcards to individuals across the country, asking them to choose who they were planning to vote for on election day. They relied on a variety of sources and lists, but most respondents came from telephone directories and registers of automobile owners. However, there was a potential problem in using those two sources at the time—individuals who were listed as having a telephone or automobile in 1936 tended to be the more affluent, and the more affluent had traditionally favored Republicans rather than Democrats in national elections. Thus, the voting sample chosen may have been skewed toward the more affluent, which resulted in a higher reported percentage voting for Landon than was the actual case in the general population. The fact that the sample was not random doomed the results.

As noted, this had been the standard explanation for 70 years. However, a recent analysis showed that there was actually a more important factor in explaining the significant amount of error. Dominic Lusinchi reanalyzed the 1936 data, and found that the fundamental reason why the *Literary Digest* poll got it so wrong had to do with what is known as nonresponse bias.[20] Of the 10 million postcards mailed out, only 2.4 million were returned for a response rate of 24 percent. If those who returned the postcards had the same preferences as those who did not, there would not be a problem. However, Lusinchi shows that those who returned their postcards were much more likely to say they were voting for Landon than those who did not. Why would this be? Lusinchi explains,

> It has been said that the 1936 contest generated "the bitterest campaign since 1896." The New Deal, which had ruffled many feathers, was accused, among other things, of being "socialistic," the ultimate anathema in the political culture of America. Feelings ran high in certain quarters of the American electorate that "America [was] in peril" as a result of the administration's policies. It is no wonder, then, that highly motivated individuals seized on the *Digest* poll to register their discontent with the direction in which the administration was taking the country. These respondents caused the downfall of the poll and, ultimately, of the *Digest* itself.[21]

Consequently, the 2.4 million individuals who returned their postcards were a more motivated group to do so, and the reason they were more motivated was their displeasure with FDR's New Deal policies. As a result, they were more likely to say they were voting for Alf Landon than the 7.6 million who did not submit their postcards. This then skewed the results to appear that Landon would be the runaway winner, when in fact it was Roosevelt who won in a landslide.

The issue of nonresponse bias is also quite relevant in today's world of internet surveys. These surveys can be found routinely on the web, often with response rates of 10 or 15 percent. The problem is that those who respond to such surveys may not be representative of the wider population that the researcher is interested in generalizing to. They may be skewed in various ways, which will then bias the results and make generalizations to the wider population problematic.

It is randomization and a high response rate that comes to the rescue. If a sample can be drawn randomly from the population of interest, if it is large enough, and if the response rate of those contacted is high, then we can be confident that what we find in our sample will be reflective of what we would find in the total population. It is the random factor that allows us to extrapolate into the social world around us.

Statistical Probability

One of the ways in which we have attempted to exert some control over the random factor is through the laws of statistical probability. Beginning with Blaise Pascal and Pierre de Fermant in the seventeenth century, continuing through to John Maynard Keynes's 1921 classic, *A Treatise on Probability,* and moving on to recent times, statistical probability has advanced as a field, allowing us a clearer window into the future.[22] In his *Analytical Essay on Games of Chance* published in 1708, the French nobleman Pierre Remond de Montmort wrote,

> [Most men] believe that it is necessary to appease this blind divinity that one calls Fortune, in order to force her to be favorable to them in following the rules which they have imagined. I think therefore it would be useful, not only to gamesters but all men in general, to know that chance has rules which can be known.[23]

More recently, financial historian Peter Bernstein notes, "The revolutionary idea that defines the boundary between modern times and the past is the mastery of risk: the notion that the future is more than a whim of the gods and that men and women are not passive before nature."[24] He goes on to write, "the most powerful tool of risk management ever to be invented: the laws of probability."[25] Or as historian Jackson Lears writes, "After acknowledging the existence of chance, statistical thinking aimed to rob it of its power."[26]

There are at least two ways of thinking about statistical probability. The first is where the probability or odds of an outcome are known definitively. This is known as theoretical probability. The tossing of a coin and the drawing of a particular card from a deck are examples of this. There are only two possible outcomes of a fairly flipped coin, and therefore the probability of a tossed coin coming up heads is 50 percent, and likewise for tails. Similarly, we know exactly what the odds are of drawing a particular card out of a well-shuffled 52-card deck. For example, the odds of drawing an ace can be determined precisely. In the deck are four aces. Therefore the odds of selecting an ace is 4/52, or 7.7 percent.

In real life, however, we rarely know the precise odds of an event occurring. Rather, we can only estimate the approximate odds based upon past data. This is known as empirical probability. The field of insurance underwriting relies upon this principle. For example, an actuary can estimate an individual's life expectancy based upon current mortality statistics. Likewise, the insurance company can calculate from past records the likelihood of a flood or hurricane occurring in a particular locality, and subsequently base their premiums upon the likelihood of such an event happening and the potential monetary damage that it may cause. Yet these probabilities are based upon historical data. Future events may very well deviate from the past record, causing the expected probabilities to be erroneous.

A different application of this principle would be the familiar heart disease risk calculators found across the internet. In using these calculators, one is asked to input various pieces of personal information, and based upon that information, the risk of having a heart attack over the next 10 years is calculated. Cardiologists use these statistical probabilities to determine a patient's 10-year risk of having a heart attack based upon factors such as cholesterol, blood pressure, family history, weight, age, gender, and smoking history.

By factoring in these variables, your doctor can give you a more targeted probability of having a heart attack in the next 10 years.

These estimates are derived from a sample of individuals who make up the Framingham Heart Study. The Framingham study has followed a very large number of individuals over several decades. During this period of time, researchers have observed who has and has not experienced a heart attack, and what factors appear associated with an elevated chance of heart failure. For example, those with high cholesterol and blood pressure, a family history of early heart disease, are overweight, older, male, and have smoked during their entire adulthood, are much more likely to experience a heart attack in the future than someone who does not have these characteristics.

Let us suppose that such an individual (person A) has a 10-year risk of 15 percent, while their counterpart who does not have these characteristics (person B) has a risk of 5 percent. What does this mean? One interpretation would be that if we were to draw from the general population a random sample of 100 individuals with the characteristics of person A, we would find that approximately 15 of those individuals would have a heart attack in the next 10 years. Likewise, if we did the same thing and drew 100 individuals with the characteristics of person B, we would find that approximately 5 of those individuals would have a heart attack in the next 10 years. Thus, the likelihood of having a heart attack is increased threefold for individuals with the characteristics of person A as compared to individuals with the characteristics of person B.

However, as we can also see, although individuals with person A's characteristics are at a much great risk of experiencing a heart attack, the vast majority of them will not. Likewise, although the risk of having a heart attack is much lower for individuals with person B's characteristics, a few of them will have such an attack.

Thus, what is being predicted are differences in the overall odds of an event occurring, as well as the changes in those odds depending on changes in the set of background characteristics. These models cannot definitely say that if you have a certain combination of these characteristics, then the event will occur—only that the odds are increased or decreased over time.

My colleague Tom Hirschl and I have used this approach to develop a poverty risk calculator.[27] Our calculator works in a similar fashion as the heart disease calculators. We are able to take five individual factors (age, race, gender, education, and marital status), and based upon a user's responses to these factors, estimate their 5-, 10-, and 15-year risk of poverty. These predictions are grounded in several hundred thousand households taken from a large longitudinal study of Americans called the Panel Study of Income Dynamics, which has followed a nationally representative sample of Americans from 1968 onward. During this period of time, we have observed what happens to individuals with respect to their risk of poverty. Assuming that these patterns hold, we are able to make an estimate regarding an individual's personal chances of experiencing poverty. In this manner, an individual can roughly assess what their economic risk of poverty in the future may be.

Robert Rubin, the former U.S. Treasury secretary in the Clinton administration from 1995 to 1999, has written several books and articles dealing with decision-making in a world of uncertainty. As he states, "At the heart of my own approach is 'probabilistic thinking,' the idea that nothing is 100 percent certain and that everything is therefore a matter of probabilities."[28] We will return to this idea in chapter 9, but suffice it to say that by using probabilities in combination with the potential payoffs of various decisions, one can arrive at a reasonable course of action.

These examples illustrate that the random factor can to some extent be reined in through the laws of statistical probability.[29] They allow us to look into the future with something akin to a rudimentary roadmap that shows what we might expect in the future based upon the patterns of the past.

Another example of attempting to rein in the random factor is through a technique known as a Monte Carlo simulation. Named after the famous casinos in Monte Carlo, it was first developed by Stanislaw Ulam, a mathematician working on the Manhattan Project in the 1940s. The approach is intended to solve the problem of having a statistical model designed to predict a particular outcome, but with the value of at least one variable in the model being unknown. In order to arrive at the best possible prediction, a random value is assigned to that variable and the model is computed. This would be akin to allowing the value or number being chosen by a roulette wheel (hence the name Monte Carlo). This is repeated many times, with a different random value being imputed each time the model is run. Once the simulations are completed (this might be 500 or 1,000 times) the results are averaged in order to arrive at an overall best estimate.

This approach is often used in the world of finance to help guide investment decisions. For example, my investment advisor relied on a Monte Carlo approach to provide me with an overall 10-year estimate as to the amount of return I would encounter given the current structure of my retirement assets. The Monte Carlo simulation predicted that I had a 95 percent probability of experiencing between x and y amount of gains after 10 years, given my current portfolio.

And yet even with these laws of probability, there is no guarantee that a specific event will correspond to its probability. For example, we are able to ascertain that the odds of drawing a particular sequence of cards out of a deck is 2 percent. We now draw the cards, and voila, it turns out that the sequence has been drawn. The odds were overwhelming that it should not have happened. And yet it did. The reason is that the element of chance is always in play. Or in the case of my investment portfolio, my returns may fall outside the 95 percent confidence interval. It is possible that I might see gains above or below what is given a 95 percent chance of occurring. The past may not always be a good predictor of the future. The reason? Our unpredictable companion called chance is never far from sight.

Serendipity in Scientific Discoveries

What do X-rays, penicillin, and Velcro all have in common? They each were discovered through what scientists refer to as serendipity. In their definitive history, Robert K. Merton and Elinor Barber traced the origin of the word back to a letter written by Horace Walpole to his friend Horace Mann on January 28, 1754. In that letter, Walpole describes a fairy tale called "the three Princes of Serendip." The princes were constantly making new discoveries as a result of chance and sagacity. Walpole himself had recently made such a discovery, and in his letter he coined the word "serendipity" to describe the process.[30]

Since Walpole's letter, the term serendipity has been used to describe new discoveries that are triggered by chance events. It turns out that any number of major discoveries have come about through the interaction of chance and perceptive observation. X-rays, penicillin, antibiotics, pulsars, radioactivity, microwaves, and many more have been the result of serendipity. A petri dish accidently left out over a weekend; an unexpected chemical reaction; a rounding error in a computer program—all of these and more can trigger serendipity. Such events may result in a researcher stepping outside their frame of reference and comfort zone to consider new possibilities and realities. In *The Serendipity Mindset*, Christian Busch writes, "Serendipity is about the ability to recognize and leverage the value in unexpected encounters and information."[31] As we saw earlier with social movements, a chance event can ignite a spark that triggers a new and important discovery.

For example, the understanding of DNA in 1953 came about through a combination of training, creativity, and hard work. But the fact that James Watson and Francis Crick were able to arrive at the structure of the double helix in DNA was also the result of serendipity. By chance, in their laboratory was a young American chemist, Jerry Donohue, who alerted them to a key mistake that was found in basically all chemistry textbooks regarding hydrogen bonds. Donohue was one of only a handful of people in the world who were aware of this mistake, and as luck would have it, his desk was in their office. Crick recalls "the unforeseen dividend of having the visiting Jerry Donohue, who next to Linus Pauling knew more about hydrogen bonds than anyone else in the world." This serendipitous event was critical in allowing Watson to finally piece together the double helix. In describing Watson's discovery, Crick writes,

> In a sense Jim's discovery was luck, but then most discoveries have an element of luck in them. The more important point is that Jim was looking for something significant and immediately recognized the significance of the correct pairs when he hit upon them by chance— "chance favors the prepared mind."[32]

Serendipity is an excellent example of how chance interacts with a larger force, in this case, scientific training. It is the two acting together that can create the magic of innovation and invention.[33] The noted physicist John Ziman puts it well in *Real Science: What It Is and What It Means*:

> The key point is that serendipity does not, of itself, produce discoveries: it produces opportunities for making discoveries. Accidental events have no scientific meaning in themselves: they only acquire significance when they catch the attention of someone capable of putting them into a scientific context. Even then, the perception of an anomaly is fruitless unless it can be made the subject of deliberate research. In other words, we are really talking about discoveries

made by the exploitation of serendipitous opportunities by persons already primed to appreciate their significance.[34]

In addition, as we saw with natural selection, chance allows for scientific discovery and innovation to progress in entirely different directions. Ziman goes on to write,

> But because serendipity is completely unpredictable in its incidence and outcome, it introduces a factor of blind variation in the production of knowledge. This factor is strongly favoured in evolutionary theories of scientific change. A serendipitous observation involves a wild leap outside the limits of what was until that moment supposed, and thereby enables science to advance into domains of understanding that were not previously imagined.[35]

Consequently, the element of chance can be extremely useful for breakthroughs in knowledge. Likewise, chance can be fortuitous in facilitating the adaptations of plants and animals to their environment, as discussed earlier. Finally, as we saw with random sampling, the random factor is an invaluable component that allows us to understand the social world around us.

4 Luck in Everyday Life

Enjoy yourself, drink, call the life you live today your own, but only that, the rest belongs to chance.

—EURIPIDES, 438 BC

It has been called one of the greatest games in baseball history. And as luck would have it, it took place in my hometown of St. Louis. It was Game 6 of the World Series, pitting the St. Louis Cardinals against the Texas Rangers on October 26, 2011. The Rangers were leading the series 3 games to 2, and with one more win would claim the World Series for the first time in their history.

The game seesawed back and forth throughout the early innings, but during the seventh inning the Rangers scored three runs to go ahead 7 to 4. The Cardinals scored a single run in the eighth, making it 7 to 5 as the game moved to the bottom of the ninth inning and the last chance for the Cards. With two outs, they had runners on second and third base when outfielder David Freese stepped up to the plate. The pitch count went to one ball and two strikes. The Rangers were now one strike away from the championship. Freese then hit the next pitch down the line into right field. Outfielder Nelson Cruz looked as if he would catch the fly ball and claim the World Series for the

Rangers. But instead it flew over his outstretched glove by no more than an inch or two, bouncing off the right field wall. Two runs scored, sending the game into extra innings.

Would lightning strike a second time? In the bottom of the tenth inning, the Cardinals were down again, this time by a run, 9 to 8, when Lance Berkman came to bat. Berkman worked the pitch count to two balls and two strikes. Again, the Rangers were one strike from the World Series title. Instead, Berkman hit a single to drive in the tying run.

Would lightning strike a third time? In the eleventh inning, who but David Freese returned to the plate. After getting the pitch count to three balls and two strikes, Freese connected on the next pitch, sending it over the center field wall for a walk-off home run and a re-markable come-from-behind win for the Cardinals. The Cards went on to take Game 7 and claim the World Series title for the eleventh time in their storied history. The Rangers were left with what if?

In this chapter we explore a few of the ways in which chance, luck, and randomness play themselves out in everyday life. These include sports, the stock market, games of chance, artistic creativity, the field of entertainment, getting into elite universities, and accidents and windfalls. It is my contention that in almost every facet of our daily life, chance is an active agent. It shows its face in ways that are unexpected and revealing. Let us consider a few.

The Sporting Life

Sports are often compared to life. The elements of skill, effort, and teamwork are emphasized by coaches at all levels as the ingredients for playing well and winning. Participating in sporting activities, particularly for children, is also felt to develop good character and preparation for adulthood.

Yet sport reflects life in another way—it is often "a game of inches." You have undoubtedly heard that expression before. It refers

TABLE 1. The Contribution of Luck in Five Professional Sports Leagues

League	Contribution of Luck
National Basketball Association	12%
Premier League	31%
Major League Baseball	34%
National Football League	38%
National Hockey League	53%

Source: Michael J. Mauboussin calculations, 2012

to the small distance that is sometimes found between winning and losing—between winning the World Series and coming up one strike short. As in life, outcomes in sports can and often are determined by pure luck and chance.

This is particularly the case when two evenly matched teams or individuals meet on the playing field. How many times have we seen a key hit in a baseball game land an inch or two in fair territory (or in foul ground) determining the outcome of the game. The same can be said for virtually any sport.

In this respect, sport does indeed imitate life.[1] The random factor is a constant companion in both. Yet exactly how much is luck responsible for winning and losing in sports? In an analysis using five years of data for the major professional sports, Michael Mauboussin was able to calculate, through a mathematical approach known as true score theory, the contribution of luck to a team's overall season.[2] This is a statistical technique that utilizes the variance in skill, luck, and outcome to determine the relative importance of each. The results are shown in Table 1.

First off, it is important to keep in mind that every player at this level is obviously highly skilled. Nevertheless, there will be differences in skill levels between teams, although they may be slight.

We can see that the sport where luck plays the smallest role is professional basketball, while the sport where luck exerts itself the most is hockey. In the National Basketball Association, it is estimated that the contribution of luck to a team's season record is 12 percent. However, in the National Hockey League, the role of luck is estimated to be 53 percent. The three other professional sports are clustered in the middle, those being soccer, baseball, and football, with about one third of their position in the standings due to luck.

How might we understand these differences? One key factor is the number of opportunities that a team has to score. The more times that a team can score, the less important the role of luck. In the NBA, an individual team may score a basket 40 or 50 times during a game, whereas in professional soccer or hockey there may be only one or two times that a team scores. Luck will play much more of a role when the chances to score are low.

One way of seeing this is with the flipping of a coin. If we flip a coin 10 times, we may very well wind up with seven or eight heads or tails, even though the overall probability on any individual coin toss is 50 percent. In the case of 10 tosses, there can be significant deviations from the overall probability due to luck or chance. However, if we flip a coin 100 times, we will probably find that close to half of those coin tosses will be heads and the other half tails. This illustrates the fact that as the number of events (in this case coin flips) increases, the more likely the final tally will reflect the underlying dynamic of a 50 percent probability.

A further illustration of this principle is the game of tennis. In a tennis match, there may be hundreds of points until the outcome is decided. Each game has at least four points played, which can often be extended to six, eight, or more. A player must then win six games to win the set. And that player must then win two out of three, or three out of five sets. The mathematician Ian Stewart calculated that if a player (because of their greater skill) has a 53 percent chance of winning any individual point, they will have an 85 percent chance of winning a three out of five set match. If their likelihood of winning any individual point is 60 percent, they are practically guaranteed to win the match. The conclusion is that a "slight advantage in skill gives you a tremendous advantage if you have enough chances to exercise that skill and to thereby nullify the effects of luck."[3]

Turning back to Table 1, the fact that hockey is the sport most influenced by the role of luck can also be explained by an additional factor. Consistent with our first principle, scoring in hockey is quite low. A typical game may be decided by a score of 3 to 2. However, in an NHL game, each team may very well have 45 or 50 attempted shots, which goes against the number of events explanation. Yet anyone who has watched a professional hockey game can quickly see the amount of randomness that is occurring on the ice. Shots are often randomly deflected from reaching the goal by players skating in the path of trajectory. Pucks can take strange bounces as they travel across the ice. In short, there is considerable randomness that occurs between the time the hockey stick hits the puck and where it eventually ends up. In addition, it is quite hard to score a goal in hockey. The net is small and the goalies are large, allowing for few shots to pass through their pads and sticks.

One final note. Because the role of luck is much more important in a sport such as baseball than in basketball, it becomes more difficult for a team to dominate the standings. In a major league baseball season, it is unusual for the best teams to win more than 60 percent of their games. On the other hand, in professional basketball, a highly skilled team might very well win 80 percent of their games.

Randomness and chance can also be found in many individual sports. Take Alpine skiing. The American skier Mikaela Shiffrin has had her share of ups and downs. A winner of Olympic gold in 2014 and 2018 and the skier with the all-time highest number of World Cup victories, she came up short in the Beijing Olympics of 2022, where she was expected to medal in four or five races. One of the most consistent skiers on the World Cup circuit, she nevertheless found herself exposed to the whims of chance. A *New York Times* story touched upon this:

> Yet for several years now, Shiffrin has been trying to explain that Alpine skiing, with its microscopic margins for error and its laundry list of uncertainties, is not that predictable. A shift as subtle as a gust of wind, or the movement of a cloud that allows sunlight to soften the snow in the middle of a race, can make the difference between a gold medal and 11th place.[4]

For those waiting a lifetime to participate in the Olympics, it can sometimes come down to the movement of a cloud or a gust of wind that is the difference between standing atop the medal ceremonies or going home empty handed.

Or take the case of Matt Rogers. Matt had been pursuing his dream of playing professional baseball in the big leagues when I interviewed him. And yet as any potential major league ballplayer will tell you, it takes not only skill, talent, and hard work, but often luck and chance to get to the highest level. For five years Matt had bounced around the Detroit Tigers minor league system, but did not have the success he had hoped for. This was partially due to several ill-timed injuries combined with a bat that seemed to go cold at just the wrong times. As Matt explains,

> You've got to be skilled to get where you are but you've got to have luck. If I would of gotten lucky and played well [during those times when his bat went cold], who knows, I could've gone to double A. I could've done a whole bunch of different things. I could be in the Big Leagues, playing at Smith Stadium right now. But you know, things didn't work out [sigh and pause]. Luck I would say gives you the opportunity but then your skills gotta take over to take advantage of the opportunity. You've got to have luck to get to the big leagues.

The Tigers eventually released him from the organization. He went on to sign minor league contracts with the Florida Marlins, San Diego Padres, and Pittsburgh Pirates, but was never able to make it all the way to the "Big Show."

The fact that Matt was making a career out of playing professional baseball was due to his skills, efforts, and talents. But the fact that he had not made it to up to any of the top major league ball clubs was at least partially due to chance and luck.

One unexplained and perplexing random event that occasionally strikes an athlete out of the blue is what is known as the "yips."[5] This can occur at all levels of a sport, but is particularly noticeable at the very highest levels. It often shows itself in pitching among baseball players, putting among golfers, field goal kicking among football players, and second serves among tennis players. The yips refers to an athlete who has successfully performed a particular task endless times, but suddenly loses their ability and control to do so. An athlete may be able to eventually get over such a loss of control, or they may never recover.

I witnessed firsthand one of the more well-known cases of the yips. It was game 2 of the 2000 National League Championship Series of the St. Louis Cardinals against the New York Mets. The starting pitcher was Rick Ankiel. Ankiel, only 20 at the time, was one of most promising young pitchers in the National League. In 1999 he was runner-up in the voting for National League Rookie of the Year. With a blazing fastball and wicked curveball, his pitching throughout the 2000 season placed him as one of the best in the league, and he was a major reason the Cardinals were in the playoffs that year.

In the first inning of the game, on the first pitch of the game, he threw the ball three or four feet over the head of Mets' hitter Eli Marrero. Of his 20 pitches in that inning, five were wild pitches. I can remember sitting in the stands wondering what on earth was happening. He simply had no control of throwing the ball, and this from a young pitcher who was at the top of his game. Ankiel never made it out the inning, and never recovered from his notorious case of the yips. To his great credit, he retrained himself to be an outfielder, and made it back to the big leagues and the Cardinals in 2007 by playing an entirely different position.

What this example illustrates is the interaction of a very random event with the psychological response to such an event. There is a dynamic that occurs between the random factor and the ability or inability to successfully process and overcome such events. In the case of Rick Ankiel and many others, the random occurrence of the yips made it extremely difficult, if not impossible, for them to control their motor skills in order to compete effectively in the game that they loved.

A Random Walk

Trying to determine when and where the stock market and individual stocks are heading in the short run has been the gold standard for many professional and amateur investors alike. If one can do so on a consistent basis, considerable money is to be had. Trying to outguess the market has been an active sport for decades if not centuries. Yet for those who enter this contest, the vast majority end up losing. The reason can be found in the random factor.

It turns out that the flipping of a coin or the throwing of darts to predict short-term movement of stocks often produces results on par with those of professional investors. Burton Malkiel is credited with popularizing the phrase "a random walk." As he writes, "A random walk is one in which future steps or directions cannot be predicted on the basis of past history. When the term is applied to the stock market, it means that short-run changes in stock prices are unpredictable."[6] The original analogy pertained to a "drunken man staggering around an empty field. He is not rational, but he's not predictable either."[7]

To illustrate this principle, a number of amusing examples can be found. During the 1990s, the *Wall Street Journal* ran a dartboard contest pitting the throwing of four darts against a professional stock investor each month. The four darts were thrown at financial pages hung on the wall in order to determine which stocks would be included in the portfolio, while the professional used their expertise to pick four stocks for their portfolio. Each month the darts were pitted against a new expert. After a decade of darts versus investors, no clear winner was declared.[8]

Even more impressive, a Russian circus monkey named Lusha was able to select an investment portfolio that "outperformed 94% of the country's investment funds." Lusha was presented with 30 blocks representing different companies, and was asked to pick eight of the blocks for investment. Her portfolio grew by nearly 300 percent over the course of a year.[9]

Such a performance is nothing new. In 1933 Alfred Cowles published a study analyzing a number of printed financial services and every purchase and sale made by 20 leading fire insurance companies over a four-year period. His conclusion was that the "best of a series of random forecasts made by drawing cards from an appropriate deck was just as good as the best of a series of actual forecasts, and that the results achieved by the insurance companies 'could have been achieved through a purely random selection of stocks.'"[10]

These examples illustrate in a light-hearted way that there is considerable randomness in how the stock market behaves on a short-term basis. Research has shown that investors are much better off with an indexed fund rather than an actively managed portfolio. And yet the belief in being able to predict short-term gains and losses persists. As Malkiel notes,

Human nature likes order; people find it hard to accept the notion of randomness. No matter what the laws of chance might tell us, we search for patterns among random events wherever they might occur—not only in the stock market but even in interpreting sporting phenomena.[11]

Yet one might object to this line of argument by pointing to a select number of investors who have beaten the market for six or seven straight years running and ask, "Isn't this evidence that some investors with superior skill can actually come out ahead?" Here again, the explanation is likely to be the random factor. Given the large numbers of professional investors, by simple chance some of them will have a lucky streak of doing well. Think back to our coin-flipping example. If we have 1,000 people flipping a coin 10 times, we are quite likely to find a few of these folks who have eight heads or tails in a row simply by chance. Similarly, it is quite possible, and in fact likely, that some professional investors will experience a hot or cold streak of six or seven years with respect to their choices. As Malkiel writes, "With large numbers of investment managers, chance will—and does— explain some extraordinary performances."[12]

For example, let us suppose that we are interested in whether an investor can pick on a weekly basis whether the stock market will go up or down at the end of the week. In this experiment, we designate five weeks of correct choosing as our measure of a savvy investor. Simply by pure chance, at least 1 in 32 individuals will probably be correct. This has nothing to do with skill or knowledge, but with the fact that each week there is a 50/50 chance of getting the prediction correct. Multiplying this across the course of five weeks gives us: $\frac{1}{2} * \frac{1}{2} * \frac{1}{2} * \frac{1}{2} * \frac{1}{2} = 1/32$. Consequently, regardless of skill, 1 in 32 individuals will likely have correct predictions for each of the five weeks.

Another way of seeing this is with a particular scam that has been used to hoodwink amateur investors into handing over their money.

It goes like this. I obtain a list of 1,024 potential investors and send them an email or text saying that I have developed a new foolproof way of predicting short-term changes in the stock market and in specific stocks. However, I realize that you are probably skeptical about such a claim. Therefore, in order to prove my ability to accurately forecast, each Monday morning for the next 10 weeks I will provide you with my prediction based on an exclusive algorithm as to whether a particular stock will be up or down at the closing bell on that Friday. On the first Monday, I send out emails to 512 individuals giving my prediction that the stock will be up for that week, while the other 512 individuals receive emails that the stock will be down. For the next week, I send out 512 emails to the group that had the correct prediction, and for 256 of those individuals my email says that the stock will be up, and for the other 256 I predict the stock will be down. I continue this process through to week nine, where I now have two individuals for whom I have been correct all nine weeks. One gets the prediction the stock will be up, the other that the stock will be down.

I then contact the person for whom my predictions have been correct all 10 weeks in a row. My email says that you can now clearly see that the algorithm is completely accurate, and that by having this advanced information, you will achieve an enormous windfall in the market. If you would like my stock prediction for this coming week, it will only cost you $5,000. Of course, this person does not know that it took 1,023 people to arrive at this point.

What is the moral of this story? The random walk theory suggests that investing in the stock market is best done through an index fund. Such a fund will mirror the overall patterns in the market. Because the long-term trajectory of the stock market has been upward, the investor whose portfolio is indexed to, say, the Standard and Poor's 500, should do fine over the long horizon. But for the investor who chooses to play the market, buyer beware![13]

Games of Chance

Perhaps the most obvious place to observe chance and luck in everyday life is within the games that we play. Some contain no luck at all, such as chess, checkers, and Go. These are games in which the players completely determine their moves on the board. Other games involve pure luck, such as roulette, the lottery, or slot machines. Here the only decision involved is choosing a number or color, or pulling a lever.

However, most games involve a combination of luck and skill. For instance, many board games involve the throwing of dice to determine the moves around the board. The skill comes in determining what to do with those placements. For example, in backgammon, the roll of the dice determines the options available in terms of moving one's pieces, but the choosing of which options to take involves judgment and skill. Similarly, card games are rooted in luck with respect to the cards that are drawn, whereas how one plays their hand takes skill and intuition. Or in Scrabble, the letters drawn are determined by chance, but the manner in which one utilizes those letters on the board is where the player demonstrates their skill.

Many of the expressions that we use in everyday life come from these games. "The luck of the draw," "the hand you're dealt," "the roll of the dice," and "the wheel of fortune" are all derived from games of chance. And perhaps it is no coincidence that many of these games combine the elements of luck with skill since they are often seen as reflections of the wider world.

No city in the country exemplifies the realm of luck more than Las Vegas, and no event dramatizes this more than the Main Event in the World Series of Poker. Held each year, thousands of players from around the world put down $10,000 for a chance to be crowned the best poker player on the globe along with a multi-million-dollar prize. Maria Konnikova was one such player. She writes about her experiences in *The Biggest Bluff*:

Poker stands at the fulcrum that balances two oppositional forces in our lives—chance and control. Anyone can get lucky—or unlucky—at a single hand, a single game, a single tournament. One turn and you're on top of the world—another, you are cast out, no matter your skill, training, preparation, aptitude. In the end, though, luck is a short-term friend or foe. Skill shines through over the longer time horizon.[14]

This reflects what we saw earlier in sports. The more opportunities that an individual or team has to score, the greater the role of skill in determining the outcome of the game.

But there is an additional component to poker that makes the game particularly interesting—the unknown factor of what your fellow players are holding in their hand. It is here that the art of bluffing comes into play. You obviously know the cards in your hand, but your opponents do not. Similarly, you are kept in the dark as to the cards that they are holding. This introduces an additional dynamic into the game—the art of deception. My betting may reflect that I have a winning hand, but do I? Perhaps I am trying to scare or bluff my opponents into folding their cards, allowing me to claim the chips in the pot.

In trying to gauge whether someone is bluffing or not, players often look for something called the "tell." This could be any number of physical signs or facial movements that the bluffer may not be aware of but can tip off the other players to the deception. In this way a poker player is looking to tilt the scales of chance in their favor.

During the last few decades, the rise of computer programs and artificial intelligence has challenged humans for game supremacy. Chess, checkers, and Go have all seen the best players lose to the latest computerized programs. But so too have the top players in games involving luck, such as backgammon, poker, and Scrabble. It would seem as if luck and chance can be mitigated over the long haul by a computer able to access the odds and potentialities of movements across a board or in a hand. Nevertheless, as Oliver Roeder writes,

> Games remain necessities of life today . . . They activate and satisfy psychological desires. Pleasure derives from immersing oneself in games' worlds, or in improving one's skills, or in benefitting from their systems of chance. The real world may from time to time offer us a chance to solve an elegant problem, and the satisfaction that comes with it, but games offer this chance constantly.[15]

The Exquisite Corpse

A very creative use of the random factor can be found across a number of artistic endeavors. One such example comes from the surrealists of the 1920s. Surrealism was built upon the technique of juxtaposing images or words that were normally not found together. These juxtapositions were thought to stimulate the unconscious mind, leading to new insights and understandings. Man Ray's photography or Salvador Dali's paintings of jarring and puzzling contrasts were typical.

For example, there is a famous 1928 image entitled *Mystery of the Street* taken by the photographer Otto Umbehr, better known as Umbo. He snapped the picture from a Berlin window to the street below and randomly captured a street scene. However, what gives the photo its subliminal power is that he has turned his overhead view of the street upside-down. The result of this inversion is a startling image of people with their elongated shadows taking on a life of their own. As Sandrine Hermand-Grisel writes, "The surrealists question the documentary value of photography. They perceive its capacity to capture the manifestations of the marvelous that can happen at random."[16]

Another specific random technique created by Andre Breton, one of the founders of the surrealist movement, came to be known as the exquisite corpse. The exercise was to gather a small group of friends together and divide the structure of a blank sentence into various parts such as nouns, verbs, adjectives, adverbs, and so on. Each part of the sentence would be assigned to one person. The first person would write down a word for their part of the sentence, fold the paper over, and hand it to the next person. The second person would then choose their word, not knowing what the first person had written down, and pass the developing sentence onto the next person. In this way the sentence would be written as it traveled around the room, without anyone knowing what the completed sentence looked like until the paper was unfolded.

According to legend, the first sentence constructed by Breton and his fellow surrealists was "The exquisite corpse shall drink the new wine." Hence, the technique became known as the exquisite corpse. Such randomizing of words results in sentences we normally could never imagine, which was one of the hallmarks of the surrealist movement.

The principle of the exquisite corpse has been applied to many other creative venues. Recently it has been utilized to create a pencil. The story goes as follows. One of the most iconic pencils of the twentieth century was the Blackwing 602 pencil manufactured by the Eberhard Faber Pencil Company. Its motto was "Half the Pressure, Twice the Speed." It was known for the quality of its graphite and the uniqueness of its rectangular removable eraser. The Blackwing had been a favorite of many writers and creative artists including John Steinbeck, Chuck Jones of Looney Tunes fame, and Leonard Bernstein. However, the digital age hit the pencil industry particularly hard and the Blackwing pencil was discontinued in the 1990s.

Fast forward to 2018. The Blackwing 602 was reintroduced in 2010 by the California Cedar Products Company under its Palomino division. In addition to the 602, beginning in 2015 Palomino began releasing limited editions of Blackwing pencils on a quarterly schedule. Each edition was inspired by "stories of people, places, and events that inspire a creative lifestyle." In March of 2018 they designed a pencil to commemorate the surrealists by using the exercise of the exquisite corpse to create the pencil.

How did they do it? They divided the parts of the pencil into five sections: graphite, barrel, imprint, ferule, and eraser. The first person of the design team choose the graphite. The second person, who was unaware of the first person's choice, selected the barrel, and so on. The result was a stunning pencil that would probably not have been created without randomization, and is certainly one of my personal favorites. The pencil has a rose barrel with teal imprint, silver ferule, blue eraser, and extra firm graphite. The pencil was given the number 54, in honor of 54 rue due Chateau in Paris, the birthplace of exquisite corpse.

Other fields of artistic creativity have also been inspired by the use of the random factor, including music, film, and graphic design. For example, the composer John Cage often used randomness and chance in his compositions. From 1951 onward, Cage consulted the *I Ching* to produce chance elements in his music. In his piece 4'33", the pianist sits silently at the piano for four and half minutes, as the listener experiences the random coughs and rustlings in the audience. In his *Imaginary Landscape* series, random elements produced by electricity are part of the performance; for instance, 12 radios are placed on stage tuned to different stations and played simultaneously. In each of these cases, randomness has been used to create art in a totally unpredictable and original way. In describing this process, Cage writes, "Chance, to be precise, is a leap, provides a leap out of reach of one's own grasp of oneself."[17]

The Big Break (or Not)

In early adulthood, my professional aspirations lay largely in music. I performed mostly original songs on my guitar in smaller clubs throughout the Midwest and Canada. During this time, I met and shared the bill with many talented musicians, including the legendary singer-songwriters Townes Van Zandt and Steve Goodman, and guitarist extraordinaire John Fahey. While one close acquaintance would go on to achieve stardom, the vast majority of my personal friends in this group would never break into the big time. Nevertheless, my sense was that many of these musicians were just as gifted and talented as those who had achieved much greater visibility.

The entertainment and artistic fields are well known for the role that luck and chance plays in providing artists with their "big break." As we will see in who gets into Harvard, there are many more talented individuals than there are slots available. Often what distinguishes those who have attained renowned status has as much to do with luck and chance as it does with talent.

Talk to just about any artist or entertainer who has achieved fame and fortune, and they will likely tell you some variation of the story about how luck had favored them early on in their career. Obviously talent and creativity are important in shaping careers, they will explain, but so too is the role of luck. For example, the actor Bryan Cranston, who became a household name by starring in the crime drama series *Breaking Bad,* talked about his career and the role of luck in an interview with *The Guardian.* Cranston explains, "Luck is a component that a lot of people in the arts sometimes fail to recognize: that you can have talent, perseverance, patience, but without luck you will not have a successful career."[18]

One individual I interviewed for my *Chasing the American Dream* book was extremely well known in the world of jazz. The founding member of the World Saxophone Quartet, Hamiet Bluiett was perhaps the most renowned baritone jazz saxophonist in the world. At the start of his career he had a talk with fellow St. Louis native and saxophonist Oliver Nelson, whose album *The Blues and the Abstract*

Truth is considered one of the most significant recordings in jazz. Nelson offered this advice,

> When I decided to go to New York I asked Oliver Nelson. I said, "Where do you think I should go?" He said, "Well, it depends on what you want to do." I said, "What do you mean?" He said, "Do you want to make a lot of money to play? All the clarinets, all the flutes, all the saxophones, all the double reed instruments should go to California." Then he said, "If you want to play, go to New York." Chicago wasn't even thought about. So I said okay. I wanted to play, so I went to New York. He was basically letting me know what I had to be involved with.

Hamiet moved to New York City in 1969. There he found work in the cutting-edge ensemble headed by Sam Rivers. Then as he recalls, he had a chance meeting on the subway with an influential musician:

> We were on the subway one day and I met this guy named Mario Rivera, who's dead now. One of the baddest baritone players I ever met. He said, "Can you read?" He knew I had a baritone. I said, "Yeah, I can read." He said, "Can you really read?" I said, "I can read Count Basie. Is that good enough for you?" He said, "Okay, good."

That led to his joining the Tito Puente band. And then he caught a huge break by being in the right place at the right time. The legendary bassist Charles Mingus happened to be looking for a baritone sax player to join his group. By a chance encounter, Bluiett came to his attention in 1972, and he wound up working with Mingus for over two years. That experience gave him the stature to start the avant-garde World Saxophone Quartet, which in turn cemented his reputation as one of the leading baritone sax players around.[19]

And of course, jazz itself is steeped in the random factor. One of its keystones is the ability to improvise. To take a theme, and then develop a one-off interpretation of that theme on a particular night, is the heart and soul of jazz. The World Saxophone Quartet epitomized this. Each performance was unique, both in terms of individual improvisation, and in terms of how each member of the group would respond to the other's improvisations. In this sense there is a random element introduced into each concert. Ralph Ellison described his style of writing in the *Invisible Man* in similar terms: "I would have to improvise upon my materials in the manner of a jazz musician putting a musical theme through a wild star-burst of metamorphosis."[20]

On the other hand, an extremely talented performer who never quite achieved that big break was an actor I interviewed named Tom Spencer. When I talked to Tom, he had just finished a local run in an Arthur Miller play. He had received the kind of reviews that an actor can only dream about. One critic raved about his performance, saying it epitomized that rare and thrilling melding of actor and role. As we gathered around a small table at a local Starbucks, we began chatting about his acting career.

Tom had committed his life to his profession. Yet the personal cost was high. He had experienced periods of depression and problems of anger management, strains in his relationships, and severe financial problems. He had devoted his life to his profession, honed his skills, perfected his craft, and yet had never had that "big break" that most performers hope for. He had certainly gotten close, appearing in movies and television, as well as acting on many prominent stages, but never quite broke into that front row seat of acting.

Spencer worked in and out of New York City for a number of years, but eventually returned to his hometown of St. Louis.

Here's what happened. In 1985, after having been in and out of New York for about 10 years, I came back here feeling very discouraged. I had a couple of near misses, film roles that didn't pan out. There was one that was going to be a World War I movie about Doughboys, and I tested for it, and I got the role. It was going to shoot in Georgia for three weeks and then go to France and shoot for five weeks, and I would've had a major supporting role. I wouldn't have been the main guy, but I would've been like the main guy's main buddy. It would have been a huge thing, and the whole thing fell through.

I came close to getting a couple of other roles and didn't quite get them. And life in New York wears you down. Anybody that has gone up there, just overall, I have a great admiration for anybody that has made a career in show business and has actually made a real living out of it. It takes an enormous amount of effort. Laurence Olivier, when they asked him what does it take to be an actor? He said, "The hide of a rhinoceros."

Two individuals. Both extremely talented. Both go to New York City to pursue their dreams. One catches a break, the other does not. One achieves the pinnacle within a career, the other comes up short.[21]

Mihaly Csikszentmihalyi has written extensively about creativity and the importance of what he refers to as "flow," or being able to totally immerse yourself in a task. But he also points out the role of luck in artistic success:

Luck is without a doubt an important ingredient in creative discoveries. A very successful artist, whose work sells well and hangs in the best museums and who can afford a large estate with horses and a swimming pool, once admitted ruefully that there could be at least a thousand artists as good as he is—yet they are unknown and their work is unappreciated. The one difference between him and the rest, he said, was that years back he met at a party a man with whom he had a few drinks. They hit it off and became friends. The man eventually became a successful art dealer who did his best to push his friend's work. One thing led to another: A rich collector began to buy the artist's work, critics started paying attention, a large museum added one of his works to its permanent collection. And once the artist became successful, the field discovered his creativity.[22]

Leonard Mlodinow, in *The Drunkard's Walk,* also gives many examples where luck and chance plays a similar role in the lives of the successful and the not so successful. Yet too often we fail to see the connection. Mlodinow writes:

> It is easy to make heroes out of the most successful and to glance with disdain at the least. But ability does not guarantee achievement, nor is achievement proportional to ability. And so it is important to always keep in mind the other term in the equation—the role of chance.[23]

Getting into Harvard

Just as achieving widespread recognition in the entertainment field can often be described as a lottery, so too is getting into Harvard University. In 2021 there were 57,435 students applying for admittance from around the United States and the world to be a part of Harvard's class of 2025. Many of these applicants had sterling credentials—a GPA at 4.00 or above; an array of advance placement courses; standardized test scores in the top 5 percent; a portfolio of volunteer and enrichment activities. Of the 57,435, 1,968 were admitted, for an overall acceptance rate of 3.4 percent.[24]

Certainly there are factors that can increase a student's chances of being admitted. Obviously having high scores and grades is a prerequisite. But one study analyzed Harvard admissions data from 2009 to 2014, and the authors found that for White students with a 10 percent chance of admission, if they were a legacy they would see a fivefold increase in their chance of admission; if a relative gave a donation to the university, they would experience a sevenfold increase; and if they were a recruited athlete, they were practically certain of admittance.[25] Consequently, a handful of nonrandom factors are very important in gaining admission to Harvard.

In addition, admissions officers will tell you that they are looking for students who are highly qualified academically and who will stand out and enrich the campus community. Furthermore, they are seeking young adults who will become leaders in their fields. And they are wanting to construct an incoming class that is diverse in terms of race and ethnicity, social class, geographical location, life experiences, and so on.

All of these are undoubtedly important factors that are considered when deciding who will be admitted into highly selective universities such as Harvard. But what they probably will not tell you is that the selection from among this group of applicants also is influenced by the random factor. To acknowledge this would be to admit that the process is not completely deliberate and systematic.

Consider the standard procedure for choosing who will be admitted into a highly selective university such as Harvard. We can think of this as a weeding-out process. The first cut will eliminate any applicants who do not meet the basic requirements that are felt necessary to succeed academically at the institution. These would include grade point average, standardized test scores, rigor of the classes taken in high school, and so on. Frequently a computer program known as an academic index will provide a weighting of these criteria in order to rank the applicants. Only those above a certain cutoff point will move to the next round.

At this stage other considerations come into play. They include the essay the student has written for their application, along with their extracurricular activities. In addition, larger university concerns are considered such as the earlier-mentioned desire of having a diverse incoming class or having students to fill a particular need (i.e., bassoon player for the orchestra or goalie on the soccer team).

Having served on graduate school admissions committees here at Washington University in St. Louis, I can attest to the fact that the element of subjectivity enters into the picture at this point. For example, when reading student essays detailing why they are interested in coming to our university, or describing an important life experience, it can be hard to distinguish among dozens of such essays. Certainly there may be some that are standouts or dropouts, but most fall within a gray area. Likewise, the judging of extracurricular activities can be quite subjective.

And it is here that the random factor is present. One way of seeing this is that a specific student may be accepted at one highly selective school but rejected at several others. One university may have been looking for something in particular that year which influenced the decision to accept the student, while another university was interested in something else.

But just as important, a final decision may have reflected the mood of the admissions officer on a particular day. The difference between two students may be virtually nonexistent. The selecting of one versus the other might as well have been decided by a coin flip. As Michael Kinsley writes about getting into Harvard, "The luck may be in your genes, in your parent's checkbooks, in their parenting skills, or in the dubious meatloaf the dean of admissions had for dinner the night before your application was considered."[26] While a highly qualified student applying to a dozen very selective universities will in all likelihood be accepted into at least one or two, the specific university that they are admitted to may be the result of luck.

Harvard political philosophy professor Michael Sandel and others have proposed introducing a lottery system to the admissions process at highly selective universities as a straightforward way of simply recognizing randomness for what it is. Such an approach would first remove from the applicant pool those who do not have the basic qualifications to succeed during their four years. This might reduce the numbers by 20 percent, leaving perhaps 40,000 applicants. At this point,

> Rather than engage in the exceedingly difficult and uncertain task of trying to predict who among them are the most surpassingly meritorious, choose the entering class by lottery. In other words, toss the folders of the qualified applicants down the stairs, pick up 2,000 of them, and leave it at that . . . This is sensible, first of all, on practical grounds. Even the wisest admissions officers cannot assess, with exquisite precision, which eighteen-year-olds will wind up making the most truly outstanding contributions, academic or otherwise. Although we valorize talent, it is, in the context of college admissions, a vague and watery concept.[27]

Whether such a procedure will ever be adopted is probably a long shot. But as Sandel points out, "Setting a threshold of qualification and letting chance decide the rest would restore some sanity to the high school years, and relieve, at least to some extent, the soul-killing, resume-stuffing, perfections-seeking experience they have become."[28]

Sandel's suggestion is reminiscent of a story often told about the investment banking company Goldman Sachs. Those applying for first-year analyst positions at Goldman are obviously a very competitive and credentialed group, with many more qualified than positions available. One year, a managing director who was overseeing recruiting randomly divided the stack of resumes into two piles on his desk. He thought for a moment, and then threw one stack into the wastebasket. A colleague standing next to him looked surprised. The managing director replied, "You have to be lucky in this business." Pointing to the resumes still on his desk, he said, "We might as well pick from the lucky ones."[29]

Accidents and Windfalls

It could have been a sheet of invisible ice, a partially covered banana peel, or a crack in the sidewalk. Hundreds of people had walked over or around or through it without incident, but his shoe touched it in just the wrong way. His right leg slid forward, his arms flailed, his body arched back, and he crashed to the ground. The sound of his skull cracking was heard for half a block, even on the busy New York City street.

He was dead because of bad luck.

Had he not slipped, he would have arrived at the Thirty-Fourth Street train station at 4:59 p.m. and shortly thereafter detonated the homemade bomb he was carrying in his briefcase. Everyone who forced their way onto the crowded cars of the northbound number 3 train eleven minutes later was extraordinarily lucky. They were lucky because their would-be assassin had been unlucky. They would never learn that they were alive because he had died. They would go about their affairs unaware that his bad luck had bequeathed them the luckiest day of their lives.[30]

So begins Martin Sherwin's *Gambling with Armageddon.* Accidents are one of the most common and dramatic ways in which luck and chance shows its hand. And yet as this example vividly demonstrates, we are often unaware of its role behind the scenes.

Luck played a dramatic role in my life years ago. I was driving home from work in my 20-year-old Toyota Corolla. It had been a typical day and the route home was one I had taken hundreds of times in the past. As I drove down a familiar side street, I approached the stoplight where I would make my usual left turn. I rolled up to the intersection and waited behind the two cars ahead of me. After a minute, the traffic light changed from red to green. The first car went through the intersection followed by the second car. At this point the light had been green for at least six or seven seconds. Normally I would have simply followed the cars in front of me, but for some reason, I quickly glanced over to the left. That turn of the head may have saved my life.

Approaching at high speed was a full-size pickup truck. I slammed on my brakes just as the truck came barreling through the intersection. As I looked at the driver, he seemed completely oblivious to anything out of the ordinary. I can remember him staring straight ahead with no idea of what he had done. I had literally been saved by an inclination to glance over to my left. Had I not, my aging automobile would have certainly been crushed on the driver's side, along with myself. I had found myself in the wrong place at the wrong time, but escaped disaster by a chance inclination and a split second. A pure twist of fate.

This is but one of countless examples of luck that each of us can probably recall in our lives. The expression "That was a close call" is one that is quite familiar. Accidents or near accidents are often a part of life. The hope is that they are not too serious if they occur.

In *The Black Swan,* Nassin Nicholas Taleb writes that his focus "concerns our blindness with respect to randomness, particularly the large deviations."[31] Those large deviations are what he terms "black swans." These are events and accidents that come completely out of the blue and cannot be imagined. Much of his analysis is derived from the world of high finance. As we saw earlier, the stock market is ruled by considerable short-term randomness. But it is also affected by large and infrequent shocks as well. The crash in 1987 and the Great Recession of 2008 come to mind. These "black swans" were off the radar screen for just about everyone.

Yet sometimes black swans can bring great fortune. The flip sides of accidents are windfalls. These are cases of good luck that also appear out of the blue. Of course the biggest personal windfall of all is you and I being here in the first place. As Taleb writes,

We are quick to forget that just being alive is an extraordinary piece of good luck, a remote event, a chance occurrence of monstrous proportions. Imagine a speck of dust next to a planet a billion times the size of the earth. The speck of dust represents the odds in favor of your being born; the huge planet would be the odds against it. So stop sweating the small stuff. Don't be like the ingrate who got a castle as a present and worried about the mildew in the bathroom. Stop looking the gift horse in the mouth—remember that you are a Black Swan.[32]

We will pick up on the lottery of birth in the next chapter, but suffice it to say that chance can bring very good fortune. As Taleb points out, the fact that you and I exist at all is a stroke of luck beyond belief. It is difficult to step outside oneself, but try to look at your existence from the perspective that Taleb provides. First off, your two parents had to find each other out of millions of people. The same is true for your grandparents on your mother's and father's side, great grandparents, and so on. The odds of you and I being here right now in this place and time are astronomical, and yet here we are. Or as the French mathematician Blaise Pascal put it 400 years ago,

> You find yourself in this world only through an infinity of accidents. Your birth is due to a marriage, or rather a series of marriages of those who have gone before you. But these marriages were often the result of a chance meeting, or words uttered at random, or a hundred unforeseen and unintended occurrences.[33]

Perhaps no greater proof of the random factor is needed.

Summing Up

In these last three chapters we have looked at how randomness profoundly shapes the world around us. Whether the focus is upon the direction of history, the natural environment, or everyday life, chance and luck are sure to be an important part of the story.

As I have argued throughout, there is an intricate dance that occurs between social and natural forces on the one hand and randomness on the other. The broader forces push the world in general directions, but randomness can influence the particulars of those directions. It is a dynamic tango as these partners make their way across the dance floor. Recognizing this dynamic provides a clearer understanding of the world around us.

Oftentimes we simply do not see this dynamic because we have but one history to reflect on. This results in a singular interpretation of how events took place. But as we have seen, the random factor opens up the possibilities to many different scenarios. History, the natural world, and everyday life can unfold in a multitude of ways depending on the outcomes of chance and luck.

Just as the random factor helps shape the world around us, so too does it influence the direction our individual lives will take. In the next three chapters we explore some of the ways in which our unpredictable companion walks beside us as we make our way along life's journey.

II   *The Patterns of Our Lives*

5   *The Lottery of Birth*

The birth lottery is the happenchance. It's the randomness of our starting point. It's the randomness of the traits and circumstances that we're born into, that we have absolutely no control over, that determine the opportunities and challenges that we're going to face in life.

—YASMINE MUSTAFA, 2015

In the next three chapters we consider some of the ways in which the random factor exerts itself in helping to shape the direction and course of our lives. We begin by examining the greatest lottery of all; that is, the lottery of birth. Much of who we are is entirely beyond our control and dependent upon chance. We have no say in our genetic composition, while the manner in which our genes exert themselves can be at least partially thought of in a probabilistic rather than deterministic fashion. Likewise, the environment in which we are raised is the luck of the draw. Finally, the size and timing of our birth cohort can impact upon our success, and once again, this effect is governed by chance.

Next, we explore in chapter 6 some of the ways in which the random factor influences the specific events in our lives. These include who we form relationships with, the career and jobs we enter into, where we live, and in extreme cases, the difference between life and death.

Finally, in chapter 7 we turn to understanding some of the dynamics and patterns in which chance plays itself out over our lifetimes. These include the topics of timing, cumulative advantage, and the interaction of the random factor with the powerful currents of class and race. Understanding these dynamics provides a fuller accounting of the forces that shape our lives.

As we concluded in the last chapter, the fact that we are here at all is a stroke of unfathomable good fortune. The odds against you or I existing right now are enormous. And yet, here we are. Our birth is totally the result of chance and luck.

Furthermore, we do not choose the family we are born into or the community that we are raised in. Nor do we decide the quality of the K-12 schools we attend, the native language we speak, or the peers and adults who we will live and learn among. We also have little say in the culture and structural arrangements which determine the rewards and punishments that will be associated with particular social positions in our society. As Raoul Martinez explains, all of this results not from our personal choices, but instead comes down to the lottery of our birth:

> We do not choose to exist. We do not choose the environment we will grow up in. We do not choose to be born Hindu, Christian or Muslim, into a war-zone or peaceful middle-class suburb, into starvation or luxury. We do not choose our parents, nor whether they'll be happy or miserable, knowledgeable or ignorant, healthy or sickly, attentive or neglectful. The knowledge we possess, the beliefs we hold, the tastes we develop, the traditions we adopt, the opportunities we enjoy, the work we do—the very lives we lead . . . This is the lottery of birth.[1]

Consequently, when we consider the role of luck in shaping our lives, it behooves us to fully appreciate just how much chance is involved from the very beginning.

Nature, Nurture, or Chance?

A perennial debate going back centuries has revolved around the extent to which who we are and who we become is the result of nature versus nurture. In other words, to what extent do we owe our makeup to our genes, and to what extent to our environment? Most evolutionary biologists today consider that on the individual level, our traits should be seen as arising from the interaction of genes with environment, and that it is extremely difficult to partition a certain percentage of an individual trait to nature and a certain percentage to nurture.[2] Researchers point out that in some areas nature may be more important than nurture, and in other areas the reverse may be the case.

Yet I would argue it is the random factor that can often trump both nature and nurture. Randomness influences the very way that both nature and nurture exert themselves upon our life outcomes and it exerts an independent effect as well.

Nature and Chance

Let us consider nature. Obviously the genes we inherit come from our mother and father. In one respect there is nothing at all random about that. It is simply a fact of nature. However, the coming together of our parents, as we discussed in the last chapter, is highly dependent upon chance. Furthermore, our inheritance of specific genes from our father or mother is due to chance. Offspring randomly inherit one of the two alleles (the discrete version of the same gene) from each parent. Thus, at the molecular level, randomness is at play. Research has also shown that random molecular events happen in both brain and physical development both before and after we are born. The way in which our genes play themselves out as we grow is also subject to considerable randomness. As psychologist Steven Pinker puts it:

Epidemiologists, frustrated by their inability to explain the pack-a-day nonagenarian and the young athlete who keels over from a heart attack (even after taking their genes into account) are starting to acknowledge the enormous influence of Lady Luck in the working of our bodies. That must apply in even greater measure to the working of our brains.[3]

Many scientists have recently argued that our genes work in probabilistic ways, not simply determinist ways. As a result, randomness injects itself into both our physical and mental development and outcomes. Pinker notes,

> The unexplained variance in personality throws a spotlight on the role of sheer chance in development: random difference in prenatal blood supply and exposure to toxins, pathogens, hormones, and antibodies; random differences in the growth or adhesion of axons in the developing brain; random events in experience; random differences in how a stochastically functioning brain reacts to the same events in experience.[4]

One way to appreciate the role that chance plays in biological outcomes is through a wide range of research studies that have looked at life span variation in genetically identical organisms that have been reared in similar environments. As a result, both nature and nurture are being held nearly constant in these experiments.[5] Consequently, if they were the entire story in terms of life span, we should expect little variation in life expectancy. Yet it turns out that life expectancy can vary by as much as threefold within such populations. The reason has to do with chance events that are occurring at the biological and molecular level. For example, epidemiologist George Smith writes:

> In genetically identical marbled crayfish raised in highly controlled environments considerable phenotypic differences emerge. These

and numerous other examples from over nearly a century demon-strate the substantial contribution of what appear to be chance or stochastic events . . . on a wide range of outcomes.[6]

Another way of appreciating the role of chance in affecting biol-ogy is why some individuals are struck by disease while others are not. Certainly there are conditions that can predispose us to being at a higher or lower risk of contracting a disease. These would include both biological and environmental factors. But the element of chance is also very much in play. As Smith writes, "Several lines of evidence suggest that largely chance events, from the biographical down to the sub-cellular, contribute an important stochastic element to disease risk that is not epidemiologically tractable at the individual level."[7]

Take the case of cancer. Why do some individuals develop cancer while others do not? Much of the answer may lie with the random fac-tor. Cancer often depends on what are known as somatic mutations, or mutations that cause a change in an individual's DNA. Your DNA can be thought of as containing the information that allows your cells to be able to perform properly. Our DNA is bombarded constantly with stressors from the environment. These include radiation, expo-sure to chemicals, and so on. The result is that DNA damage can oc-cur. If this damage occurs in the coding regions of our DNA, it be-comes more serious. Normally this damage is carefully repaired, but once in a great while it is not. Such a mutation can create a situation where the cells are no longer able to function correctly. This can lead to unregulated cell growth that in turn can lead to cancer.[8] Environ-mental factors influence the likelihood of somatic mutations, but there is also a clear random element to these events. Medical re-searcher Richard Doll, who was writing on the fiftieth anniversary of his classic article on the multistage theory of carcinogenesis, observed:

Whether an exposed subject does or does not develop a cancer is largely a matter of luck; bad luck if the several necessary changes all occur in the same stem cell when there are several thousand such cells at risk, good luck if they don't. Personally I find that makes good sense, but many people apparently do not.[9]

Other diseases and medical conditions are also strongly impacted by the random factor operating on the biological and cellular levels. Whether it be a blood clot breaking loose or being exposed and coming down with Covid-19, the element of luck is very much in play. Consequently, although nature is certainly important in affecting life outcomes, the way in which it exerts itself is often mediated by the random factor.

Nurture and Chance

If we turn to nurture, here too we see the hand of chance playing her cards. As the earlier quote from Martinez indicates, the environment in which we are raised is simply the luck of the draw. We do not choose our parents or the neighborhood we grow up in. Nor do we typically choose the schools we attend or the teachers who instruct us.

This aspect of our lives is filled with streams of randomness. Think back to your childhood and the environment in which you were raised and you will undoubtedly be able to recall a number of events and occurrences in which the random factor may have played a role. Consider elementary school. In fifth grade you were in all likelihood randomly assigned to a particular teacher rather than the other two or three who might have been teaching that grade. Your fifth-grade teacher may have had a specific interest that in turn had a profound effect upon igniting in you a particular passion which in turn influenced the direction your life took. Or perhaps that teacher turned you away from a subject matter as a result of poor teaching.

Perhaps in that fifth grade you happened to meet a new friend who was instrumental in piquing your interest in music or art. Perhaps across the street from the house you grew up in was a basketball court where you and the neighborhood kids would gather nearly daily for a round of shooting hoops. Perhaps as a result you became quite good at the game that then led to making the high school team and a college athletic scholarship. Or perhaps you suffered a freak injury on that court that changed your life completely.

There are literally thousands of happenstance events which occur during childhood that can have an effect upon life outcomes. The environment itself is clearly important in helping to shape our life outcomes. But the random factor is constantly at play in terms of how that environment impacts upon us. As we will discuss later, we can think of the environment as representing a current or stream that tends to push us in particular directions. But within that current are the ripples of randomness affecting the specifics of where we might be headed.

Take the situation of a child growing up in an affluent neighborhood versus a child growing up in a poverty-stricken neighborhood. These two environments will each exert an effect upon each child's future outcomes. The child in an affluent neighborhood will be exposed to more resources and fewer anxieties than the child in a poverty-stricken neighborhood. But the random factor will play out differently as well. The types of random events that each child experiences, and the probability of those events occurring, may very well differ. The child in an affluent neighborhood will likely have more experiences of being in the right place at the right time, while the child in a poor neighborhood may have more encounters of being in the wrong place at the wrong time. In this way nurture interacts with the random factor in order to produce potentially different life outcomes.

We have seen in the last few pages some of the ways in which the random factor exerts itself through both nature and nurture. Epidemiologist George Martin, in reviewing the research on health span and life span, concludes that among nature, nurture, and chance, chance has the most important influence on health and long life. Martin writes that "the most important variables underlying the striking differences in human patterns of aging involve stochastic events, particularly age-related drifts in gene expression."[10]

Similarly, in a review of psychological research, Stephen Rice and colleagues conclude that human behavior is affected not only by nature and nurture but also by randomness:

> Given that there is substantial randomness in human behavior, why should we care? One reason for caring is that the fact is interesting in its own right, particularly as it contradicts the common intuition that all human behavior is determined by systematic factors. A second reason harks back to the issue of nature versus nurture. The evidence from the review suggests that the issue needs to be reframed: It is not about nature plus nurture, but rather about nature plus nurture plus randomness.[11]

The nature versus nurture debate therefore needs to be revised in order to accommodate the third key element in the equation—chance. The random factor exerts itself in both of these domains. The result is that from our very beginnings we are partially beholden to the unpredictable spinning of the mythical wheel of fortune.

What's in a Name?

On the day we are born, one of the first decisions made by our parents is the name that they place on our birth certificate. Our last name has already been determined—either our father's last name, our mother's, or a hybrid of the two. On the other hand, our first and middle names are left up to the discretion of our parents. Could the name we are given actually have an effect on certain outcomes?

The answer is yes. Research has shown that the spelling of your first and last names can have an influence upon particular outcomes. Perhaps what immediately comes to mind would be having the last name of a well-known person and being related to that person. But researchers have found something much more subtle.

The first letter of your last name has been demonstrated in certain cases to lead to a positive or negative advantage. Specifically whether you are near the front or back of an alphabetical listing of names can be important. Two examples illustrate. In a study conducted in the Czech Republic, Stepan Jarajda and Daniel Munich looked at the odds of being accepted into the university system depending on where your last name fell in the alphabet.[12] The admissions process in the Czech Republic is highly competitive, with only 29 percent of applicants accepted. What the researchers found was that many universities went through their applications in alphabetical order. For those students who were clearly most or least qualified, the authors found no effect of name placement. However, they hypothesized that "marginal cases at the top of such a list may obtain a more favorable treatment compared to marginal applicants toward the bottom of the list where constraints on total number of possible admissions become more binding."[13] In other words, if you happen to land at the top of the list, and your qualifications place you somewhere in the middle of the pack, you are more likely to be accepted into the university than your counterpart whose name falls at the end of the alphabet. The reason is that there are more potential openings available at the start of the process, and therefore more leeway to admit students compared to when the admissions team has arrived at the bottom of the list.

The researchers found just such an effect. They estimated that for those with marginal applications, moving from A to Z reduced the admission chances by 3 percent. This was actually a fairly large effect. For example, increasing an applicant's mathematical test score by one standard deviation raised their chances of admission by 1 percent.

A second example comes from the field of economics. Specifically, the tradition of listing authors' names on academic papers in alphabetical order. Approximately 85 percent of all multi-authored peer reviewed journal articles by economists list the authors' names in alphabetical order.[14] Consequently, an economist with a last name starting with a B will always be listed before an author with a last name starting with a K. This is in contrast to the vast majority of other disciplines where the name ordering of multiple-authored papers will be determined by the contributions that each of the authors has made to the paper—if Professor K did most of the work on the paper, they will be listed ahead of Professor B. Not so in economics. No matter the contributions of the authors, they are listed alphabetically.

As a result, those who are lucky enough to have a last name at the beginning of the alphabet will be listed first on all multi-authored articles. This could result in a professional advantage in at least two ways. First, for those unfamiliar with the economic norms, many might assume that the first author has made the greatest contribution to the paper. As a result, greater prestige will be given to that author. And second, when there are three or more authors, citation metrics often just list the first author's name followed by an "et al." As a result, first authors receive more name recognition.

But could this placement actually result in greater academic rewards for authors at the beginning of the alphabet? In the article "The Benefits of Being Economics Professor A (Rather than Z)," economists Mirjam Van Praag and Bernard Van Praag found that the answer is yes. They report a significant effect of the alphabetical rank of an economist's last name on scientific production: "Scientific productivity grows faster for A-authors than for Z-authors, because

A-authors have been more visible on previous publications and have therefore built more of a reputation, which in turn increases productivity."[15] They conclude: "Being an A-author, and hence often the first author, is beneficial for someone's reputation and academic performance."[16] In further support of the importance of name placement, Liran Einav and Leeat Yariv found that economics faculty with earlier surname initials were more likely to receive tenure at top departments of economics in the United States, more likely to become fellows in the Econometric Society, and more likely to receive the Clark Medal and the Nobel Prize.[17]

A third example illustrating the importance of name spelling has to do with the ability to pronounce one's name. Psychologists Simon Laham, Peter Koval, and Adam Alter conducted a series of experiments in which they demonstrated that individuals with easy-to-pronounce names were evaluated more positively than those with more difficult-to-pronounce names. This effect was "independent of name length, unusualness, typicality, foreignness, and orthographic regularity."[18] The authors argue that the reason for this effect is that easy or difficult-sounding names contribute to what psychologists refer to as processing fluency, or the experience of ease or difficulty associated with a cognitive process such as name pronunciation. If we have difficulty pronouncing someone's name, that difficulty then subtly exerts a negative influence upon our overall opinion of that person. The authors also point out that in educational settings, students with names that are hard to pronounce may be called on less often by their teachers, resulting in lowered feelings of affirmation and support, which in turn can reduce that student's ability to learn.

Finally, there have been several studies looking at the effect of having a "White-sounding" first name versus a "Black-sounding" first name. One of the best known of the recent analyses was conducted by two economists, Marianne Bertrand and Sendhil Mullainathan.[19] The researchers sent out similar resumes to various job ads in Chicago and Boston. The one difference was that some of the resumes had "White-sounding" names such as Emily or Greg, while the others had "Black-sounding names" such as Lakisha or Jamal. Even though the resumes were virtually identical, the White-sounding-name resumes were 50 percent more likely to be contacted by the employer than the Black-sounding-name resumes. This racial name effect has been found to occur in many other areas as well.[20]

Each of these studies indicates that the name we are given can have an effect upon life outcomes. The name that is ours is very much the luck of the draw. With the exception of those in the entertainment field, very few people will change their name to one that they like better. And yet as with so many other aspects of life, it turns out that the randomness involved in the spelling of our name can and does exert an influence upon our lives.

The Randomness of Birth Cohorts

A third way of thinking about the lottery of birth is to consider the timing of when we were born. This can and does exert a profound impact upon our success in life, yet it is one that we rarely think about. It is also one in which the random factor is very much in play. Our parents may have wanted to conceive a child during a specific period of time, but the exact month and day we were born is left up to chance. And yet, although the point in the year we enter this life is the luck of the draw, it nevertheless can exert an early impact upon life outcomes.

The Month We Are Born In

The idea that the exact date and time of one's birth being important goes back centuries. The field of astrology is rooted in the belief that the positioning of the sun, moon, stars, and planets at the time of birth is critical in understanding our personality and future. In Western astrology, the year is divided into the 12 astrological signs that align with the 12 months of the year. The sign we are born under is thought to provide insights into who we are and where we might be heading. Obviously these ideas have no scientific basis for support and yet many still consult their daily horoscope before going about the day.

It turns out that the month we are born in is indeed important, but not because of the Zodiac. Rather, it has to do with whether we are early or late with respect to the groupings that we find ourselves in during childhood. Two examples illustrate this. The first deals with sports, specifically hockey.

Recall that in the last chapter we explored the role of luck with respect to various professional sports. Of the five major sports, hockey is the one with the most luck involved in terms of team outcomes. Yet luck plays itself out in hockey in quite another way as well.

Malcolm Gladwell draws attention to a puzzling pattern. Within the elite levels of Canadian hockey, "40 percent of the players will have been born between January and March, 30 percent between April and June, 20 percent between July and September, and 10 percent between October and December."[21] This is true from the junior levels all the way up to the National Hockey League. Why should this be?

The reason has to do with the way in which young hockey players in Canada are divided by age. The eligibility cutoff for age-class hockey is January 1. The result is that a boy whose birthday is January 2 could be competing against his counterpart born 12 months later on December 31. The difference of up to a year during the early stages of playing hockey can be significant. By the ages of 9 or 10, coaches are looking to put together all-star or "rep" teams. Players with a few extra months of maturity are more likely to be chosen for these teams since they might be slightly bigger, faster, and more skilled. Once on such a squad, they receive better quality coaching and more ice time resulting in greater practice time (in Canadian hockey, finding playing time on a rink is at a premium). By the time these players reach the age of 13 or 14, the better coaching and greater practice time results in better-skilled players, with greater chances of making it into the Major Junior A league or playing on the collegiate level, and then perhaps in the National Hockey League.

This example illustrates the process of cumulative advantage that we will explore in the next chapter. The initial advantage of being a few months older than one's teammates then leads to further advantages, which in turn leads to even further advantages. But the process is jump-started by the random factor. The month of one's birth is simply up to chance, and yet it represents a highly important factor in predicting the likelihood of becoming an elite hockey player.[22]

A second example may be even more impactful. It has to do with where a child's birth date falls within a particular school year. School districts around the country establish cutoff points for children's eligibility into a particular grade. Oftentimes this will be around the middle to end of August. Children going into kindergarten who were born in September will be nearly a full year older than children whose birthdays are in July. Gladwell notes,

> But most parents, one suspects, think that whatever disadvantage a younger child faces in kindergarten eventually goes away. But it doesn't. It's just like hockey. The small initial advantage that the child born in the early part of the year has over the child born at the end of year persists.[23]

Although the research on age and academic achievement is somewhat mixed, it does tend to indicate that children who are older when they enter kindergarten tend to do somewhat better than their counterparts who are younger. It may be the case that teachers are at times confusing maturity with ability. Like our hockey example, older children with a bit more maturity may be getting extra attention and praise from their teachers.

Economists have also looked at the question of season of birth and later outcomes. Again, although the evidence is somewhat mixed, several research studies have found that those born later in the school year tend to do worse.[24] In reviewing this literature, Kasey Buckles and Daniel Hungerman write, "Economists have long recognized that the month of a child's birth is associated with outcomes such as test performance, wage, and educational attainment. These studies overwhelmingly show that children born in the winter months (or in the first quarter of the year) have relatively low educational attainment, wages, and intellectual ability."[25]

An even more dramatic example of timing pertains to the exact date of birth. During the height of the Vietnam War, on December 1, 1969, the Selective Service Committee instituted a draft lottery for men born between the years of 1944 and 1950. At the time of the lottery these men would have been between the ages of 18 and 26. The rationale behind the lottery was to address some of the inequities in terms of who had been called up to serve, as well as to increase the number of soldiers available for the war.

The way the lottery was conducted was that each of the 365 days of the year were printed on slips of paper. These slips of paper were then inserted into blue plastic capsules. They were mixed in a large box and then poured into a spacious glass jar. New York representative Alexander Pirnie drew the first capsule from the jar, which was September 14, and therefore those with this birth date were assigned lottery number 1. The event was held at the Selective Service National Headquarters in Washington, DC, and was televised nationally. The first 195 birthdays chosen were later drafted in the order that they had been drawn.

In addition, a second lottery was also held on December 1 for the 26 letters of the alphabet. This then determined the order in which those with the same birthdays would be called up. Last, first, and middle initials of one's name were assigned a rank order based upon this drawing.

The draft lottery in many cases resulted in the difference between life and death. Those who were unlucky to have had their birthdays drawn early were often sent to Vietnam, with some never to return, while those with high-number birthdays were exempt. This is an extremely stark example of randomness completely determining one's fate, and possibly one's life.[26]

The lotteries continued through 1975, although no one was drafted after the 1971 lottery. I was in the 1975 lottery, and my birthday was the sixteenth drawn for that year. Had the war not been winding down, I might very well have found myself either fighting on a foreign shore or put in the position of resisting the draft. From 1972 to 1975, men with the first 215 numbers drawn were asked to report for an armed forces physical examination.

Size Does Matter (Smaller Is Better)

A second manner in which the randomness of one's birth cohort exerts an effect on life outcomes relates to size. Specifically, there is an advantage to being in a smaller birth cohort and a disadvantage to being a member of a larger cohort. We can see this effect in at least two areas—the job market and the marriage market.

With respect to the job market, being in a larger birth cohort means that you are likely facing greater competition in terms of securing a job—there are more individuals your age who are graduating from high school or college and beginning their careers. The result is greater numbers of people competing for entry-level jobs, making it more difficult to secure such a job.

The opposite is true for smaller birth cohorts. Because of fewer numbers, individuals looking for entry-level jobs face less competition and therefore will find themselves in greater demand. They will also find themselves with less competition when it comes to landing highly desirable jobs.

The marriage market is a second area in which cohort size can make a difference. Research has indicated that in the United States as well as most other countries, men tend to be several years older than women at age of first marriage.[27] In the United States there is a preference among men to marry women who are one to three years younger than them, and for women to prefer marrying men who are one to three years older than them. The result of these preferences is that there can be an imbalance in the sex ratio of the numbers of men and women in the marriage market. This results when birth rates are increasing or decreasing over time.

For example, the height of the baby boom was the year 1957. From 1947 to 1957, birth rates steadily increased, and from 1958 to 1964 they steadily decreased. The result was that for women born in 1957 who were looking to marry someone two years older (the 1955 birth cohort) there were fewer men than women, putting women with birth dates of 1957 at a disadvantage compared to men with a birth date of 1955.

The opposite was the case for women born in 1959. For this cohort, there were more men born in 1957 than women born in 1959, putting men with birth dates of 1957 at a disadvantage in the marriage market.

In both of these cases—the job market and the marriage market—individuals may experience advantages or disadvantages simply as a result of the actual size of their birth cohort. As with the month in which we are born, this is a completely random event over which we have no control.

Timing Can Be Crucial

A third manner in which the randomness of birth cohorts plays itself out is through the element of timing. Specifically, the lucky (or unlucky) combination of a birth cohort entering early adulthood during a particular historical moment, resulting in a particular fortuitous or not fortuitous outcome. As the sociologists Roland Neil and Robert Sampson write,

> What if individuals born into the same socioeconomic conditions or who experience similar childhoods nonetheless face significantly different social worlds growing up or entering early adulthood? What if two groups of individuals, whose only early life difference is the year in which they are born, have immensely varied experiences over the course of their lives, not because of who they are, but because of when they are?[28]

The authors here are referring to the happenstance of coming of age during a particularly unique point in history, which can then impact the course of one's life.

Several examples illustrate this dynamic. The first comes from the demographer Richard Easterlin. Easterlin was interested in explaining why the baby boom of the 1950s occurred when it did. Birthrates had been falling throughout the twentieth century, and yet they increased dramatically during the 1950s (the height of the baby boom). Demographers were puzzled in attempting to explain this increase.

Easterlin proposed an ingenious explanation.[29] Children who were born in the 1930s grew up during the dire economic conditions of the Great Depression. As a result, their economic expectations formed during childhood were quite low. In addition, the size of these cohorts was small as a result of these economic conditions. When the children of the Great Depression entered early adulthood during the economic boom years of the 1950s, their economic expectations were far exceeded. Furthermore, because of their relatively small numbers, they were in greater demand with respect to the labor market.

Research has shown that individuals who marry and have children generally wish to be economically secure before they do so.[30] Young adults in the 1950s were fortunate to be coming of age during a particularly prosperous time. When combined with their frugal upbringing during the 1930s, and that they were highly competitive with respect to the labor market, they were able to marry at an earlier age and have more children than they might have had under different economic circumstances. Easterlin thus argues that the baby boom was the result of the fortuitous coming-together of individuals from a small birth cohort who had low economic expectations entering adulthood during a robust economic period.

Easterlin then uses this cohort dynamic explanation to explain the baby bust of the 1970s and 1980s. Birthrates during the 1970s and 1980s fell to historic low levels. According to Easterlin, children born in the prosperous 1950s had formed high economic expectations. In addition, there were large numbers of children comprising these cohorts. As they entered young adulthood during the 1970s and 1980s, economic conditions were challenging, and because of their large numbers, they were at a disadvantage in the labor market. In addition, their high levels of economic expectations were not matched by their own economic realities. The result was that childbearing was both delayed and reduced.

A second example illustrating the importance of the historical timing of birth cohorts comes again from Malcolm Gladwell.[31] Many have argued that January 1975 represented the dawn of the personal computer age. Up until that point, computing had been done on large mainframe computers. When I began graduate school, punch cards were still being used to feed a program into the IBM computer, which easily filled up a very large room. One had to wait their turn (often a day or more) in order to get time on the computer.

In January 1975 the magazine *Popular Electronics* published a cover story on a do-it-yourself home computer called the Altair

8820, which at the time cost $397. The headline read, "PROJECT BREAKTHROUGH! World's First Minicomputer Kit to Rival Commercial Models." Rather than having to rely on a university or business mainframe computer, the possibility now arose of being able to have your very own computer. Gladwell poses the question that if January 1975 was the start of the personal computer age, who might be best able to take advantage of it?

He argued that it would be individuals who were both highly interested in computing (which is obvious) and who were born roughly between the birth cohort years of 1953 and 1957 (which is not so obvious). Such computer-savvy individuals were young enough not to be established in jobs within traditional firms such as IBM where their thinking would be shaped by the old paradigm of mainframe computing. On the other hand, they were old enough and of college age to be able to take advantage of the new opportunities and ideas that had arisen. These would be individuals roughly between the ages of 18 to 22 in 1975.

So when were many of the leaders in the field of personal computing born? It turns out that many were indeed born between 1953 and 1957. They include Bill Gates (October 28, 1955), Steve Jobs (February 24, 1955), and Paul Allen (January 21, 1953). Others include Eric Schmidt, who built Novell and became chief executive office at Google (born April 27, 1955), Steve Ballmer of Microsoft (born March 24, 1956), and Bill Joy, who founded Sun Microsystems (born November 8, 1954).

Obviously not everyone who was instrumental in creating the personal computing industry was born between 1953 and 1957, but Gladwell argues many in fact were. And a key reason lay in the fortuitous timing of when they came of age.

A third example illustrating the role of the timing of birth cohorts within particular historical periods comes from the earlier-mentioned sociologists Roland Neil and Robert Sampson. In an academic article entitled "The Birth Lottery of History," Neil and Sampson analyze the likelihood of arrest during early adulthood at different historical periods of time.[32] In order to do so, they focused on over 1,000 children born up to 17 years apart who came of age between 1995 and 2018 in the city of Chicago.

In their analysis they were able to statistically control for any differences that might have existed between the various cohorts. In this fashion they could analyze the effect that the different historical periods exerted upon coming of age. Their findings indicated that those who were unlucky to enter later adolescence from the mid-to-later 1990s to the early 2000s (which represented the height of the war on drugs, mass incarceration, and proactive policing) were significantly more likely to be arrested than their counterparts who came of age later.

For example, when comparing adolescents and young adults from disadvantaged socioeconomic backgrounds, for those entering early adulthood during the late 1990s and early 2000s, 70 percent had been arrested by the time they reached their mid-20s. For those coming of age during the 2010s, only approximately one quarter had been arrested by the same point in their lives. The only difference between these groups was the historical period during which each of them were coming of age. They found a similar pattern when looking at other factors often associated with a greater propensity for arrest. The authors write,

> We should be looking not only at what was wrong (or virtuous) with the individuals of a particular cohort, as is common, but also what was wrong (or virtuous) with the larger social environment during the historical period through which they happened to come of age. By this way of analyzing the life course, individual characteristics like self-control are less stable or, in effect, less individual than commonly conceived, with manifestations that vary by sociohistorical context. Socioeconomic disadvantage, a mainstay of sociological

theories of crime, is even more dependent on history. Individual differences and social inequality in life experience are thus fundamentally in interaction with the birth lottery of history and should be studied as such.[33]

Here again we have an example of how the luck of when one enters early adulthood plays out. In our first two examples fortune shines upon those who were in the right place at the right time, while in this latter example, fortune casts a spell of bad luck for being in the wrong place at the wrong time. In all three cases it is the random factor that significantly contributes to the outcomes. Had Bill Gates or Steve Jobs been born a few years earlier or later, we may very well have never heard of them. Had a youth not come of age during the late 1990s, they may well have avoided the criminal justice system.

A final example demonstrating the unlucky timing of a historical event upon young adults has been the Covid-19 pandemic. In the first study of its kind, medical researcher Angelina Sutin and colleagues analyzed the impact of the environmental conditions imposed by Covid upon a handful of personality traits.[34] The rise of the pandemic itself might be thought of in terms of chance. In order for Covid to have begun and spread, certain conditions and factors had to come together in very specific ways.[35]

Be that as it may, the fact that young adults experienced the pandemic when they did has been shown to have had a negative effect upon their personalities. Sutin used a standard five-factor model of personality traits comprising measures of neuroticism, extroversion, openness, agreeableness, and conscientiousness. These five traits are thought to be relatively impervious to environmental conditions across adulthood.

During 2021 and 2022 young adults showed a significant increase in their levels of neuroticism and a decrease in their levels of agreeableness and conscientiousness. The magnitude of these changes that were "observed during the short time of the pandemic approximated the degree of change usually observed over a decade."[36] The authors go on to write that these changes in personality are particularly worrisome because they "may ripple throughout their adult lives."[37]

Consequently, the happenstance of coming of age during the isolation, stress, and anxiety of the Covid-19 pandemic is a particularly unlucky occurrence for younger adults. It has had a detrimental impact upon their personalities that may last a lifetime.

As we will see in chapter 7, an early lucky or unlucky break can set in motion a cascading effect of cumulative advantage or disadvantage. For example, an early arrest may put in motion a series of blocked opportunities in the job market, resulting in a downward trajectory with respect to economic and social well-being. On the other hand, a fortuitous event may open up a particular pathway to success that could only be accessed early in one's life. As Ed Smith writes,

Nor does luck "even out", as the adage holds. An early lucky break stays lucky throughout your life. Once you're in a good job, advantages accumulate: you are surrounded by better colleagues, an enhanced network and greater challenges.

Chance events are not like weights, balanced in a scale, with good luck on one side and bad luck on the other. Instead, the intervention of luck is like a boulder that diverts the course of a stream: the course is changed—and stays changed forever, whatever happens downstream. By then, it is a different life that is being altered. Luck not only intervenes; it persists.[38]

Conclusion

In this chapter we have considered the role of chance in the early stages of life. Beginning with the month and year that we are born and the name we are given, and continuing through childhood, our genes and environment are mediated through the stochastic process of randomness.

Like currents in the water or air, our genetic background and social and physical environments tend to push us along in particular directions. These are unquestionably strong forces that propel each of us forward in life. But within those strong currents exist the many ripples of randomness. These ripples are often key in determining the specifics of our lives. And at times they may throw us into a different current or direction. We now turn to exploring several of these dynamics in the next two chapters.

6 Who, What, Where, and When

I returned, and saw under the sun, that the race is not to the swift, nor the battle to the strong, neither yet bread to the wise, nor yet riches to men of understanding, nor yet favour to men of skill; but time and chance happeneth to them all.

—ECCLESIASTES, Old Testament

As I mentioned at the beginning of the book, an impetus behind this project was the frequent references made to chance events during interviews with individuals for *Chasing the American Dream*. Over and over I would listen to folks across many walks of life tell me about random occurrences that had shaped the specifics of their lives. In this chapter we examine a few of the ways in which the random factor impacts upon the particulars of our lives.

In the prior chapter we heard cognitive psychologist Steven Pinker discuss the role of luck in affecting our biology. Pinker goes on to note,

> But once we allow Lady Luck into the picture, she can act at other stages in life. When reminiscing on how we got to where we are, we all can think of forks in the road where we could have gone on very different life paths. If I hadn't gone to that party, I wouldn't have met

my spouse. If I hadn't picked up that brochure, I wouldn't have known about the field that would become my life's calling. If I hadn't answered the phone, if I hadn't missed that flight, if only I had caught that ball. Life is a pinball game in which we bounce and graze through a gauntlet of chutes and bumpers. Perhaps our history of collisions and near misses explains what made us what we are.[1]

The specifics of our lives are where we often see the random factor's influence most explicitly. There are powerful currents that push our lives in particular directions. But within those currents, chance and luck exert themselves. In one of the first social science articles specifically focusing on the role of chance, psychologist Albert Bandura writes,

> The central thesis of this article is that chance encounters play a prominent role in shaping the course of human lives. In a chance encounter the separate chains of events have their own causal determinants, but their intersection occurs fortuitously rather than through deliberate plan. Some fortuitous encounters touch only lightly, others leave more lasting effects, and still others branch people into new trajectories of life.[2]

In this chapter we focus on three particularly important aspects of our lives—who we form relationships with, what we do in terms of work and income, and where we live. In each of these cases, the random factor plays a significant role in shaping the details of these domains. In addition, we will also look at the question of when. Specifically, two stories of when a second chance comes along.

Who We Form Relationships With

Of all of the places where the random factor can be found, perhaps most apparent is in who we form relationships with. Ask just about anybody how they met someone they are close to, and luck is likely a part of the story. Whether it be friends, significant others, marriage partners, work colleagues, or any number of relationships, the random factor has probably played a major role.

A theme running throughout this book is the intersection of the random factor with the powerful currents that push our lives along. This is most certainly the case here. Who we meet is both random and nonrandom. It is not random in the sense that who we interact with is strongly influenced by factors such as class, race, gender, religion, and political and ideological preferences. Other factors that influence who we might encounter include our specific interests and pursuits. It is therefore not the case that our interactions with people simply reflect a random sample of the population. Far from it.

Within these various currents of who we encounter, however, are strong ripples of randomness. For example, although children from a middle-class background will likely attend a college or university, the specific people they meet at school are very much the luck of the draw (as we discussed in chapter 4). Many of these students will be from similar economic backgrounds, but the specific individuals they encounter on campus is one of chance. A long-term friendship might be formed with a randomly assigned roommate in a residence hall, or a fellow student who happens to be sitting in the next seat in a large classroom. In both of these cases that person could just as easily have been someone different. As Albert Bandura noted earlier, "In a chance encounter the separate chains of events have their own causal determinants, but their intersection occurs fortuitously rather than through deliberate plan."

In addition, there is the element of agency that interacts with randomness. True, who we encounter has a strong streak of randomness to it. But who we choose to become involved with reflects agency on the part of both persons. I may randomly interact with a variety of people, but I can actively make decisions on who I might want to spend more time with. In this way there is dynamic interaction between chance and agency. Similar to what we saw in chapter 3 with respect to serendipitous discoveries, the random factor presents us with opportunities that we may or may not choose to take advantage of.

Let us first consider the case of our work colleagues. Although the workplace during the last few years has become more remote as a result of the Covid pandemic, it nevertheless is still the case that most jobs require their employees to be in person at the work site. This may be an office building, a retail store, a school, a factory, or hundreds of other places.

Those who we work with are very much the luck of the draw. When we interview for a job, we may meet a handful of employees, but for the most part, we are in the dark regarding who are work colleagues will be. Where we happen to situate in an organization will determine who are fellow workers are, thereby introducing the random factor into our work lives.

In my work building, my next-door neighbors assigned to the offices adjacent to mine have changed over time. I have seen people come and go. Some of them I have become friends with, and others not. But in all cases, the specific person assigned was simply random. An office space had opened up and there was someone in need of an office. The result was that who I would see on a daily basis was simply up to chance.

In companies that are on the cutting edge of invention, randomness has been used to encourage greater innovation and productivity in the workplace. The idea is to foster chance interactions and conversations between individuals with differing but complementary areas of expertise. Ben Waber and colleagues writing in the *Harvard Business Journal* note that "our data suggest that creating collisions—chance encounters and unplanned interactions between knowledge workers, both inside and outside the organization—improves performance."[3]

Creativity can be stirred by bringing people together with different perspectives and allowing them to improvise regarding ideas and solutions. In order to facilitate this, office space is designed in such a way that leads to such serendipitous encounters. These include placing individuals with different areas of expertise in closer proximity, having communal and open spaces where employees can freely interact, and designing work spaces such that they allow both privacy and collaboration.[4]

Bell Labs and IBM were early practitioners of this approach.[5] More recent companies such as Apple, Microsoft, Facebook, and Google are among the corporations that have redesigned their office spaces in order to facilitate more random improvisations and happenstance interactions. For example, Google's campus in Mountain View, California, known as Googleplex, is specifically designed to maximize chance encounters.[6] As Natalie Engels writes,

> The chance encounter is a cornerstone of any company looking to foster creative and innovative workplace environments, and this is especially true in the tech world. That's because we know that some of the best ideas and discussions happen spontaneously—in the lunch line or waiting for the elevator—rather than in a conference room.[7]

In addition, as researchers Keith Pennington and Myles Shaver note, the move to more remote work arrangements triggered by the Covid-19 pandemic carries a drawback. As they write,

> Our research, and the research of others, suggests that the primary rationale for returning to the office is that we miss something that is important for long-term performance but hard to observe— unplanned serendipitous interactions among co-workers. For example, running into a co-worker in the elevator who knows the answer

to that question you have struggled with or the unplanned conversation while getting a coffee that generates a new business idea. Serendipitous interactions are important for creative, innovative or non-formulaic activities; however, they rarely occur in virtual interactions because these interactions are highly structured.[8]

The workplace is therefore one area of our lives where we encounter randomness both in terms of who our co-workers are, and in terms of the way in which we may interact with these workers.

A second area where the random factor plays a very large role is who we form close and intimate relationships with. I have yet to encounter someone who, when asked how they met their partner, did not mention some element of chance and luck. This appears to be an almost universal happening. Think back on the relationships that you have been involved in, and chances are that luck played a role in the two of you coming together.

Much of the social science research on intimate partners has focused on who is likely to marry whom. The bulk of this work has found support for what is known as marital homogamy, or better put, "Birds of a feather flock together." Research has indicated that individuals tend to marry other individuals with similar characteristics.[9] These include education, race, socioeconomic status, age, religion, ideological preferences, height, and many more. In other words, on a population level, who we marry is most certainly not random. However, on an individual level, the specific person we marry is often due to chance or luck.

The way in which the random factor exerts itself is through who we have the opportunity to interact with. One of the ways in which we meet new people and potential marriage partners is within our places of work as discussed above. Other settings for meeting new people include schools, organizations we belong to, family or friends, bars or other public areas, events, dating apps, and more. The people found through these means are unlikely to be a random sample of the population. Rather, they will tend to reflect our own makeup. Hence, the individuals we are likely to interact with will probably have backgrounds fairly similar to our own.

The specific persons we meet and encounter on a one-to-one basis, however, will be highly random. Social scientists have almost completely ignored this element. An economist colleague of mine notes that from an economic perspective, who we enter marriage with assumes no luck at all—"who you marry is determined by the requirements of equilibrium in the marriage market."[10] On the other hand, novelists and playwrights from Shakespeare to the present have introduced the random factor as a key component to their stories. Albert Bandura, who we heard from earlier, gives this example:

> One can similarly document the influential role that initial chance encounters often play in the formation of partnerships of marriage. Let me cite but one example with which I have some personal acquaintance. Seeking relief from an uninspiring reading assignment, a graduate student departs for the golf links with his friend. They happen to find themselves playing behind a twosome of attractive women golfers. Before long the two twosomes become one foursome and, in the course of events, one of the partners eventually becomes the wife of the graduate golfer. Were it not for this fortuitous constellation of events, it is exceedingly unlikely that their paths would ever have crossed. Different partnership create different life courses. The graduate student in this particular case happens to be myself.[11]

Consequently in this most important aspect of our lives, chance and luck are active players. As mentioned earlier, we certainly exert agency in this process. In the above example, Bandura could have chosen not to get better acquainted with the member of the twosome in front of him. Likewise, his potential partner could have expressed no interest in his overtures. In this way chance and agency come together to help steer the direction that our lives will take.

What We Do and What We Earn

Just as who we form relationships with is often a matter of chance, so too is the career and job that we find ourselves in. No doubt there are strategic decisions that are made regarding career choices. But there are also chance events that help determine the occupation or field we go into along with the specific job we find ourselves in. The decision to pursue a particular line of work may hinge on various contingencies that interact with our preferences and deliberate strategies.

In a very early study looking at career decision-making, Anne Roe and Rhonda Baruch found that rather than individuals describing their career choices as a series of logical decisions, most referred to chance events and external influences that impacted and shaped the course of their careers.[12] In more recent research, psychologist Jim Bright and colleagues found that among a large sample of young adults, "Chance events were reported as influencing the career decision making of 69.1% of the sample."[13] They go on to argue that "a clear pattern of chance events having frequent and profound influences on careers emerges that cannot be adequately accounted for in terms of attributional disposition."[14]

One can see this pattern play out in a variety of ways. For example, take the field of study that undergraduate students decide to major in. This decision often leads to the specific profession that a student will enter into. The choice of a major can hinge on enrolling in an introductory course that triggers a student's interest in the subject. But the taking of that specific course may have been because it just happened to be the one that fit into the student's weekly schedule. Had it not been offered at that particular time, they would have gone in a different direction.

Furthermore, whether the student continues taking courses in the field may rest on who was assigned to teach that course that semester. Depending on whether the professor was an excellent teacher or not could be crucial in sparking the student's interest in the subject. Suppose Professor A was teaching the course in that semester rather than Professor B who normally would have taught the class but was on a sabbatical leave. Professor A was considered one of the department's best teachers while Professor B was not. Our hypothetical student is then exposed to Professor A, which in turn leads the student down a particular career path. This scenario is but one among hundreds in which chance exerts itself upon a career trajectory.

Chance assumes an even larger role in the specific job that we might find ourselves in. One of the first studies analyzing the process of job searching came from the sociologist Mark Granovetter. His groundbreaking book, *Getting a Job*, looked at the process by which individuals located jobs. He notes that "the central theme of *Getting a Job* involves the explication of one element of what is usually considered 'luck' in job-finding: having the right contact in the right place at the right time."[15] He goes on to note that "personal contacts are of paramount importance in connecting people with jobs. Better jobs are found through contacts, and the best jobs, the ones with the highest pay and prestige and affording the greatest satisfaction to those in them, are most apt to be filled in this way."[16] Having the right contact in the right place at the right time is most certainly the case of being very lucky.

In a more recent study looking at job locating within an engineering firm, Steve McDonald also found a strong influence of chance events on locating specific jobs:

The findings presented here highlight the unpredictable character of the processes by which people become aware of job openings. Serendipity abounds in job finding, as people often receive job information without engaging in a job search. Even when a search is utilized, people frequently receive job leads in unexpected ways.[17]

Other research has found similar patterns.[18] In an early study looking at the careers of school superintendents in Wisconsin from 1940 to 1972, James March found that the movement up or down the career ladder was almost entirely random and disconnected from measures of ability. Those at the top of the career ladder were nearly indistinguishable in their behaviors, performances, abilities, and values from those further down on the career ladder. He concludes that the moral of the research

> is that the same behaviors, abilities, and values that produce successful careers at the top will, on the average, produce unsuccessful ones also; that little can be learned about how to administer schools by studying successful high-level administrators that could not be learned by studying unsuccessful ones; and that the stories we tell each other about success and failure in top management, like the stories we tell about success and failure in gambling, are in large part fictions intended to reassure us about justice and encourage the young.[19]

The landing of a particular job in a field is therefore very often due to the random factor. An example illustrating the role of chance in the job market is one that I know quite well—my own. Tenure-track academic jobs have been hard to come by over the years. This is particularly the case in the humanities and social sciences. In a given year there are only a select number of jobs in a given discipline for newly minted PhDs. The specific universities offering jobs during any one year is very much the luck of the draw. Some years there may be more job openings, other years there may be less, and their locations will vary accordingly. In addition, the specialty areas sought within disciplines will change from year to year, which will further narrow down the field of available jobs. It is quite common for there be a hundred or more applications for any assistant professor opening at a major university.

The year that I was on the job market, I was fortunate to have three campus visits to Cornell University, Purdue University, and Washington University in St. Louis. Each school was quite different, and I wound up taking the assistant professor position at Washington University. Landing in St. Louis was certainly the luck of the draw, but here is where the story becomes even more interesting.

My appointment at Washington University was in the sociology department. During the autumn of my fourth year, I ran into a social work faculty friend of mine in the hallway of my building. She was on her way to an appointment, and only had time to chat for a couple of minutes. As we said goodbye, she mentioned in passing that the social work school had a job opening that perhaps I might be interested in. Up to that point, I had never considered applying for a social work professor position, and I was quite happy where I was. However, on a whim I decided to apply. To make a long story short, I was offered and accepted the job in March of that year. Two weeks later, the university announced that they were closing the department of sociology and that all junior faculty would be terminated. That announcement took everyone, myself included, quite by surprise. Had I not accidently run into my friend in the hallway, had she not mentioned as an after-thought the job opening, I certainly would have found myself out of a job and searching for a comparable position somewhere in the United States. The direction of my research and scholarship might also have taken a different course had it not been for this twist of fate.

The result was that had my three-minute happenstance meeting with my social work friend not taken place, my life undoubtedly would be much different than it is today. Would it be better or worse?

Impossible to say. Would it be different? Most definitely. I would be at another job, probably in another part of the country, with completely different work colleagues. And I very well might not be writing this book right now.

An empirical illustration of how luck interacts with other forces to influence the landing of a job, is a labor market simulator that I have developed for my website dealing with poverty, titled "The Musical Chairs of Poverty."[20] The simulation is based on the game of musical chairs. All the information in the simulator is from actual Bureau of Labor Statistics (BLS) data. At the center of the screen is a circle of chairs representing the number of livable-wage jobs for every 100 workers in the labor force. This varies from year to year but tends to be around 65 chairs. The 100 players on the outside of the circle of chairs are color coded to represent the percentages in the working population between the ages of 25 and 59 by levels of education, race, and gender. When you hit the start button, the players begin to circle the outside of the chairs, sometimes being a bit closer to the chairs and sometimes further away. When the music stops, they are at slightly different distances to the nearest chair. This represents the element of chance. In other words, it is random where one might find oneself at the moment the music stops.

However, the speed at which the players then travel to attempt to land a chair is determined by their education, race, and gender. This speed is derived from imputing actual BLS data. Those with greater levels of education and are white and male have greater speed in racing toward a chair, reflecting their greater likelihood of securing a job. This then represents the larger forces that have an effect on landing a good-paying job. In this way, both luck and structural forces are in play in terms of who winds up with one of the chairs in the game. If one plays the simulation again, the results will be slightly different as a result of the random factor at work. The simulator thus illustrates the dynamic interaction between chance and demographics.

A third manner in which the random factor exerts itself is with respect to what we earn at our job. Just as chance and luck influence the specific jobs we find ourselves in, so too can they affect our pay. As sociologist Christopher Jencks writes in his book, *Inequality*,

> Income also depends on luck: chance acquaintances who steer you to one line of work rather than another, the range of jobs that happen to be available in a particular community when you are job hunting, the amount of overtime work in your particular plant, whether bad weather destroys your strawberry crop, whether the new superhighway has an exit near your restaurant, and a hundred other unpredictable accidents . . . In general, we think luck has far more influence on income than successful people admit.[21]

Obviously there are a handful of factors that directly influence how much we are paid. These include seniority, education, age, occupation, and credentials. In addition, structural variables such as race and gender have also been shown to exert an influence in terms of what people earn. However, in studies that have utilized these factors in order to predict an individual's income, only approximately 35 percent of the variance in earnings can be explained.[22] For example, economist Samuel Bowles writes that although

> similar individuals receive quite different earnings: a person's age, years of schooling, years of labor market experience, parents' level of schooling, occupation, and income tell us surprisingly little about the individual's earnings. In standard earnings equations for individuals of the same race and sex in the United States, between two-thirds and four-fifths of the variance of the natural logarithm of hourly wages or of annual earnings is unexplained by the above variables.

In other words, more than 65 percent of the differences in income cannot be explained through the array of factors that we normally think of as critical to earnings. Part of this 65 percent is most assuredly chance.[23]

Take the case of who becomes wealthy and who experiences poverty. It turns out the random factor is very much in play. In a fascinating research article entitled "Talent Versus Luck: The Role of Randomness in Success and Failure," Alessandro Pluchino and colleagues were able to empirically quantify the relative importance of talent versus luck in terms of acquiring great wealth over a 40-year working age life span. What they found is that

> if it is true that some degree of talent is necessary to be successful in life, almost never the most talented people reach the highest peaks of success, being overtaken by averagely talented but sensibly luckier individuals. As far as we know, this counterintuitive result—although implicitly suggested between the lines in a vast literature—is quantified here for the first time. It sheds new light on the effectiveness of assessing merit on the basis of the reached level of success and underlines the risks of distributing excessive honors or resources to people who, at the end of the day, could have been simply luckier than others.[24]

Their research results splash quite of bit of cold water on the myth of meritocracy and wealth. Certainly individual attributes such as talent and determination are important ingredients for material success, but just as important is the role of luck. We might think of having a baseline level of talent and determination as a necessary but not a sufficient condition for getting economically ahead in life. What is often needed beyond just talent and determination in order to be highly successful is luck. As Pluchino and colleagues write, the idea that we live in a strict meritocracy is patently false because it "underestimates the role of randomness among the determinants of success."[25]

The economist Robert Frank has written extensively about the role of luck with respect to earnings. He notes that although there are certainly cases of highly skilled and extremely hard-working individuals who become wealthy, "Far more numerous are talented people who work very hard, only to achieve modest earnings. There are hundreds of them for every skilled, perseverant person who strikes it rich, disparities that often stem from random events."[26] Frank observes that the United States has become much more of a winner-take-all society over the past 40 years. This has resulted in a very small number of people seeing incredible gains in wealth while the rest of society has experienced economic stagnation. What separates the fortunate few from other equally talented individuals is being blessed with good luck. Frank writes, "The upshot is that with far greater frequency than ever before, seemingly trivial chance events give rise to spectacular differences in economic reward."[27]

Let us now consider poverty. Much of my research over the years has focused on the question of why people experience poverty.[28] Again, there are many reasons, but one of the most important has to do with bad luck. This plays out in many different ways—a sudden health emergency, a factory shutting its doors, an unannounced cutting back of work hours, a car breaking down, and on and on. When these events happen, often out of the blue, they can send households in a downward spiral and into poverty. For individuals who are struggling to keep their heads above water, such unlucky happenings often trigger a spell of impoverishment.

My life course research has shown that over the span of adulthood, 75 percent of Americans will experience at least one year in poverty or near poverty.[29] The reason this percentage is so high is that over the course of 40 or 50 years, many unanticipated and unlucky events can happen to people. When these occur, poverty often follows. Similarly, in the Pluchino analysis, those at the bottom of the wealth distribution were those who had the most number of unlucky events happen to them.

In previous work I have described the lives of those living near poverty as one in which they may be barely able to scrape by and keep their heads above water. However, should something unexpected happen (as it often does), it can set in motion a domino effect that ripples through these lives, catapulting them into poverty. Take the case of Mike Abbot, a 31-year-old husband who had recently suffered a serious back injury while on the job. I interviewed Mike and his wife, Susan, for my *Living on the Edge* book. The injury had thrown the Abbots into poverty, forcing them to rely on workers' compensation and food stamps. I asked them how life had treated them? They responded that life had been good until the last year and a half when Mike's injury happened quite unexpectedly. Mike went on to say,

> What did it do to deserve that? No! You get a little bitter. I do (pause). You know, you worked all your life. Made a good home, good . . . (long pause), and everything, and then all of a sudden that happens. Something you had no control. I could see if you went out and blew it all. It would be your fault. Or, you know, somethin' like that. But somethin' you had no control over, you're bound to feel a little bitter about it. And it's been a lot of pain. I spent a lot time in the hospital . . . Which isn't fun (pause) . . .[30]

It is again the case that the random factor plays an important role in terms of our financial well-being. Upward and downward swings in income are often the result of events that are beyond our control. And many of these events are triggered by the random factor.

Where We Live

Just as with forming relationships and finding jobs, where we live is also influenced by chance. Certainly there are factors that shape our residential options and directions. The most important of these are income, race, and personal preferences. The size of your income will largely determine what neighborhoods are viable options. No matter how much you might want to live in a particular neighborhood, if you cannot afford the housing or rental prices, you simply will not be able to reside there.

Likewise, race has unfortunately been shown to be a major factor in determining where people reside. Because of historical and current discrimination in the housing industry and elsewhere, patterns of racial residential segregation are found across the United States.[31] Redlining, steering practices, and differences in loan approval have all limited the options of where individuals of color may reside.

Finally, where we live is also influenced by our personal preferences with respect to what we are looking for in a neighborhood and in housing. Perhaps we prefer living in a historical neighborhood with older homes. Or maybe our ideal housing situation would be in a high-rise condominium close to our work. We might want to live in a neighborhood that has young children and good schools. These preferences will shape where we choose to look for housing.

But once these factors have been accounted for, the particular dwelling and street where we end up living is very much due to chance. This is because there are only a small number of housing units up for sale or rent at any specific time. When people are looking to move to a new location, the amount of time for house hunting may be limited. During that window, only a select number of potential housing options may be on the market. As in our discussion of relationships, individuals have the choice to pursue a particular option or not. In this sense agency is of course a part of the process. But this agency is bounded by the options that are available to us during any window of time. And those options are very much the luck of the draw.

Let us suppose that you have decided that you want to buy a house in a particular neighborhood. The housing in the neighborhood fits your budget, and you are very much drawn to the charm of the homes lining the streets.

The question now becomes, what house will you reside in? Only a few will be up for sale at any point in time. There may be homes that you would have liked to have purchased, but they are not on the market. Likewise, some of the houses being offered for sale have problems that you cannot overlook. That may leave just a handful of choices. You finally settle on one, and your offer and loan has been approved.

Congratulations! You have now purchased your new home. But of course you probably have no idea who your next-door neighbors are. Perhaps you will become great friends with them, or perhaps great enemies. Likewise you have no idea who will be your child's teacher in the upcoming school year. The teacher may be terrific or perhaps not. You may also not know the recent environmental history of your new neighborhood, and/or some of the long-term history behind your particular home.

In this sense, our hypothetical individual enters into the home-owner world with many unknowns in which the luck of the draw could be important. For *Chasing the American Dream*, I interviewed a very successful real estate agent. As we sat down to talk over coffee, she spoke about the ins and outs of the trade. One of the things she emphasized is the ongoing dynamic process between the number of homes available at any point in time and the number of potential buyers. This ratio fluctuates over time. Sometimes it is a buyer's market and sometimes it is a seller's market. Where you happen to fall in this dynamic is the luck of the draw. If you are looking to buy a home during a buyer's market, good fortune has smiled upon you. On the other hand, if you happen to be buying during a seller's market, you are likely to experience greater difficulties in purchasing that home. Again, this is very much the luck of the draw, as we saw in chapter 5 when we discussed the timing of birth cohorts.

A dramatic example of the random factor influencing the residential location of poverty-stricken families was the Moving to Opportunity demonstration project and experiment in the 1990s.[32] A group of randomly drawn public housing residents in five major U.S. cities were offered housing vouchers that could only be used in low-poverty neighborhoods (less than 10 percent poor). The experiment was designed to assess the effect of moving from a high-poverty to a low-poverty environment upon overall family well-being. Those who received these vouchers and the opportunity that came with them were chosen completely by chance. The Moving to Opportunity program was a striking example of how pure luck played out in improving the residential environments for a small group of low-income households.

A further interesting aspect of luck in the housing market is that the address of a housing unit can have an effect on how desirable it may be to buyers. Within Chinese culture, the number 4 is considered bad luck because when pronounced it sounds very similar to the word for death. On the other hand, the number 8 is considered one of particularly good luck because it is associated with wealth. Research has shown that among Chinese buyers of housing units, addresses that end with an 8 rather than a 4 tend to sell faster and command a higher price. Housing units that are on the eighth floor of a building are also more likely to sell or rent. In one study of Chinese residents in the Vancouver, British Columbia area, researchers found that houses with an address ending in 4 sold at a 2.2 percent discount while those ending in 8 were sold at a 2.5 percent premium.[33] This translated into an average discount of $8,000 and an average premium of $10,000. Likewise, in a study of the real estate market in

Chengdu, China, secondhand apartments located on floors ending with 8 commanded a higher price and sold faster than apartments on other floors.[34]

When a Second Chance Occurs

Having looked at aspects of the who, what, and where in our lives, we now turn to the question of when. When does the random factor play its cards and how might we react? Chance events occur across all points in a lifetime. But the specific timing of such events can be particularly important in terms of the impact they might have. In the first story I am about to recount, the "when" specifically occurred on May 18, 1939, in a small town in Nazi Germany. And in this particular case, the "when" became a question of life and death.

How often are we given a second chance to live? For Hedy Epstein, she was given just such a gift. Hers was a remarkable story of adversity, a twist of fate, and a second chance in life. Meeting Hedy for the first time had, in turn, been a complete random encounter. I had gotten up early to go to a downtown breakfast event sponsored by an organization I recently joined. My friend Denise came by to pick me up, but mentioned that we also needed to pick up a friend of hers who was attending the breakfast as well. I asked Denise who it was, and she started to tell me a bit about Hedy Epstein and the extraordinary life she had lived.

Born in Germany in the mid-1920s, Hedy had grown up in a small village during the rise of Adolf Hitler and the Nazi movement in the 1930s. After experiencing increasing levels of terror and violence, she was the only Jewish child in her village to have escaped out of Germany by train in 1939 on the Kindertransport, or children's transport. Denise mentioned that Hedy had spent the war years in England with two different foster families, and then returned to Germany after the war to assist in the Nuremberg Trials. Since coming to the United States in 1948, she led an equally remarkable life, being involved in various social justice movements and human rights causes. She had recently been stopped in Turkey while trying to join a group of protesters seeking to draw attention to the conditions among Palestinians.

As Hedy climbed into the car, she was even more impressive in person. Although very small in stature and 86 years old, she had the energy and spirit of someone half her age. As we chatted I asked if she would be interested in being interviewed, she agreed, and two weeks later I found myself in her modest apartment on an older, tree-lined street.

As the interview began, Hedy talked in careful but chilling detail about growing up as a child in Nazi Germany. It was both a privilege and spellbinding to hear such living history unfold over the next several hours. Hers was a story of how a twist of fate had saved her life and eventually led her to America and a second chance.

She began by describing how the conditions for Jews quickly deteriorated after Hitler came to power in 1933. In particular, she talked about her schooling becoming increasingly oppressive for her and a handful of Jewish classmates. Her math teacher in his black SS uniform and knee-high boots would ridicule whatever answers she volunteered in class, calling them "Jewish answers" and "garbage."

Things took a dramatic turn for the worst on November 9, 1938, known as Kristallnacht or "Night of Broken Glass."[35] On that day across Germany and Austria, 7,500 Jewish-owned businesses were smashed, over 1,000 synagogues set on fire, Jewish homes looted and ransacked, and the police rounded up approximately 30,000 Jewish men and forced them into concentration camps until their families could ransom them out. Hedy described what happened to her that day:

I left for school that morning just like any other day. And I remember it was a cold but very sunny day. As I passed the home of a Jewish dentist or it could have been an attorney . . . all the windows in that building were broken, and I didn't know why. I assumed it was because the family was Jewish because they also lived in the same building.

I went on to school. Classes started promptly at 8:00, and at about 8:30 the principal walked in. And he talked to all of us. Then he suddenly stopped and he pointed his finger at me, and he said, "Get out, you dirty Jew!" I heard what he said, but I just couldn't believe that this man, who I thought was a very kind, gentle person, would say something like this.

So I asked him to repeat it, and he did. He came over, grabbed me by the elbow, and shoved me out the door. As I was standing outside in the hallway, all kinds of thoughts raced through my head like, "What did I do? Did I fall asleep? Did I not pay attention? What am I going to tell my parents?"

Before I could answer those questions, the children came running out of the classroom, put on their coats or jackets, some pushed and shoved me and called me dirty Jew. Then they all left. Where were they going? I had no idea.

Hedy went back to her empty classroom along with a younger Jewish classmate and tried to study, but of course could not concentrate. After an hour of sitting at her desk, she heard a loud commotion outside and went over to the window to look out. She saw dozens of Jewish men and boys being marched down the street by the SS who were hitting and yelling at them to walk faster. At that point Hedy tried to call home from a bookstore next door. She first called her mother, then her father, grandmother, and aunt. Each time a strange voice answered by saying that telephone service was no longer being provided. Hedy then left school and walked home. When she arrived, her house had been boarded up.

She eventually found her mother at her aunt's house. She told Hedy that 10 minutes after she had left for school that morning, her father had been arrested and dragged out of their house in his paja-mas. He along with the other Jewish men and boys in the village were being sent to a concentration camp at Dachau.[36]

Four weeks passed before her father returned home, badly beaten, head shaven, and suffering from a mild heart attack. After he had finally begun to recover, the family decided to do whatever they could to get out of Germany.

Once my father was relatively well again, the efforts to leave Ger-many were resumed, but the decision was that unlike until now, when we hoped to leave as a family unit, if one of us has the opportu-nity to leave, that person will leave and hopefully the others can fol-low soon thereafter. And the opportunity came for me to leave on May 18, 1939, on a children's transporter, Kindertransport as it has been referred to.

There were almost 500 children on this transport that I was on. The youngest were twins that were 6 months old, the oldest were 17, and I was 14 1/2. We all went to England. Some of us were placed in foster homes. I was in a foster home. England, by the way, took in al-most 10,000 mostly Jewish children in the nine months preceding World War II and would have taken more except the war broke out.

That Hedy was able to escape from her village via the Kinder-transport was a twist of fate she would never forget. The window of time to get out of Germany was extremely precarious and narrow, and the paperwork necessary was laborious. How her parents had managed to get her on the list, Hedy to this day does not know. Her twist of fate also lay in an unknown administrator's hands, who de-cided on one day that Hedy would be included on the Kindertrans-port. That decision was in all likelihood one of life or death.

Hedy's story was repeated in case after case for those children lucky enough to have gotten out of Nazi Germany, while ending tragically for most who did not. In *Sons and Soldiers,* Bruce Henderson describes these twists of fate for a select number of teenage boys who were able to escape from Germany to America as a result of their parents being at the right place at the right time. They then returned to Europe to fight as American GIs, helping to defeat the Nazis.

What Hedy knows is that she was given a rare second chance in life.

> I think one huge opportunity came for me, which was a life-changing and life-saving opportunity—my parents' decision to send me on a children's transport to England. Had they not done this, I don't know, my fate might have been the same as theirs and I might not be sitting here. So by sending me on a Kindertransport or children's transport to England, they literally gave me life a second time. What an opportunity. So thank you to my parents.

While Hedy's direction on the Kindertransport had been to the west, her parent's direction would ultimately turn to the east. After England declared war on Germany on September 3, 1939, Hedy could only communicate through brief letters. Three years into the war she received two final letters and a postcard from her parents.

> I received a letter from my father dated August 9, 1942, saying, "Tomorrow I'm being deported to an unknown destination, and it may be a long time before you hear from me again."
>
> I never heard from him again. I then received a letter from my mother dated September 1, in which she essentially says the same thing and expresses the hope to me that my father is somewhere and that we will carry our lot with dignity and with courage. And she's urging me to be a good girl, to be always honest, keep my head high, hold my head high, and never give up hope.

I asked Hedy about her mother's final admonition to hold her head high and never give up hope. How did those words shape the course of her life after that?

Because I became an eternal optimist, not afraid, willing to risk things, risk myself. There's also other things that had a profound influence on the path I chose. A couple times in my life I see I'm coming at a crossroads. I could go this way, I could go that way. And I sometimes wish I could go back and try the other way, not because I don't like the way I chose, but I just wonder what would happen if I did this other thing, you know. But you can't do that.

After the war was over, she returned to Germany and assisted the Americans in researching the medical atrocities that the Nazis had performed on the Jews and others. Her work was part of the background research that was done for the Doctors Trial at Nuremberg, in which former high-level Nazi doctors were tried and convicted for war crimes and crimes against humanity.

In 1948 Hedy immigrated to the United States. She worked in a variety of settings helping fellow immigrants and the disadvantaged. In addition, she led an equally remarkable life working for social change and social justice around the country and the world. She has been honored by the likes of former German chancellor Gerhard Schröder and Prince Charles, appeared in a film documentary, and continued to work tirelessly toward improving the living conditions of the Palestinians. She noted that although she cannot thank some of those who helped her, she can do something to help other people in need, to whom she has devoted her life.

One of the things that is so striking about Hedy Epstein's life is the pure twist of fate that allowed her to escape from Nazi Germany. Had her name not been put on the list for the Kindertransport by some unknown administrator, she may very well have lost her life in the Holocaust. Perhaps if this administrator had skipped his breakfast or lunch that day, her fate may have been different.

For Hedy Epstein, that she became an international advocate for social justice was largely shaped by the horrors she witnessed as a child in Germany. As she says, she took her mother's advice and "became ... not afraid," willing to risk things, including herself. At the age of 86 when she was interviewed, she remained actively engaged in various causes designed to help the human condition. Although she has since passed away, her legacy only continues to grow.

A second dramatic example of a second chance was the case of Seid Girma, who I also interviewed for my American Dream project. Born into a very poor family in rural Ethiopia, Seid was only three years old when his father died. Through the help of several sponsors, he was able to complete his primary and secondary school education. Seid then began a promising teaching career in his early 20s. Yet his life changed completely in 1974. That was the year the long-standing emperor of Ethiopia, Haile Selassie, was overthrown by a military coup d'état. According to Seid, the military pledged to return control back to the civilian population in six months, but failed to do so. Seid, along with many others, protested, and they were subsequently targeted as a serious threat to the government.

> So there was a tense relationship between teachers, students, and factory workers with the military government. But they are strong because they have the army. And finally when the situation was so intense, the military government decided to take everybody who is against (them) into the prison. So I was one of them. I was thrown into the prison. You can imagine how scary that was.

He went on to describe the horrific conditions he was exposed to.

I was in one (of) the worst cells in the city. There were like 80 different prisoners, and the room was not enough with maybe that much
area [pointing to a small space in the conference room where our interview was being conducted]. It was terrible.

But the worst thing is every evening, the military they came and
they call names, five from each class, maybe ten, it depends. Once
you are called that time, it's sure, it's definitely sure, we will not see
you again. That's it.

So people were executed?

Yes. No judgment, nothing. Nobody told me that I was arrested before and this was the reason. Nobody told me that I was released because of this. The number, nobody knows for sure the number, but
some documents attest that there were over 500,000 people who
were killed by the military government. And the bodies were thrown
in the street, and they write on the top, "Red Terror."

After two years of being exposed to these conditions, Seid was
eventually released. In 1987 he left Ethiopia, becoming a refugee in
Sudan. He then made his way in 1993 to the United States looking for
a better life.

After settling into his new country and community, Seid worked
at a number of jobs, including founding a taxi cab service designed to
provide jobs for immigrants and minorities. He was currently working in a social service agency that provides legal services for immigrants. In addition, he has also earned an MBA degree along the way.
I asked Seid about his American Dream.

And when you come here, yes, you have a dream. The dream is first
you have to settle yourself, of course. There is no chance to go back
home. Then once you come here, you think about, "Okay, how do I

live my life?" And then you start to study, and you hear about the American Dream. And that's really one of the things that I just got very quickly. You can be anybody in America.

Seid Girma has experienced a remarkable journey from terror and refugee status, to eventually helping fellow immigrants and refugees in the United States. He looks back on his life with a sense of humility and gratitude in being able to have the chance to gaze upon a new horizon.

But had his name been called out in that prison cell in Ethiopia, his life would have been over. The judgment of who would live and who would die on a particular day in 1974 was most likely the result of pure chance. How many millions have been in the position of Seid, waiting each day, wondering if this was the day that their luck would run out? Or perhaps for those who were mercilessly tortured, hoping that that day would come soon.

The element of randomness can be found throughout each of our lives, although rarely with the consequences that it held for Hedy and Seid. Chance encounters, accidents that occurred, conversations that changed lives, being in the wrong place at the wrong time, being in the right place at the right time—all of these and more are a part of the randomness that life often presents us with. This randomness can be disconcerting because it is something that we basically have no control over. But although these events help to shape who we are, perhaps just as important, the manner in which we respond to them helps to shape who we will become.

Tallying Up the Chances

In this chapter we have looked at some of the ways in which the random factor exerts itself into the specifics of our lives. Who we form relationships with, what we do and what we earn, where we live, and when chance events occur are all strongly influence by the random factor.

These are but a few of the specifics of our lives, and it is here that the random factor is most apparent. Given a stronger gust of wind, given a chance telephone call, given a last-minute cancellation, our lives would look different. As law professor Edward Kleinbard writes in *What's Luck Got to Do with It?*,

> Like gravity, brute luck is a universal force that cannot by itself be turned off. We like to think that we control our destinies through the decisions we make, but in fact our careers and our happiness are shaped to a large extent by the consequences of luck, favorable or unfavorable, that are not only out of our control, but often are unobserved by us. Many successful people expend enormous energy denying this fact.[37]

The details of each life are very much driven by the fickleness of chance and luck. Were we to replay our lives at the same starting point, how might they look given that randomness itself could play out differently? My hunch is that the answer would be—significantly different.[38]

7 Shortcuts, Detours, and Forks in the Road

But most of us are afraid of chance, happy or otherwise, and like to put it out of our nice airtight frame of things. We are not flattered by the thought that our successes are in large part due to it, and, as has been noticed before, we don't like to think of our failures at all. Nevertheless, chance is in the air we breathe, an incalculable wind blowing from somewhere, where nothing is or can be explained, often with a tang of irony in it which searches the marrow.

—LEONARD BACON, 1946

Let us now take a step back and consider several of the dynamics and patterns whereby luck and chance play themselves out in our lives. As we have seen in prior chapters, the random factor is a constant companion as we make our journey across a lifetime. It reveals itself in ways both small and large. But there are also tendencies with respect to how these cards are played. In this chapter we look at four such features: (1) the timing of a chance event; (2) the process of cumulative advantage or disadvantage; (3) the wider structural context in which randomness occurs; and (4) the fact that luck does not necessarily even out over time.

Timing Is Everything

An initial way to consider the dynamics of randomness is with the particular timing of a lucky or unlucky event. In chapter 5 we discussed the issue of timing with respect to birth cohorts. Specifically, the fact that a group of individuals who were born in a particular year and then entered adulthood during a particular historical period. The coming together of these two streams or paths could lead to an advantageous or disadvantageous situation.

Here we examine the timing of chance events with respect to individual lives. First off, the importance of being in the right place at the right time, or conversely, being in the wrong place at the wrong time. These are expressions that we have heard throughout our lives. But what do they actually mean?

In the case of being in the right place at the right time, the implication is that something positive or lucky has occurred as a result. The opposite is true of being in the wrong place at the wrong time, the outcome being some unfortunate or unlucky event has happened.

In both cases the elements of time and place must come together. It is here that the random factor shows its hand. The coming together of these separate streams is often the result of luck or coincidence. They have to align with each other such that they intersect at the same point.

Imagine the elements of time and place as two trains proceeding down their separate but perpendicular tracks. When the Place and Time trains meet at the intersection point (Point A), it can be thought of as the right place at the right time (such as being able to transfer smoothly from one train to the other), or the wrong place at the wrong time (such as when the two trains collide).

The Place train can be at the right location of Point A but not at the right time. The Time train has either not yet arrived at Point A or has gone past it. Similarly, the Time train might be at the intersection point, but the Place train is either ahead or behind that point. The time is correct but not the place.

These two trains have to be on an intersecting schedule to arrive at a similar point. Again, this is where the element of chance comes into play. There are many times when we are at the right time but the wrong place, or as Dr. John sang, "I've been at the right place, but it must have been the wrong time."

In order for timing to work, each of the two trains must intersect at the same point and at the same time. There will be many more misses than connections. In addition, the Place train does not know the schedule of the Time train and vice versa. It is by pure chance that they bisect.

In our lives there are numerous examples of time and place coming or not coming together. In the case of being in the wrong place at the wrong time, this is often expressed in terms of accidents and disasters. Whether it is being on the bridge of San Luis Rey at noon on July 12, 1714, the Twin Towers on 9/11, or some other catastrophe, it is the unfortunate coming together of place and time that can result in disaster. Similarly, other accidents such as being hit on the head by a chunk of ice or being struck by an automobile are the result of being in the wrong place at the wrong time.

On the other hand, being at the right place at the right time generally refers to time and place coming together in a fortuitous coincidence. You will often hear this phrase around the entertainment field. Perhaps a novice actor decided to go to a party, and by chance she met a movie producer who just that week was looking to cast an up-and-coming actor in a new production. They were introduced by a mutual friend at the party, and after talking for a few minutes, the producer suggested that the young actor try out for the part. She wound up getting the role, which then facilitated getting her next role, which in turn led to a successful acting career. Hers was an example of being in the right place (the party) at the right time (a producer looking to hire a new actor)

Or take my earlier example of the saxophonist Hamiet Bluiett discussed in chapter 4. Hamiet happened to run into a fellow musician on the subway who mentioned that a well-known musician, Tito Puente, was looking for a baritone saxophonist to join his band at that moment. This serendipitous meeting then lead to Hamiet trying out and joining the band. That opportunity then lead to another chance meeting, in which he found himself being asked to join the quintet of jazz legend Charles Mingus. But it was the earlier chance meeting on a subway that jump-started a career-altering experience.

On the other hand, we are usually unaware of the many times that we are in the wrong place at the right time, or in the right place at the wrong time. The schedules of these two trains are generally operating behind our backs, leaving us unaware of how close we may have been to a disaster or a success. Occasionally we become aware of these near misses. For example, when a disaster strikes, individuals may be able to trace their steps to see just how close they were to experiencing the catastrophe.[1] Or in a sporting event, an athlete may be able to see just how close they came to victory but for a difference of a second or two.

A second way of thinking about timing is with respect to the period in life when chance events occur. Does it matter if a lucky break occurs earlier or later in one's life? The answer is that generally a critical chance event that happens earlier in a lifetime will be more profound and influential than one that happens later on. The reason is simple. You have many more years to live at a younger age than at an older age. Consequently, there is simply more time in which such an event can shape your life. In addition, because individuals are starting out their careers, an early lucky or unlucky break can carry more weight than one that occurs later on. I particularly like the way that Ed Smith describes an early lucky break as a "boulder that diverts the course of a stream: the course is changed—and stays changed forever, whatever happens downstream."[2]

Similarly, a negative chance event will generally be much more profound if it occurs early in life. Recall in chapter 5 the discussion of young men coming of age at a time of heightened rates of arrest and incarceration. This particular timing sequence may result in an arrest and criminal record for a youth that might not have happened at a later historical time. This then will have repercussions throughout their life. They will find it harder to get a job, locate housing, acquire credit, and many more. These, in turn, could lead to a downward spiral in terms of the quality of life.

The Matthew Effect

A second way in which the random factor exerts itself is through what is known as cumulative advantage and disadvantage. The dynamic is that as a result of the position one starts in life, particular advantages or disadvantages may be present. These initial advantages or disadvantages can then result in further advantages or disadvantages, producing a cumulative process in which inequalities are widened across the life course. This perspective has been used to understand various inequities and how they can multiply throughout a lifetime.[3]

One of the earliest discussions addressing this topic was an analysis of scientific productivity by the sociologist Robert Merton.[4] Merton argued that early recognition, placement, and advantage in the career of a young scientist often led to exponential gains and rewards over time, which in turn further solidified the status and reputation of the scientist. Scientists who did not experience these key early advantages (although they were often as capable) generally saw their careers stall and plateau. Merton described cumulative advantage as "the way in which initial comparative advantage of trained capacity, structural location, and available resources make for successive increments of advantages such that the gaps between the haves and the have-nots . . . widen."[5]

Merton labeled this process as the Matthew Effect, referring to the book of Matthew in the New Testament where it is said, "For unto everyone that hath shall be given, and he shall have abundance; but from him that hath not shall be taken away even that which he hath." Since Merton's initial discussions, this concept has been applied in a wide array of subjects, including differences in schooling, work and career opportunities, and overall health status.[6]

Of course, a much more familiar example of cumulative inequality is found in the classic 1939 song "God Bless the Child," written by Billie Holiday and Arthur Herzog Jr. The well-known verse goes, "Them that's got shall get, them that's not shall lose. So the Bible said, and it still is news." The dynamic of cumulative inequality has been observed and commented upon over a very long period of time.

As we discussed in chapter 5, where we start in life is very much the luck of the draw. We do not choose our parents or our genetic background. Likewise our socioeconomic background is left to chance. In this way the random factor jump-starts the process of cumulative inequality.

Cumulative advantage also relates back to our prior discussion on receiving a lucky break early in one's career. As in Merton's example of scientific productivity, those who receive a fortuitous event early in their career may then see that benefit multiplied over time. The converse is true for those experiencing an unlucky occurrence early in life. As in the example from chapter 5, an early criminal conviction can set in motion a downward spiral across the life course.

In the past I have used a game analogy to help illustrate this process.[7] The quintessential American board game is that of Monopoly. The objective of the game is to acquire properties, build houses and hotels, collect rent, make money, and eventually put the other players out of business. The rules themselves are straightforward. Normally, each player is given $1,500 at the start of the game. The playing field is in effect level, with each of the players' outcomes determined by the roll of the dice and their own skills and judgments.

This notion of a level playing field is largely the way that we like to imagine the economic race in America. Each individual's outcome is determined by their own skill and effort, and by taking advantage of what happens along the road of life. Our belief in equality of opportunity as a nation underlies this principle.

Let us now imagine a modified game of Monopoly, in which the players start out with quite different advantages and disadvantages, much as they do in life. Player 1 begins with $3,000 and several Monopoly properties on which houses have already been built. Player 2 starts out with the standard $1,500 and no properties. Finally, Player 3 begins the game with only $250.

The question becomes, who will be the winners and losers in this modified game of Monopoly? Both luck and skill are still involved, and the rules of the game remain the same, but given the differing sets of resources and assets that each player begins with, these become much less important in predicting the game's outcome. Certainly, it is possible for Player 1, with $3,000, to lose, and for Player 3, with $250, to win, but that is unlikely given the unequal allocation of money at the start of the game. Moreover, while Player 3 may win in any individual game, over the course of hundreds of games, the odds are that Player 1 will win considerably more often, even if Player 3 is much luckier and more skilled.

In addition, the way each of the three individuals is able to play the game will vary considerably. Player 1 is able to take greater chances and risks. And if they should make several tactical mistakes, these probably will not matter much in the larger scheme of things. If Player 3 makes one such mistake, it may very well result in disaster. Player 1 will also be able to purchase properties and houses that Player 3 is largely locked out of, causing the rich to get richer and the poor to get poorer. These assets, in turn, will generate further income later in the game for Player 1 and in all likelihood will result in the bankrupting of Players 2 and 3.

Consequently, the initial advantages or disadvantages at the start of the game result in additional advantages or disadvantages as the games progresses. These, in turn, will then lead to further advantages or disadvantages, and so the process goes.

The other point to be made with this analogy is that the impact of luck will be much different for our three players. Each player takes their turn to roll the dice to determine where they will land next on the board. In this sense all players have the exact same amount of chance affecting them. However, the negative and positive impacts of those chance events are much different for the players. For Player 3 with limited resources, the bad luck of landing on a property owned by one of the other players could be catastrophic. Likewise, Player 3 may not be able to take advantage of the good fortune of landing on a property not owned by the other players. Although Player 3 may want to purchase that property, they likely will not be able to do so given their limited resources.

On the other hand, should Player 1 have the unlucky outcome of landing on another player's property, this bad luck is blunted by the fact that they can easily pay that player the rent that is due. If Player 1 has the good fortune of landing on an unowned property, they can just as easily take advantage of their good luck and purchase it. Such a purchase will, in turn, amplify their already substantial advantages.

This analogy illustrates the cumulative process that compounds advantages or disadvantages over time. Differences in parental incomes and resources exert a major influence over children's ability to acquire valuable skills and education. These differences in human capital will, in turn, strongly influence how well children compete in the labor market, and therefore help to determine the extent of their economic success during the course of their lives, as well as their risk of poverty.

The analogy also demonstrates the fact that chance affects each player differently. Although each player is exposed to a similar amount of chance, the way that luck plays itself out differs considerably given each player's different levels of resources. In addition, as a result of earlier advantages with respect to resources for Player 1, bad luck can be blunted and good luck accentuated. In this manner chance and luck amplify the process of cumulative inequality.

Ripples and Currents

One of the major themes throughout this book is the intersection of randomness with the various structural forces that push our lives forward. There is a dynamic interplay between these two partners. One way to conceptualize this dynamic is through the image of currents and ripples. There are strong currents that tend to push our lives in particular directions. But within those currents are the ripples of randomness. These ripples have much to say about the specifics of our lives. As we saw in the preceding chapter, the particular job we find ourselves in, the street we live on, who we form relationships with— all of these and more are influenced by chance.

Structural forces have long been analyzed by social scientists. They are influential in pushing our lives in particular directions and in having a profound impact upon life chances. Three of the most important are class, race, and gender. These attributes influence many things, such as our income, occupation, education, health status, life expectancy, and family patterns.

The manner in which the random factor and these structural forces interact is of particular interest for our purposes. One point of intersection is that structural conditions such as class or race may set boundaries around the types of chance events which are likely to occur. For example, children growing up in a wealthy environment are likely to experience different chance events than children in a poor environment. In both cases the random factor is present, but it will present itself in very different ways.

A second point of intersection is that similar chance events may have quite different repercussions depending upon the current that one is in. In our Monopoly analogy, the impact of Player 3 rolling the dice, landing on Boardwalk, and having to pay rent will be much different than if Player 1 rolls the dice and lands on Boardwalk.

A third point of intersection is that it is possible for a chance event to throw an individual into a different current. A ripple of chance may turn out to be a wave which can alter the trajectory that one is on. In this way chance can at times override the influence of the structural currents in our lives. This is particularly the case when such an event occurs early in one's life.

Several examples illustrate these dynamics. The phrase "driving while black" is one that is unfortunately all too familiar. Research has shown that Black drivers are much more likely to be stopped by the police for traffic violations than White drivers.[8] Often this is the result of racial profiling, with the intention of using traffic stops as a pretext for investigating other possible criminal offenses such as drug trafficking.[9] Or it may involve a local community looking to bring in revenue from those seen as easy targets of opportunity.[10]

Being pulled over for a traffic violation involves several ripples of chance coming together. First, you have to be driving your car along a path that intersects with the location of where a police officer is. Second, the officer needs to be traveling along a route or is stationed in a spot that intersects with your path. These two events must obviously coincide at the exact same time. And third, at the moment of this intersection, you generally must be violating a traffic law—going too fast, not signaling a turn, running a red light, having a tail light out, not wearing a seatbelt, and so on. When these three things come together, there is a likelihood that you will be pulled over.

However, given what we know about the racial differences in traffic violations, the structural currents that are pushing Black drivers along are much different than the structural currents pushing White drivers along. For Black drivers, their driving routes are more likely to be intersected by police officers. Because of patterns of racial residential segregation, Black residents are more likely to live in poorer areas that are predominately Black. As a result, the police presence may be greater in such areas, which are seen as "problematic." Second, the cars that African Americans are driving may be older and therefore more likely to have something wrong with them. Third, the police officers may be more attuned to be looking for traffic violations as an excuse to pull individuals over. This is the by-product of the dynamics of racial profiling mentioned above. Consequently, the chances of a traffic arrest are much greater in the currents that Black drivers travel than in the currents that White drivers travel.

In addition, the consequences of a traffic arrest may be much more consequential for Black drivers than for White drivers. *St. Louis Post-Dispatch* reporter Tony Messenger has written extensively about this in *Profit and Punishment: How America Criminalizes the Poor in the Name of Justice.*[11] What can happen is that an individual is arrested for a minor, nonviolent offense such as a traffic violation. Bail is set at $500. The defendant is poor and does not have the cash. She is then placed in jail for days or weeks until her court hearing, but all this time the dollar clock is ticking.

Most states have what are known as "pay-to-stay" statutes. This means that the individual is being charged for her room and board as long as she is behind bars. Eventually she is encouraged to enter a guilty plea for a probationary sentence of one or two years. But now she must return to court each month and begin paying back her court fines and fees and pay-to-stay costs. Judges serve as debt collectors for the county government. And if the guilty party fails to show up or make a monthly payment, she often finds herself back in jail, with her debt rising even higher.

As Messenger writes, "In most jurisdictions, the largest of these fines is the bill for time in jail, as if one has spent a year in a hotel."[12] Charles Dickens wrote about such debtors' prisons in nineteenth-century England, and Messenger's book shows that they are alive and well in twenty-first-century America. The result of this process is that individuals may lose their jobs, their homes, and their cars as a result of failing to pay the court costs. Many will never recover. In this way a chance event such as a traffic stop will have much different consequences depending upon the structural forces of race and class.

A second example illustrates how a strong wave within a current can push an individual into a different current. For decades, women have been subtly and not so subtly steered into certain occupations, and steered away from other occupations. Gender preferences and norms have reinforced these patterns. The result is what is known as occupational segregation in the labor market. This refers to the fact that within many of the jobs where women are employed, the vast majority of their co-workers are also women. Over the past few decades these patterns have been breaking down, but nevertheless remain strong.

Consequently, gender is a powerful current that pushes women into particular directions with respect to a career. However, there are many instances where a chance event is powerful enough to completely lift someone into a different current and direction. This often takes the form of a random event that triggers an interest or curiosity about an untraditional career, and it generally happens early in one's lifetime.

In *Chasing the American Dream*, I talked with several women for which this was very much the case. They had not considered a particular career option until something quite by chance crossed their path. This chance occurrence had opened their eyes to an option that they had been unaware of, and it put them on an entirely different path. It may have been a happenstance conversation with a friend of one's mother or father. It could have been accidently discovering a newspaper or magazine article that had been lying in the trash. It may have been an email that for some reason had been sent by mistake. Or in the example given in chapter 6, it may have been an undergraduate course that was enrolled in because the time fit into a schedule, and turned out to be a career-changer. Similar to what we saw earlier in chapter 3 with regard to serendipitous discoveries, these events may have sparked an interest that had been lying in wait.

The result was a strong wave that pushed these women into a different current and career trajectory. They still had to manage the considerable baggage and struggles that come with being a woman in a male-dominated field, but they became determined to make their way. And make their way they did. One was the chief financial officer at a major university. Another was a principal member of the low brass section (traditionally male dominated) in one the country's finest symphony orchestras. And a third was a U.S. district judge. In each case a chance event had been important in redirecting the trajectory of their lives.

A third example illustrates the way in which economic class can blunt or accentuate a chance event. In chapter 5 we discussed some of the research findings dealing with the random factor and disease. Contracting a specific disease may be a combination of environment and genes, but it may also be very much dependent upon chance as well. Good or bad luck can be important in terms of who does and who does not develop a particular disease.

Take the case of cancer. Research has indicated that for many cancers, randomness plays an important role in who does and who does not develop cancer. In two key studies published in the journal *Science*, medical researchers estimated that approximately 66 percent of "cancer-causing genetic mutations arise from the 'bad luck' of a healthy, dividing cell making a random mistake when it copies its DNA."[13] Lead author Bert Vogelstein also found that 29 percent of mutations were due to the environment, and 5 percent due to heredity. Of course, these percentages will vary depending on the type of cancer. Vogelstein reports that 60 percent of skin and lung cancer mutations are caused by the environment, compared with only 15 percent for breast cancer. But the point being that the occurrence of cancer is often a random, unlucky event. It can strike anyone.

Particularly pertinent examples are those who develop nonsmokers lung cancer, known as small cell lung cancer. This type of cancer is primarily caused by random mutations. It occurs across the population, and is not influenced by lifestyle choices or genetic background. Consequently, it is the random factor that chooses who will come down with this disease.

Nevertheless, it is here that social class plays a significant role in how this unlucky diagnosis will impact the individual. First off, for someone from a wealthy background, they are likely to have excellent health insurance and access to very good doctors. As a result, they are more likely to have received an earlier diagnosis than someone from a poor background. This is critical in terms of one's prognosis. The earlier a cancer is discovered the better with respect to recovery. They are more likely to have a team of doctors who are highly regarded in the profession and as a result their treatment procedure should be excellent. In addition, new research has shown that between 78 and 92 percent of such cancers can be treated very effectively with precision drugs to target specific mutations in a patient's tumor.[14] However, these drugs are expensive and a patient must have good health insurance to access them. The individual from a wealthy background is much more likely to be able to utilize these drugs as part of their treatment.

On the other hand, individuals in poverty may not even have health insurance and are therefore unable to afford any treatment whatsoever.

They will probably be diagnosed with the cancer much later in its progression leading to a less hopeful prognosis. In addition, the use of precision drugs is unlikely to be a part of their treatment. The result of all of this is that given a similar cancer diagnosis, the wealthy individual can expect to live a much longer life than the poverty-stricken individual. A similar stroke of bad luck, yet very different outcomes.

These are but three examples that illustrate some of the ways in which the ripples of randomness intersect with the currents of structural forces such as class, race, and gender. I find this analogy quite helpful in thinking about how randomness exerts itself as we make our way on life's journey. There are particular forces that push us in general directions. But within those strong currents are the ripples of randomness that often decide the specifics of our life stories. And at times, some of these ripples can fundamentally change the very direction of our lives.

Finally, there is an additional set of currents that also help shape the direction of our lives. These are what we might call personal attributes. They include traits such as intelligence, determination, creativity, inquisitiveness, cooperation, assertiveness, optimism, and many more. This group of personal attributes can influence the direction our lives can take.

For example, a highly motivated and driven person may have a particular trajectory that is influenced by these traits. Their choices in terms of an occupation and career may be partially shaped by these characteristics. Perhaps they are drawn to a very competitive and challenging work environment, one in which individual success is encouraged and economically rewarded. Or an extremely creative and innovative individual might be drawn to the world of avant-garde art or music. Personality traits can and do influence the directions our lives might take.

But within these currents of personality traits, the ripples of randomness are again ever present. Similar to our discussion of the structural forces of class, race, and gender, randomness interacts with personal traits. For instance, the types of random events one is exposed to may differ within these different currents of personal traits. A person strongly motivated by greed may have quite different random encounters than an individual motivated by compassion. Or someone who is very inquisitive may be more open to recognizing a fortuitous random event when it occurs than someone less curious.

In sum, the currents of larger forces and characteristics interact with the element of randomness to create a dynamic interchange. Like the currents in a stream, our lives are pushed forward by the particular traits that we possess. But the many ripples within those currents will influence the specifics in our lives. Those ripples are very much the result of the random factor.

Does Luck Even Out and Can It Be Influenced?

A final dynamic of randomness revolves around the question, Does luck even out over time and can it be influenced? There is a widely held assumption that somehow good and bad luck events will in the end even out. That if you have experienced a string of bad luck then you are due to have some good luck. We might imagine the Roman goddess Fortuna weighing good luck and bad luck on a scale and making sure that they are somehow balanced at the end of one's life. And in fact, this was what Fortuna was accomplishing by spinning her wheel of fortune. If you had your time of riding the wheel to the top then you must also ride the wheel to the bottom. As quoted in the first chapter, she tells Boethius,

> This is my art, this the game I never cease to play. I turn the wheel that spins. I delight to see the high come down and the low ascent. Mount up, if you wish, but on the condition you will not think it a hardship to come down when the rules of my game require it.[15]

In other words, what goes up, must come down. In this way good and bad fortune are evenly divided.

There is also a belief that luck itself can be influenced. For millennia, people have believed in various superstitions in order to sway luck in their favor. More recently, self-help books often promise that you can create your own luck.

Let us first consider the question, Does luck even out? In many situations, the answer is no. In chapter 9 we will discuss the gambler's fallacy. At the heart of this fallacy is the belief that luck must even itself out. That a gambler on a losing streak should keep playing because their luck is bound to change. Or that after five spins of the roulette ball landing on red, it is now more likely to land on black because it is overdue.

These beliefs are simply fallacious. The chance of the roulette ball landing on black on the sixth spin is 50 percent, not 60, 70, or 80 percent. It makes no difference what the past spins have turned up. The roulette ball does not think to itself, "Well, it's time for me to choose to land on black since I haven't been there for some time." And yet this is precisely what people are thinking when following the gambler's fallacy.

In fact, given our earlier discussion of the Matthew Effect, there are reasons to believe that good luck follows good luck and bad luck follows bad luck. Rather than luck evening out, it can become more bifurcated over time. Likewise in our discussion of currents and ripples, it may be the case that depending on which current you find yourself in, you may be exposed to many more good luck chance events than bad luck events, or vice versa. Consequently, although we may like to believe that luck evens out over the long run, there is no evidence to suggest it is so.

One of the reasons that we cling to this belief is our hope that we live in a just and fair world (discussed in chapter 9). It seems only fair that luck should be evenly distributed—that one person should not be saddled with only bad luck, or blessed with only good luck. The notion of balance lies at the heart of many conceptions of justice. In a just world, what you put into something should reflect what you get back from that effort. But the random factor flies in the face of a just world. It does not abide by notions of balance or evening out.

Certainly it will be true that if events have a 50/50 chance of occurring, then over a long period of time they will tend to even out. A coin that is flipped repeatedly will end up with an overall tally that will be roughly half heads and half tails. However, in life as it is lived, the likelihood of chance events occurring is largely unknown. By their very nature they cannot be predicted with an overall odds percentage. The result is that good and bad luck are not on a path that they will even out in the end. They may, but then again they may not.

Let us now consider the idea that we might be able to influence luck. Certainly this was the idea in Roman times of making offerings to the goddess Fortuna. By doing so, Romans were hoping that she would smile upon their futures by bringing good luck their way.

A whole chapter could be devoted to the various superstitions that people hold in order to court good luck and forestall bad luck. The list of good luck charms is long: discovering a four-leaf clover, carrying a rabbit's foot, throwing salt over your left shoulder, wishing on a falling star, finding a lucky penny, hanging a horseshoe over a doorway, crossing your fingers, knocking on wood, and many more. Across the globe there are equally long lists of charms and customs believed to sway the fortunes of luck. Likewise, the list of behaviors thought to ward off bad luck are just as long: avoid walking under a ladder, not breaking a mirror, staying clear of the number 13, not crossing the path of a black cat, being careful on Friday the 13th, not stepping on a crack, and countless others.

Various superstitions became adopted and continue to this day in the hope that we mortals can somehow influence how chance and luck may play out. Part of the reason for their popularity is that they relieve some of the anxiety surrounding chance and luck. Bad luck can be frightening, and by believing in the ability of good luck charms to ward off such troubles, stress and anxiety might be somewhat relieved.

Suffice it to say that none of these charms and superstitions have any effect on influencing luck. Obviously, this should go without saying. And yet, as with astrology, many people continue to abide by various superstitions. The random factor is much too savvy to be swayed by such wishful thinking.

Of more recent origins are books promoting the idea that individuals can create their own luck. For example, on my bookshelf sits *The Serendipity Mindset: The Art and Science of Creating Good Luck*.[16] Many of these books deal with taking advantage of chance events that come our way, rather than actually making chance or luck appear. And indeed, I will discuss in chapter 9 that this is an important lesson we can learn from the random factor. It introduces the idea that although we may not be able to control chance events, we can exert some agency in terms of how we respond to such events. In addition, we can become more perceptive to hidden opportunities that could come to our attention via the random factor. It is in this sense that there is once again a dance between these two partners. Similar to our discussion regarding currents and ripples, there is a dynamic interchange between randomness and agency. Our lives are without a doubt influenced by chance and luck, but we also have the ability to respond and react to these elements of randomness.

In addition, as we saw earlier, the types of chance events are influenced by the currents that one finds themselves in. Moving into a different stream or current could affect the kinds of luck that one is be exposed to. For example, by increasing one's education, new opportunities may arise with some of those opportunities being the result of chance and randomness. Or by working hard at something, one may be able to influence the types of chance events that come one's way. This is what underlies the familiar statement "I make my own luck." In this sense one may be able to alter some of the chance events that we might encounter.

Summary

We have looked at several of the ways in which the patterns of chance and luck play themselves out in our lives. While predicting when and where a chance event will occur is fruitless, we can nevertheless observe some tendencies in terms of how the random factor plays its cards.

First, the issue of timing is critical. In order for many fortunate and unfortunate chance events to strike an individual, the time and place must coincide. The individual must be at both the right time and the right place, or the wrong time and the wrong place. In addition, a fortuitous or not fortuitous chance event will generally be more monumental if it occurs early in one's life.

Second, the process of cumulative advantage and disadvantage often ensures that good luck will follow good luck just as bad luck may follow bad luck. Advantages or disadvantages at the early stages of life will tend to lead to additional advantages or disadvantages resulting in a cumulative process. The types of luck that one is exposed to will be influenced by this process.

Third, we can think of the larger forces that push our lives along in particular directions as strong currents, whereas the random factor often operates as ripples within those currents. In this way there is an interaction between these two life forces. In addition, the types of chance events that one is exposed to will often vary depending upon the current that one is in.

Finally, there is no reason to assume that luck evens out across a lifetime. One may be blessed with much good luck, or cursed with much bad luck. The random factor is not in the business of evenly dividing out equal amounts of good or bad luck. Likewise, our attempts to influence luck are basically useless. On the other hand, we can and do exert agency in terms of how we might respond to chance and luck. In fact, this is one of the important lessons that we can learn from the random factor. We now turn to how we can use randomness to improve our lives and our policies.

III *Lessons Learned*

8   Retooling Policies

Waiting for God to reveal himself, I believe that his prime minister,
Chance, governs this sad world just as well.

—STENDHAL, 1830

In this final section of the book we ask, What can be gained from a
heightened recognition of the random factor? How might these insights inform our policies and programs, and how might this awareness positively impact the way we see ourselves and others around
us? In this chapter we take up policies and programs, while chapter 9
explores positive personal impacts.

Within the political world, the perceived importance of luck and
chance has varied somewhat between those on the right and left of
the political spectrum.[1] Conservatives have tended to downplay the
role of luck in affecting life outcomes. This is consistent with the
dominant ideology of rugged individualism and meritocracy.
Through hard work, effort, skills, and talents, individuals are viewed
for the most part as controlling their life outcomes. It is within this
context that Americans are seen as making their own luck.

On the other hand, liberals or progressives are somewhat more
likely to recognize the role of chance and luck in affecting lives. There

is an awareness of unexpected events occurring that can have a profound influence upon people's outcomes. The traditional liberal support of a strong social safety net is consistent with this recognition.

The perspective taken throughout this book is that chance is very much a central part of life. Recognizing the importance of chance in our lives can help establish a robust set of policies designed to ameliorate some of the negative effects of luck and amplifying their positive attributes. In particular, the understanding that bad luck can strike anyone at any time implies that social policy should be guided by an overall concept of universal insurance.

We begin our discussion by reviewing and then extending the insights of the philosopher John Rawls. At the heart of Rawls's theory is the notion of luck.

The Veil of Ignorance

John Rawls is generally considered the most significant moral philosopher of the twentieth century. His work has had a profound influence upon philosophy, as well as political science, sociology, economics, social work, theology, and law. For much of his career he was a faculty member in Harvard's department of philosophy.

Rawls's major work was his 1971 *A Theory of Justice.*[2] In it he details the basic components of a just and fair society. He begins with what he refers to as the original position. Imagine, Rawls writes, that "no one knows his place in society, his class position or social status, nor does anyone know his fortune in the distribution of natural assets and abilities, his intelligence, strength, and the like."[3] Behind such a veil of ignorance, Rawls asks, what would be an acceptable social contract for most people? His argument is that individuals in this original position would likely choose two fundamental principles.

The first is that each of us would want to be guaranteed access to the most basic liberties. These would include "political liberty (the right to vote and to be eligible for public office) together with freedom of speech and assembly; liberty of conscience and freedom of thought; freedom of the person along with the right to hold (personal) property; and freedom from arbitrary arrest and seizure as defined by the concept of the rule of law."[4] Consequently, nearly all citizens, no matter where they fall in society, would want to be entitled to these rights.

The second chosen principle according to Rawls would be to allow social and economic inequalities to exist, but only under two conditions: (1) "if they result in compensating benefits for everyone, and in particular for the least advantaged members of society;"[5] and (2) that offices and positions in society are open to all. The reason that inequalities would be tolerated in the first place is because such inequalities often provide incentives to greater production, which can benefit all citizens. According to Rawls, a just society therefore does not necessitate that the distribution of income or wealth has to be equal, but rather that an unequal distribution is to everyone's advantage, particularly those at the lower end of the income distribution. For example, from a Rawlsian perspective, a just society would be one that provides a strong social safety net to protect the economically vulnerable, with the funding for such programs coming through a redistribution of some of the gains earned by those at the middle and upper ends of the income gradient.

These two principles, referred to as the "liberty principle" and the "difference principle," form the core of Rawls's conception of "justice as fairness." In his later work, Rawls elaborated and extended the ideas laid out in *A Theory of Justice*. In particular, his 1993 *Political Liberalism* dealt with addressing how the liberty and difference principles can exist and be applicable within democratic societies, given the wide variety of ideological and religious viewpoints within such societies.[6] He argued in *Political Liberalism* and in his final book, *Justice as Fairness: A Restatement*, that his principles of justice should be understood as a political guideline rather than as a moral doctrine.[7] Consequently, the plurality of religious, philosophical, and moral viewpoints within democracies can successfully coexist under a political interpretation of justice as fairness.

Let us step back for a moment and consider in greater detail the Rawlsian veil of ignorance. What is clear from his discussion is that chance, luck, and the random factor are fundamental to this concept. Rawls proposes that we consider the kind of society we would want to live in given that we could end up anywhere in the social structure, or to put it in the vernacular of this book, that we might be randomly assigned. We might be at the top, at the bottom, or somewhere in between. In other words, chance or luck will determine where we fall. Our race and gender will also be randomly assigned. Furthermore, our natural abilities and talents will be randomly distributed. Given this uncertainty, what would we insist that society should provide to all?

Rawls is pointing out the importance of the lottery of birth, as discussed in chapter 5. We have no control over who are parents are or what their economic standing is. Likewise we have no control over our genetic background. Rather, it is chance that determines where we begin our lives. Certainly in hindsight we know now where in the social structure we started off, but this is only after the fact. Thus, Rawls's veil of ignorance incorporates many of the concepts reviewed in chapter 5.

Given that chance and luck determine our starting points and abilities, and given that these starting points are critical in determining our life trajectories, what might this suggest that a good society should provide to all of its members? Take a minute and consider this personally. Not knowing where in society you might land, not knowing what your talents and abilities might be, not knowing your gender or race, what would you want to make sure that you were entitled to regardless of where you fell in society? It is both an intriguing and important question to ponder, and it is one where the random factor is front and center.

The Two Rawlsian Principles

Of course, you and I may not completely agree, but I would assert that we would likely come to some general agreement over a handful of conditions and prerequisites that each of us would insist on. Let us begin with Rawls's two principles.

The Liberty Principle

My sense is that we would find strong support among Americans regarding the first Rawlsian principle that everyone should be entitled to certain basic liberties. Survey research indicates strong support for this principle. Americans firmly believe in the principle of fundamental rights and liberties for all, and that each individual should have the freedom to partake in those rights no matter who they are.[8]

These would include a number of basic political and human rights such as voting, trial by jury, freedom of speech, freedom of religion, and so on. Many of these rights were specified in the Bill of Rights that was added to the U.S. Constitution in 1791. Over time, additional rights have been added and others have been strengthened through amendments to the Constitution and through various decisions handed down by the Supreme Court.

The general understanding has been that a society which fails to guarantee such basic rights to all of its citizens, represents an unjust society. Only in a few cases might the denial of some rights be warranted, such as the situation where an individual was incarcerated. But other than these very narrow circumstances, all citizens should be entitled to these rights.

In looking back over our history, the denial of people's basic political and human rights has been a major force for change. It was the argument for why the colonists felt justified in declaring independence from Great Britain (e.g., the issue of taxation without representation). Because of the denial of certain basic rights laid out in the Declaration of Independence, the colonies proclaimed the right to secede from the mother country. In a sense, the nation was created in order to rectify the injustice of Great Britain's disregarding the rights of the colonists.

This notion of certain inalienable rights belonging to all Americans has continued throughout our history, for example through various rights movements. Nearly all of these movements have sought to increase the number and groups of people who are entitled to particular rights. The most blatant of rights being denied was of course that of slavery, which led to the abolitionist movement. The women's suffrage movement at the turn of the twentieth century was premised on correcting the injustice of women being denied the right to vote. The civil rights movement in the 1950s and 1960s was premised on the idea that Black Americans were being denied certain basic rights, and that this was a blatant violation of the concept of justice.

Other rights movements have also been largely built on the idea that particular rights were being denied, and therefore the country was in violation of its sense of justice. These have included the women's movement, gay and lesbian rights movement, persons with disabilities movement, and so on.

One right that has also been discussed within this justice context has been the idea that there should be a basic economic floor that no one should fall below—that in a wealthy country, everyone should have a right to a minimum standard of living. President Franklin Roosevelt introduced this idea within his economic bill of rights in 1944.[9] However, this concept has had less traction than many of the other rights movements. I will come back to this idea shortly.

In sum, the protection and enforcement of certain fundamental rights is generally viewed as an essential component of American justice. The belief has been that every citizen should be entitled to the full protection and enjoyment of those rights.

The implication of Rawls's liberty principle is that social policy should be reinforcing every Americans right to engage freely in these liberties regardless of where one falls in society. Unfortunately, this is still not the case. Although certain rights are guaranteed by the Constitution and Bill of Rights, lower income or poverty in particular reduces an individual's ability to fully partake in those rights, even though they are still guaranteed under the law.

Take the judicial right that citizens are assumed innocent until proven guilty. A strong argument can be made that the ability to fully benefit from this right is directly affected by the amount of financial resources one is able to bring to bear upon the legal system. For example, assume a hypothetical case of two individuals—Peter who is wealthy and lives in a suburban setting, and James who is impoverished and lives in an inner city. Both are accused of an identical crime with incriminating circumstances surrounding their cases, yet both are innocent. The question becomes who will have the greater likelihood of receiving a verdict of not guilty.

Peter will be able to hire an eminently qualified and experienced lawyer, or perhaps a team of expert trial lawyers. The lawyer(s) for Peter will be able to devote considerable time, energy, and resources to the case since Peter can afford for them to do so. James in all likelihood will have to depend upon the public defender, already burdened with a heavy caseload that has stretched them to the limit. By necessity, far less time and energy will be spent preparing for James's defense.

These factors, along with others related to economic class, increase the odds that Peter will receive the proper verdict of not guilty, while they decrease the odds that James will receive the same

verdict. Certainly there will be many times when individuals in James's position will receive a verdict of not guilty, and times when individuals in Peter's position will receive a verdict of guilty. However, if we were to repeat this experiment over and over, it is quite probable that taken as a whole, individuals in Peter's situation would have a significantly higher percentage of receiving not guilty verdicts when compared to those in James's situation.

As Derek Bok further points out, a case such as James's may not even reach the point of trial. Bok uses the right to attorney to illustrate how economic reality infringes upon guaranteed liberties:

> Surely there is no other nation where the nature of individual freedom has been elaborated in such detail, or any other society that is so well organized to ensure that essential liberties are defended and preserved. At the same time, freedom in the United States may be more limited by other forces than it is abroad. For example, the government in America often makes less effort than others to make sure that all or most Americans have the means to exercise important rights they formally possess. To choose but one example, it is impressive to grant everyone accused of a serious crime the right to qualified counsel, but the right may not be worth much in practice if the lawyers assigned turn out to have so little time that they can scarcely do more than hastily agree to exchange a guilty plea for a slightly reduced sentence. Yet this is the situation that exists in many jurisdictions of this country.[10]

Many other rights can also be seen in this light as well. For example, it is legally guaranteed that anyone who meets certain basic qualifications such as age and residency can run for public office. Yet in reality, economics has a profound impact on the ability to mount such a campaign and even more so on the ability to win. For example, who is it that can afford to take time off from work and run for office?

Generally it will be those who are either independently well off or who have jobs that allow them the luxury of doing so (e.g., higher-status occupations). Consequently, individuals with the fewest economic resources are the least likely to engage in such a right.

Or take the basic right to vote. Although all citizens have the right to vote, in reality, economics plays a role in influencing overall voter participation rates. The fact that the U.S. conducts its elections on Tuesdays rather than on weekends, combined with our cumbersome registration procedures, tends to disproportionally create barriers for the poor. As Leonard Beeghley notes,

> In sum, while any individual can presumably go to the polls, the structure of voting means that middle-class and rich people dominate this form of participation. The poor and working class are least capable of voting on a working day, getting registered, coping with voting procedures, and overcoming the problem posed by separate and frequent elections. These facts exist externally to individuals, decisively influencing rates of participation. Thus, for those at the lower end of the stratification hierarchy, the political system may seem open but it is closed in fact.[11]

These examples illustrate the more general point I am making regarding liberty in the sense of rights guaranteed under the law. Although in principle such rights apply to all, in reality, economics, and particularly poverty, can infringe upon the full realization of those rights. From the perspective of Rawls's veil of ignorance, one would want to be able to fully partake in these rights regardless of where one might fall in society as a result of the lottery of birth.

Social policy should therefore be directed toward reinforcing the ability for all Americans to engage in their legal rights. For example, rather than making it harder to vote, particularly for persons of color and/or lower-income individuals (which has been the case in recent years), policy should be focused on creating greater access to voting. This would include voter registration drives, developing easier procedures for voting online or absentee, moving the day of voting to a weekend, and other policies that would increase voter participation.

Likewise, other liberties should be strengthened such that the disenfranchised in society are able to fully take advantage of these rights. These would include the earlier-mentioned right of being assumed innocent until proven guilty, the right to protest, the right to live and reside in any residential community regardless of race, and many others. From a Rawlsian and a random factor perspective, social policy should ensure that all Americans can fully partake in the rights guaranteed under law.

The Difference Principle

Regarding the second principle that Rawls details (known as the difference principle), here I feel we would likely find much less agreement. It is not clear that we would agree that inequalities should be permitted only to the extent that such inequalities are to the benefit of all. America is steeped in the ethos of individualism. This works against the notion that one's economic gains must be connected to benefitting society as a whole. My hunch is that behind of veil of ignorance, many Americans would not tie economic gains to the proviso that those gains must be to be benefit of all.

The dominance of individualism in American society, and the uniqueness of the ideology's extreme popularity in the U.S. compared to elsewhere in the world, has been apparent throughout our history. Martin Marger explains,

The place of individualism as the most basic component of the American creed and its pervasiveness throughout American culture have been recognized almost since the country's founding. Scholars and social commentators have repeatedly shown this aspect of American society to be truly exceptional in comparison with other societies.[12]

Individualism is a core part of what it means to be an American. One notable American National Election Study survey from the 1990s asked respondents how important "trying to get ahead on one's own effort" is in making somebody a "true American." An overwhelming majority, 80 percent, agreed that it is either very (45 percent) or extremely (35 percent) important, while only 5 percent said it was not at all important.[13]

Survey data from throughout the twentieth century demonstrates the persistent popularity of individualism. Even toward the end of the Great Depression in the late 1930s, with unemployment falling but still very high, 74 percent of Americans opposed a top limit on incomes, and only 35 percent supported the redistribution of taxes levied on the wealthy.[14] By the early 1950s, 88 percent of Americans agreed that anybody who worked hard could go as far as they wanted.[15]

From the middle of the twentieth century to today, this individualism has persisted. As Robert Putnam notes, "In the past half century we have witnessed, for better or worse, a giant swing toward the individualist (or libertarian) pole in our culture, society, and politics," as "roughly two thirds of Americans from all walks of life told pollsters that as a matter of fact, anyone who worked hard could get ahead."[16] Judith Chafel, summarizing the results from multiple nationwide surveys since the 1960s, similarly argues that in subsequent decades,

an ideology of individualism prevailed in American society. That ideology emphasized a number of beliefs: first, the personal responsibility of each individual for his or her place in life; second, the opportunity afforded by the "system" to improve one's circum-stances; third, the social utility of economic inequality in motivating achievement; and finally, the existing system as equitable and fair.[17]

Given these deeply held beliefs, it is unlikely that behind a veil of ig-norance most Americans would tie economic inequality to only be-ing acceptable if it was to the benefit of everyone in society. Rather, I would argue that most would assert that as long as the tools are avail-able for individuals to get ahead on their own, economic inequality is permissible.

Those tools would include two additional conditions. The first would be that we would want to ensure that there should be an eco-nomic floor that no one should fall below. The second stipulation would be that society provides equality of opportunity for everyone. In each of these cases there is an emphasis that no matter where one might fall in society, one should be entitled to these basic rights and goods, and that the mechanism of social insurance ensures that this can be accomplished.

A Robust Universal Safety Net

A first stipulation beyond the liberty principle that I feel most of us would agree to behind a veil of ignorance would be that there should be an economic floor that no one should fall below. Not knowing where we might land in society, and understanding the possibility that bad luck could strike at any time, I believe many of us would want to be assured there was adequate protection to blunt the negative impact of dire economic poverty and hardship. The existence of a social safety net is designed to provide such pro-tection.

The stipulation of a social safety net is also tied to the importance of equality of opportunity (which will be discussed shortly). Individuals who fall below a basic economic floor may find it much harder to be able to take advantage of the opportunities available to them.[18] In previous research, I and others have shown that poverty stunts the ability of individuals to develop and reach their full potential.[19] In this sense we should think of a robust safety net and equality of opportunity as intertwined. The protection provided by an economic floor allows individuals to take fuller advantage of the opportunities provided to them.

And as we saw earlier, poverty and low income can also result in creating barriers for individuals to fully take advantage of their rights and liberties. Those in poverty are much less able to take full advantage of their legally entitled rights. Thus, a basic economic floor reinforces the earlier-mentioned liberty principle as well.

The mechanism underlying a safety net is that of insurance. And the idea behind insurance is that of moderating the random factor, particularly the occurrence of bad luck. Consider home insurance. No one plans to have a disaster strike their home. Yet homeowners are willing to invest in insurance because they recognize that at some point their home may be struck by the unfortunate event of a fire or flood that could result in sizable expenses. Hence, we are willing to pay for insurance today in order to minimize the risks in the future. As law scholar Edward Kleinbard notes,

> Insurance is an effective tool whose entire purpose is to mitigate the financial consequences of bad luck. It is a subtle financial instrument, honed over the last 700 years, from the time of medieval Italian merchants forward to today. If equality of opportunity is the great organizing principle of American economic life, and bad brute luck the unresolved universal force that knocks too many people off course in their pursuit of their economic dreams, then the application of insurance principles is the response that can be used to make equality of opportunity more than a hollow phrase.[20]

A social safety net includes various programs designed to offer economic protection to those facing temporary or longer-term economic hardship. Behind our veil of ignorance, I believe that most of us would want to have such protections in place. Theodore Marmor explains,

> Social insurance . . . rests on the widespread acceptance of the proposition that protecting workers and their families from dramatic losses of economic status brought on by common risks to labor market participation is what a decent society should do. Across virtually all advanced industrial societies, these risks are taken to include . . . birth into a poor family, the early death of a family breadwinner, ill health, involuntary unemployment, disability, and outliving one's savings. Indeed, there is a strong historical case that, beginning with Otto von Bismarck's social insurance income protection against these risks has been a fundamental precondition for the flourishing of industrial capitalism. Looked at historically, social insurance is a deeply conservative idea, the major viable alternative to state socialism.[21]

Social insurance is able to be successful through the concept of risk pooling. If large numbers of people with a low risk of calamity enroll in an insurance program and pay a modest fee for their participation, should a calamity strike one of its members, the funds will be available to protect them. Likewise, in social safety net programs, the general population pays into these programs through federal and state taxes, which then provide the resources to protect those who at some point might fall into poverty. By having large numbers of individuals enrolled in such programs, the magic of insurance is possible.

This magic is intended to counteract the influence of bad luck. As we have seen throughout this book, many unforeseen and random events can happen to individuals as they make their way across the life course. The random factor strongly implies that one important component of an effective and humane social policy is an array of programs rooted in the principle of social and economic insurance.

Consequently, I believe that behind a veil of ignorance most of us would want to know that there are social policies and programs in place to protect us if and when economic catastrophe strikes. This would include a robust social safety net that provides enough cash assistance to provide families with the ability to access essential resources such as food, shelter, health, and the other basic human necessities.

Nevertheless, our veil of ignorance is but a hypothetical thought experiment. We already know where we fall in society. For the well-do-do or the middle class, they may not feel that social safety net programs are important or relevant to them. Yet is this the case?

Obviously there is considerable difficulty in predicting personal well-being in the future. But what if we somehow knew that the risk of economic hardship was quite real? What if we could look into our future and understand what that risk and probability was?[22] Might this not change our thinking on the relevancy of a social safety net?

My colleague Tom Hirschl and I have engaged in research over the years to empirically assess this risk. Using over 40 years of longitudinal data from the longest-running panel data set in the world (the Panel Study of Income Dynamics), we have been able to estimate the percent of the U.S. population who will encounter various years of economic insecurity between the ages of 25 and 60.

In order to do so, we used four different measures of economic insecurity. First, how likely is it that an individual will reside in a household that uses a social safety net or welfare program at some point during the year? Second, to what extent will individuals find themselves in households falling into poverty or near poverty (below 150 percent of the official poverty line)? Third, does the head of

TABLE 2. Cumulative Percentage of American Adults Experiencing Various
Dimensions of Economic Insecurity by Age

	Economic Insecurity Measures			
Age	Safety Net Use	Poverty / Near Poverty	Unemployment	Combined Measure
25	11.9%	16.8%	14.4%	29.6%
30	27.3%	35.8%	38.9%	57.9%
35	33.7%	42.2%	48.3%	65.7%
40	37.9%	46.3%	54.8%	70.3%
45	40.4%	48.9%	58.5%	73.3%
50	42.4%	50.9%	62.0%	75.9%
55	43.2%	52.5%	64.0%	77.3%
60	44.8%	54.1%	66.8%	79.0%

Source: Rank and Hirschl calculations

household experience a spell of unemployment at some point during the year? And finally, how likely is it that one or more of these events will occur to individuals during the course of a year?

In Table 2 we can observe the cumulative likelihood of these events occurring for the U.S. population as they age across the prime working years. As is readily apparent in this table, economic insecurity is a very real risk and component of the American experience. We can see that the incidence of these events rises rapidly during the early years of the life course and then begins to slow down from the 40s onward. By the age of 40, 37.9 percent of Americans have experienced at least one year of welfare use, 46.3 percent have encountered poverty, 54.8 percent have experienced the head of household being unemployed, and 70.3 percent have experienced one or more of these three events. By age 60, the cumulative percentages are 44.8 percent, 54.1 percent, 66.8 percent, and 79.0 percent. Consequently, approximately four-fifths of Americans will experience at least one year of economic insecurity between the ages of 25 and 60.

TABLE 3. Cumulative Percentage of American Adults Experiencing Various
Dimensions of Economic Insecurity Across Age Categories

	Economic Insecurity Measures			
Age	Safety Net Use	Poverty / Near Poverty	Unemployment	Combined Measure
25–34	32.3%	41.3%	46.8%	64.7%
35–44	29.8%	32.0%	34.8%	53.3%
45–54	25.7%	25.8%	28.2%	48.2%
55–64	27.5%	29.3%	21.7%	50.3%

Source: Rank and Hirschl calculations

In Table 3 we see the occurrence of economic insecurity over separate 10-year age intervals across the life course. In general, research
has shown that economic insecurity is somewhat more likely to occur
during the earlier and later periods of the prime working years. Nevertheless, we can see that it is very real threat throughout each of
these periods of time as found in Table 3. Consequently, between the
ages of 25 and 34, 64.7 percent of individuals will encounter at least
one year of economic insecurity, 53.3 percent will do so between the
ages of 35 and 44, 48.2 percent between the ages of 45 and 54, and
50.3 percent between the ages of 55 and 64. Thus, during any 10-year
age period across the prime working years, at least half of the population will experience one or more years of significant economic
insecurity.

The reason the percentages in Tables 2 and 3 are so high can be
traced back to our unpredictable companion, the random factor. As
we have seen throughout the earlier chapters, unanticipated events
can and do happen to many people, particularly when looking over
longer periods of time. Some of these may be quite good, while
others can be quite damaging. In the case of economic insecurity,
these may include losing a job, families splitting up, or getting sick.
All of these events can and do throw individuals into poverty or near

poverty. The randomness across the life course implies that a social safety net is a very good investment. Most of us at some point during our lives will need some kind of assistance from a safety net program.

What then might a robust social safety net look like? Again, let us place upon ourselves a veil of ignorance such that we have no idea of where we might fall in society. Given this position, and given what we actually know about the very real risk of economic insecurity at some point in our lives, what might we insist upon for a safety net?[23]

From this point of view, universality takes on great importance. Access to a robust safety net should be available to everyone who falls below a particular income level. People have paid their taxes in the past, and will pay their taxes in the future, and therefore they are entitled to receive economic support to help them traverse a particularly challenging point in their lives brought about by the random factor.

Yet as it currently stands, the U.S. social welfare state is quite weak in terms of the assistance it provides.[24] In addition, it is largely targeted at a handful of specific groups (e.g., single parents, the incapacitated, the elderly). It is a system in which many people fall through the cracks. Yet as we have seen, the random factor and bad luck can strike anyone at any time.

Furthermore, it is a system that is premised on the idea that people need to prove that they are deserving of such assistance. It is by design difficult to access and difficult to use. And yet these barriers and stigma surrounding the safety net are simply counterproductive once we acknowledge the role of the random factor in economic downturns.

By recognizing the importance of the random factor, the premise of the deserving and undeserving poor largely falls by the wayside. As I have written in prior work, most poverty is the result of a failure at the structural rather than the individual level.[25] Structural failures are events in which individuals have little control, such as getting laid off from work or developing a sickness. A new social safety net would be based upon the premise of insurance, and that all are entitled to that insurance.

Perhaps the most straightforward way of providing an effective safety net is through what is known as a guaranteed minimum income (GMI). Somewhat similar to a negative income tax and a universal basic income, a guaranteed minimum income can be structured such that all Americans would be eligible for a minimal amount of income regardless of their circumstance. A variation of this idea nearly became law in 1972 with President Richard Nixon's Family Assistance Plan.[26]

The manner in which this would operate would be that for an individual or family that is earning below a certain level of income, the government would provide the necessary amount to lift them up to a minimal threshold. In this fashion no one would be allowed to fall below a basic level of income. For example, if an individual was earning $15,000 a year and the GMI was set at $25,000, they would receive a supplement of $10,000 to get them up to that level. The minimum amount would be set at a level high enough to purchase the necessary amount of food, shelter, and other necessities to maintain a household adequately during their period of economic uncertainty. Such a program could be administered through the Internal Revenue Service, with benefits supplied on a monthly basis. In addition, such a program might be structured in such a way as to reduce some of the work disincentive effects that could be present.[27]

The advantages of such a system in light of the random factor is that it recognizes the fact that bad economic luck can strike virtually anyone, and when that happens, a protective safety net is in place to prevent an individual from falling further. It represents a form of economic insurance—taxpayers pay into the system, and when needed, they are able to draw upon the resources of the program.

There is a second crucial element of any robust social safety net that must also be in place. And that is universal health coverage. The

United States is one of the very few industrialized countries that does not offer universal health care coverage for its citizens. Health care for those under age 65 is primarily provided through one's job. However, since the 1980s, a growing percentage of jobs have been lacking in health benefits. In addition, for those under the age of 65 but out of work, health coverage is unlikely except through the Medicaid program, which may be hard to qualify for.

A strong case can therefore be made that health care coverage should be universal. Most countries view health care as a basic human right—that it should be available regardless of where you might fall in society. This perspective lines up quite well with the veil of ignorance. Having access to good quality health care is a fundamental ingredient to a strong social safety net.

But universal health care coverage also reflects the importance of the random factor. A stroke of ill fortune and bad luck can send a critical illness or disability anyone's way at any time. As a result, there is a need for good quality health care to be available whenever it may be needed. It should not depend on whether your job provides a health care plan, or that you are a senior citizen. It is a crucial resource that is made all the more important because of the negative reach of the random factor.

Equality of Opportunity

A third policy that I believe must be in place, given the veil of ignorance and the random factor, would be the strengthening of policies that allow equality of opportunity to flourish. Americans have long supported the central importance of equality of opportunity. Yet what is meant by this phrase? The best definition that I have come across regarding equality of opportunity is from, no surprise, John Rawls: "Those who are at the same level of talent and ability, and have the same willingness to use them, should have the same prospect of success regardless of their initial place in the social system, that is, irrespective of the income class into which they are born."[28] This seems quite sensible and one that I believe many Americans would agree with behind a veil of ignorance.

Equality of opportunity is rooted in the belief that everyone should have access to the tools and resources that allow them to achieve success and the American Dream, and that certain things that enable one to do so, like a good education, should be available to all. Furthermore, equality of opportunity includes the notion that individuals should be judged and rewarded on the basis of their abilities. Robert Haveman notes in his *Starting Even* that "it has to do with having the same chance to run the race for economic success as others with similar talents and drives. Equality of opportunity exists if a black youth and a white youth have the same access to education, training, jobs, earnings, and incomes according to their abilities."[29]

Equality of opportunity is meant to counteract some of the undue influence that the lottery of birth exerts (discussed in chapter 5). Some children are born into wealthy families, some into middle-class families, and some into lower-class or poverty-stricken families. Equality of opportunity is a tool that attempts to combat the disadvantages that may be associated with being raised in a family with limited economic resources. It is a means of alleviating the negative effects of the random factor.

A just or fair society as seen through the prism of the veil of ignorance and the random factor should provide equality of opportunity to all of its citizens. Individuals who work hard, regardless of their economic position, should be able to achieve success by taking advantage of the opportunities available to them. This is certainly one of the key ideas behind the American Dream. President Johnson talked about the meaning of America in his inaugural address of 1965:

Conceived in justice, written in liberty, bound in union, it was meant one day to inspire the hopes of all mankind; and it binds us still. If we keep its terms, we shall flourish. First, justice was the promise that all who made the journey would share in the fruits of the land. In a land of great wealth, families must not live in hopeless poverty. In a land rich in harvest, children just must not go hungry. In a land of healing miracles, neighbors must not suffer and die unattended. In a great land of learning and scholars, young people must be taught to read and write.[30]

The idea is that of a level playing field, in which there are certain key opportunities that are open to all upon that playing field. What you then do with those opportunities is up to you. As a result, America has never believed that equality of outcome was just, only equality of opportunity. It is therefore a fair and just society that strives for equality of opportunity among all of its citizens.

The level playing field analogy reflects the importance of the random factor. Because of chance and luck, you might land anywhere on that field. As a result, you should not have to compete on an upgrade while the next person is fortunate to be playing on a downgrade. Rather, the field should be level for all who are competing. In addition, the rules of the game should be level and evenly applied to all competitors.

Given this discussion, perhaps the most direct way to improve the reality of equality of opportunity in the United States is to make certain that all children receive an excellent education regardless of where they might fall in society. The ability to receive a quality education is one of the most vital assets that an individual can acquire. Indeed, a key motivation behind the introduction of public education in the mid-1800s was the importance of making education accessible to the general public, rather than to only the wealthy and privileged. Horace Mann, the well-known nineteenth-century educator, spoke of public education as the "great equalizer" and as a place where both disadvantaged and advantaged children would be taught under one roof. The expansion and access to public education has had a profound impact upon the well-being of Americans and American society. It has contributed to an effective and productive work force, a more informed citizenry, and countless other benefits.

Public education remains the avenue through which most Americans acquire their educational training. The vast majority of today's students attend public schools. In 2019, 90 percent of all primary and secondary students were enrolled in public schools, while 74 percent of students going on to college attended public institutions.[31] As a result, public education is the dominant vehicle for the vast majority of American students.

Unfortunately, as a result of the way that public education is funded at the primary and secondary levels, the quality of that education varies widely depending on the wealth of the community that one resides in. The bulk of U.S. school funding for elementary, middle, and high schools comes from the local tax base, primarily property taxes. Well-to-do school districts with a richly endowed property tax base will generally have ample funding to operate quality public schools. This involves paying teachers competitive salaries, keeping student / teacher ratios low, purchasing the necessary educational resources such as books for libraries or computer equipment for instruction, and so on.

On the other hand, residing in a poor community with a diminished tax base often results in schools that are financially strapped. Teachers are frequently underpaid and overstressed, the physical facilities may be severely deteriorated and outdated, class sizes are often quite large, along with a host of other disadvantages. These children, who are predominately low income and frequently of color, wind up being denied a quality education as a result. Linda Darling-Hammond and Laura Post write,

Few Americans realize that the U.S. educational system is one of the most unequal in the industrialized world, and students routinely receive dramatically different learning opportunities based on their social status. In contrast to most European and Asian nations that fund schools centrally and equally, the wealthiest 10 percent of school districts in the United States spend nearly ten times more than the poorest 10 percent, and spending ratios of three to one are common within states. Poor and minority students are concentrated in the less well funded schools, most of them located in central cities and funded at levels substantially below those of neighboring suburban districts.[32]

As a result, many of these children receive an inferior education, which in turn will dramatically reduce their ability to effectively compete in the labor market.

Travel to any U.S. city and you are likely to observe a similar pattern over and over again. Begin your trip with a visit to an affluent suburb. The schools you encounter there are likely to be impressive with respect to their physical facilities, the quality of their instruction, and the depth of their curriculum. Next, turn the car around and visit a poor neighborhood, perhaps in the central city, and there you are likely to see quite the opposite—decaying schools, demoralized faculty, and districts facing a loss of accreditation. Finally, take a much further drive out into the remote countryside and you may discover a school district with the fewest resources of all.

Right outside the door of my home such patterns can be easily found. Within a 10-minute drive is a highly regarded public high school in an affluent school district. In that district, the average amount of money spent per pupil is around $16,000. The education that students receive is among the best in the nation's public schools. Drive a few minutes further, and you may notice a private high school that could very well be mistaken for a small university campus. There the spending per pupil averages out to $30,000. The quality and options of courses offered to students is almost unlimited. Finally, travel 20 minutes in the opposite direction and you will reach a high school that is literally falling apart, where the average money spent per pupil is around $9,000. The school district has lost its accreditation, and its students are nearly all poor and children of color.

In each of these different schools we find American children, all in the same metropolitan area, yet it is clear that some are entitled to a first-rate education, while others are not. It is simply the luck of the draw that some students have access to superior opportunities while others are denied such opportunities. Ill fortune has placed some children in difficult situations while good fortune has allowed others to prosper. The irony of this is that those who are most in need of an excellent education are the ones who are most likely to be receiving a substandard education. This is completely the result of the random factor. The children themselves had nothing to do with this. Social and educational policy should be structured to help ameliorate the negative consequences brought about by ill luck.

To say that these children are experiencing equality of opportunity or a level playing field is simply absurd. Rather, cumulative inequality is clearly operating within the system of education that we have in the United States. Where one lives and the size of one's parent's pocketbook largely determine the quality of education that children will receive. Over three decades ago, Jonathan Kozol referred to this situation as the "savage inequalities" of America.[33]

Unfortunately it is as true today, if not more so, than it was 30 years ago. A report by the Department of Education begins with the following statement, "While some young Americans—most of them white and affluent—are getting a truly world-class education, those who attend school in high poverty neighborhoods are getting an education that more closely approximates schools in developing countries."[34]

As mentioned, one important reason for this is the way that public education is funded in this county. The United States is one of the very few industrialized countries where the bulk of funding for public schools comes from local and state tax dollars rather than from the federal government. In particular, the overall value of real estate in a school district is the key determinant of the amount of resources a district will have available. Consequently, children living in lower-income neighborhoods tend to be enrolled in schools with far fewer resources and a lower quality of instruction than children living in well-to-do neighborhoods.[35]

In *The American Dream and the Public Schools,* Jennifer Hochschild and Nathan Scovronick note,

> School district boundaries help to provide such an advantage when they follow neighborhood lines that separate wealthy children from those who are poor and often nonwhite; school financing schemes have this effect when they are based on local property value and thereby create or maintain a privileged competitive position for wealthier children at the expense of the others. Tracking provides advantages when the best teachers or the most resources are devoted to a high track disproportionately filled with wealthier students.[36]

Research also indicates that since the mid-1970s, schools have actually become more segregated on the basis of race and income. As Erica Frankenberg and colleagues observe, "Segregation for black students is rising in all parts of the U.S. Black students, who account for 15% of enrollment, as they did in 1970, are in schools that average 47% black students."[37] Furthermore, Latino students are even more segregated. The authors find that "the segregation of Latino students is now the most severe of any group and typically involves a very high concentration of poverty."[38]

Schools that are predominately minority are also highly skewed in the direction of poverty and low income. Rather than reducing the differences and disadvantages that some children face, the structure of schooling in the United States further increases and exacerbates those differences.[39] As Hochschild and Scovronick state,

Public schools are essential to make the American dream work, but schools are also the arena in which many Americans first fail. Failure there almost certainly guarantees failure from then on. In the dream, failure results from lack of individual merit and effort; in reality, failure in school too closely tracks structures of racial and class inequality. Schools too often reinforce rather than contend against the intergenerational paradox at the heart of the American dream.[40]

The authors go on to explain the intergenerational paradox: "Inequalities in family wealth are a major cause of inequality in schooling, and inequalities of schooling do much to reinforce inequalities of wealth among families in the next generation—that is the intergenerational paradox."[41] Indeed, research has shown that the amount of education and wealth of parents is highly correlated with the educational levels achieved by their children.[42]

The cumulative advantages and disadvantages at the K through 12 level become further extended into the likelihood of graduating from high school, and then completing a college degree.[43] Children from wealthier families are often able to attend top-flight private universities, children from middle-class backgrounds frequently enroll at public universities, while children from lower-class backgrounds will probably not continue on to college at all, or if they do, are likely to attend a community or two-year college. As Daniel McMurrer and Isabel Sawhill note, "Family background has a significant and increasing effect on who goes to college, where, and for how long. With the reward for going to college greater than ever, and family background now a stronger influence over who reaps those rewards, the United States is at risk of becoming more class stratified in coming decades."[44]

In summarizing the research on education, neighborhood, and income, Greg Duncan and Richard Marmame write, "As the incomes of affluent and poor American families have diverged over the past three decades, so too has the educational performance of the children in these families. Test score differences between rich and poor children are much larger now than thirty years ago, as are differences in rates of college attendance and college graduation."[45] Unfortunately, it appears that we may be moving even further afield of a level playing surface when it comes to education.

To deny children the fundamental right to a good education is both morally wrong and bad social policy. But it is also ignoring the enormous role that the random factor plays in determining the outcomes of children. It is simply the luck of the draw where students find themselves in terms of their primary and secondary school education. Countless studies have documented the immediate and lingering effects of high quality versus inferior quality education upon later life outcomes. Improving public education for low-income children is absolutely essential for addressing the ill effects that the random factor exerts upon many.

It is clear that although money in and of itself is not the complete answer, it nevertheless represents a large part of the solution. This is particularly the case for school districts unable to provide the necessary educational tools for its students (qualified teachers, educational materials, etc.). Evening out the vast financial differences currently found across school districts, and then spending the additional money wisely by hiring qualified teachers and building strong curricula, can make a significant difference. As Craig Jerald, a senior policy analyst at the Education Trust, puts it, "The picture has become crystal clear. If you do both of those things you can really solve the problems."

Emphasis should be placed upon the federal and state governments to address the gaping disparities in school financing. Several states have begun to move in this direction, but many more need to follow their lead. As noted above, differences in spending per pupil can vary by thousands of dollars, with wealthy students who are blessed by a myriad of social and economic advantages enjoying the most in terms of public per pupil spending, while students from poor backgrounds and possessing the fewest advantages wind up receiving the least in terms of public tax dollars.

Through the lens of the random factor, equality of opportunity becomes a key ingredient that I would argue most Americans behind a veil of ignorance would want their social policy to reflect. Not knowing where one might fall in society, being guaranteed a first-rate education is perhaps the most important tool in providing such equality of opportunity.

Summing Up

The prism of the random factor is a novel way to view and consider social policy. It is certainly not the only way in which to consider policy, but I would argue that it is an important one in which to think about social programs. In this chapter we have taken the Rawlsian tool of a veil of ignorance to explore what policies we might want to have in place not knowing where we might fall in society. At the heart of this thought experiment is the element of luck. My argument is that there are at least three sets of policies that most Americans would insist upon given this situation.

First, certain fundamental liberties should be entitled to all. The idea of basic freedoms and rights being central to the American experience goes back to the beginnings of the country. In declaring independence from Great Britain, Thomas Jefferson laid out the many injustices that the Crown had inflicted upon the colonists. Most detrimental of all was the denial of the colonists' rights to engage in "life, liberty, and the pursuit of happiness."

Our history is one marked by a strong adherence to the importance of individual liberties and rights. Not knowing where we might land in society, I am confident that nearly all Americans would want to be ensured that they were entitled to the basic rights and liberties that are enshrined in the Constitution and judicial court decisions.

A second policy that would emerge behind a veil of ignorance would be to ensure that no one should fall below a basic economic and social floor. This policy is closely tied to the concept of insurance. As Kleinbard notes, "Insurance is an effective tool whose entire purpose is to mitigate the financial consequences of bad luck."[46] Because of the unpredictability of the random factor, a robust safety net takes on significant importance. In addition, an economic floor that no one would fall below helps individuals to take fuller advantage of the opportunities and liberties available to them.

And a third set of policies that I believe we would want to adhere to behind a veil of ignorance would be initiatives that reinforce the ideal of equality of opportunity. Without knowing where we might land in society, the overwhelming majority of us would want to have access to the tools that can improve our lot in life. The most important of these tools is a good education. Given the luck of the draw, a very good education becomes an essential commodity.

There are certainly many other policies and program that might be designed to help address the negative effects of the random factor. But my sense is that the ones discussed in this chapter are the most important with respect to ameliorating the effects of bad luck. The random factor provides what I feel is a very innovative way to reconsider and rethink our social policies. It also enables us to rediscover some important personal lessons. We now turn to several of those lessons.

9 *Reflecting and Assessing*

How lucky it is that the future itself consistently frustrates those who purport to unravel it. For, if the future could be predicted, what fun would remain in life?

—ARTHUR SCHLESINGER JR., 1993

The ability to reflect on and reevaluate one's beliefs can be both challenging and rewarding. As we gain new insights about ourselves and the world around us, such an understanding helps further our sense of who we are. Recognizing the role of the random factor can reveal a number of valuable lessons. Here I reflect on several of the lessons to be learned from our unpredictable companion.

I should begin by pointing out the obvious—this is not a self-help book. I certainly claim no special expertise pertaining to self-improvement. However, what I can offer are some thoughts and reflections on what might be some of the benefits of recognizing the randomness in our lives.

Humility and Empathy

As Americans, we tend not to be a particularly humble lot. We often pride ourselves and our nation as being exceptional. The term *Amer-*

ican exceptionalism has been coined to describe this widely held belief.[1] Of course, there is nothing inherently wrong in taking pride in one's accomplishments or that of one's country. But there is also a danger that this pride can quickly devolve into arrogance and belligerence. Too often Americans are seen through the eyes of those in other countries as demanding and full of self-importance. The term *ugly American* has been used to describe this unfortunate trait.

Appreciating and recognizing the role of the random factor provides an important wake-up call to this tendency. As we have seen in prior chapters, chance and luck exert an influence in shaping our lives and the world around us. The fact that we are born American is one of pure chance. If we begin to acknowledge and recognize this fact, it can help instill a bit of humility into our lives. In *The Tyranny of Merit*, Michael Sandel writes,

> For why do the successful owe anything to the less-advantaged members of society? The answer to this question depends on recognizing that, for all our striving, we are not self-made and self-sufficient; finding ourselves in a society that prizes our talents is our good fortune, not our due. A lively sense of the contingency of our lot can inspire a certain humility: "there, but for the grace of God, or the accident of birth, or the mystery of fate, go I."[2]

On the other hand, some might argue that showing humility is a sign of weakness. Certainly former president Donald Trump made this argument, epitomizing a lack of humility.[3] Yet those who are able to recognize the fact that fortune may have smiled on them tend to appreciate the worth and value of their lives and those around them. The spiritual teacher Meher Baba wrote, "True humility is strength, not weakness. It disarms antagonism and ultimately conquers it."

Interestingly, the major religions of the world all emphasize humility as an essential virtue. Judaism, Christianity, Islam, Buddhism, and Hinduism each stress that humility is key to appreciating the gifts that have come our way, and serves to properly place ourselves in the grander scheme of things. They all emphasize the sheer wonder and mystery of life, and that one cannot help but be humbled and awestruck by such revelations.

Grasping the importance of randomness can instill such a sense of humility. The impact of chance and luck shapes all of our individual lives, no matter who we are. This was emphasized early on in the book of Ecclesiastes from the Old Testament,

> I returned, and saw under the sun, that the race is not to the swift, nor the battle to the strong, neither yet bread to the wise, nor yet riches to men of understanding, nor yet favour to men of skill; but time and chance happeneth to them all.

By recognizing the universality of chance, we begin to appreciate that we are but one small cog in the wheel of life.

Another way in which randomness fosters a sense of humility is through a recognition that much of life cannot be predicted. We like to think we are in control of our lives at all times, but this is clearly not the case. Chance and luck will have their say regardless of our protests to the contrary.

This is also the case within the sciences and social sciences. These disciplines have enabled us to gain considerable knowledge and insight into a wide range of phenomena. Yet there remains much that we do not know, and may never know as a result of randomness. The old saying "The more I know, the less I know" is reflective of this sense of humility. Nature and the social world are quite adept at putting us in our place. And that place is one of humility by recognizing our inability to completely understand the world around us.

The outward expression of humility might well be empathy. The ability to realize and appreciate someone else's situation and problems is an extremely important skill and virtue. I would assert that many of the misunderstandings we have about others are rooted in a lack of putting ourselves in another's shoes. This lack of empathy can often result in stereotypes and prejudice governing our perceptions of each other.

By appreciating the ubiquitous reach of the random factor, we become better able to empathize with someone else's troubles. The familiar saying "There but for the grace of God go I" captures this spirit. Because randomness can strike anyone at any time, it allows us to imagine ourselves in the position of someone less fortunate. In doing so we begin to build more meaningful connections with each other.

These connections help reaffirm our basic human nature. At our best we are caring and supportive of one another. The random factor enables us to understand the fragile line we walk and the resulting need to have each other's backs as we move forward along life's pathway.

Gratitude

Like humility and empathy, gratitude is a virtue that can be greatly enhanced through our awareness of the random factor. Much has been written in recent years about the role of gratitude in fostering a fulfilling life. The field of positive psychology has found that psychological well-being can be greatly enhanced through a sense of gratefulness and appreciation.[4]

We might think of gratitude as an appreciation for those things in life one is fortunate to experience. This obviously encompasses many things—good health, the love of one's family, a roof over one's head, close friends, or a rewarding career. It can also entail the smaller things in life as well—a beautiful sunset, an act of kindness, or a captivating performance. In ways both large and small, the random factor allows us to appreciate the fact that these blessings are not to be taken for granted. They could just as easily be taken away by the fickleness of chance. Recall the Romans' image of the goddess Fortuna, who would spin her wheel of fortune, causing some to rise and others to fall. Her delight was in reversing the fortunes of us mortals.

The recognition of randomness in our lives ensures that we do not take the good things in life for granted and it allows us to understand the precarious nature of good fortune. As we gain an appreciation of randomness in our own life and the world around us, we realize that we might just as easily find ourselves in less favorable conditions than we currently are. Of course this is similar to the saying "count your blessings," but it is slightly different in that it recognizes the precarious nature of those blessings.

Yet what about individuals who may have very little to be grateful for—those living in dire or worse conditions? How can an understanding of the random factor enhance gratitude under these conditions? Granted, this is an uphill climb. But it may be the case that even under these conditions there are small things to be grateful for. More importantly, the random factor may begin to tilt in one's favor in the future. There is always the hope that given the fickleness of fortune, the wheel may turn upward, carrying us with it. As I shall discuss in an upcoming section, the random factor is quite capable of having unforeseen opportunities up its sleeve.

A Healthy Skepticism about Meritocracy

As mentioned in the opening chapter, America has long been steeped in the doctrine of rugged individualism. Closely connected to this has been the belief that the United States is best described as a meritocracy—people get ahead in life due to their merit, skill, and accomplishments, while those who fail have only themselves to blame. As Michael Sandel writes,

> Meritocratic hubris reflects the tendency of winners to inhale too deeply of this success, to forget the luck and good fortune that helped them on their way. It is the smug conviction of those who land on top that they deserve their fate, and that those on the bottom deserve theirs, too.[5]

This faith in meritocracy is tied to the viewpoint that America constitutes a land of opportunity. As a country we believe in the importance of equality of opportunity (as discussed in the prior chapter). Everyone should be able to go as far as their efforts and talents will take them. Consequently, for those willing to work hard, plentiful opportunities exist that allow one to climb a ladder of success.

The importance of the random factor introduces a dose of skepticism into this mindset. As the Yiddish expression succinctly puts it, "Man plans and God laughs." While there is no denying that hard work and skills are important in life's journey, there is also no denying that luck and chance may be every bit as important in helping to shape the course of our lives, as we have seen in prior chapters. These elements fall outside the reach of meritocracy. They have nothing to do with merit or deservedness. Edward Kleinbard notes,

> By marrying a more honest acknowledgment of the critical importance of luck in our lives to its implications for the cherished national credo that America is a place of equal opportunity, we can begin to confront how invidiously important forms of bad brute luck work to strip millions of their fair chance. We also can develop a little bit of humility about ourselves and our individual accomplishments, and a stronger identification with other Americans. Perhaps, if we take the

exercise seriously enough, we might even get to the point where we understand that great material success is not simply a sign of unique inner merit, and material disappointments not simply evidence of moral failure.[6]

A healthy skepticism about the influence of meritocracy due to the random factor has important ramifications for how we see ourselves and others. It serves to splash a bit of cold water on the credit we take for our successes as well as the blame we assign to our failures. As Jackson Lears writes in *Something for Nothing*, "A recognition of the power of luck might encourage fortunate people to imagine their own misfortune and transcend the arrogance of the meritocratic myth—to acknowledge how fitfully and unpredictably people get what they deserve."[7]

Robert Rubin has led a highly successful life. From 1995 to 1999 he served as U.S. secretary of the treasury in the Clinton administration. Before that, he had risen to co-senior partner at Goldman Sachs. In his *The Yellow Pad: Making Better Decisions in an Uncertain World*, he discusses the fact that luck has been just as important as merit in his life.

> One element that shaped my career is easy to identify: good luck. In my experience, many people are reluctant to recognize the role that fortune, good or bad, plays in life. I suspect that if I gave you a list of fifty people who'd been very successful by external metrics, and you asked them, "How important do you think luck has been in your life?" the vast majority would underestimate it.
>
> I think some people are uncomfortable acknowledging the importance of serendipity because they feel it diminishes the role their talents and work ethic played in their success. I disagree with that. I don't think being honest about the role of luck takes anything away

from anybody. I think it helps ground people with a sense of appreciation and, perhaps even more important, humility.[8]

By acknowledging that we do not live in a strict meritocracy, we may also become less harsh in our judgment of others as well as ourselves. Life is full of good and bad breaks, and by recognizing this randomness we can begin to properly place accomplishments and failures within this broader context.

Such a realization is noteworthy in terms of both social policy and our collective responsibility toward each other. As discussed in the prior chapter, understanding the importance of the random factor in everyday life implies the need for social policies that can address emergencies when they arise. These include a range of programs, some of which we reviewed in chapter 8.

In addition, the importance of chance suggests that our collective responsibility toward each other is much stronger than often thought. Why should this be? The reason is that personal responsibility is generally felt to be pertinent when individuals are able to exert control and agency over a situation. In these circumstances we hold the person accountable for their behavior. However, in cases where such control is beyond the purview of the individual, we generally absolve them of such responsibility. In these cases the wider community is often charged with providing some form of protection against negative outcomes. The prevalence of the random factor implies the need for an active engagement by the wider community with respect to the well-being of its members.

Don't Be Fooled by Luck

As found in our discussion of statistical probability in chapter 3, there can be a tendency to be fooled by luck and the random factor. One of the most common ways is through what is known as the gambler's fallacy. The term was first coined by the French mathematician Pierre-Simon Laplace. In his 1814 book, *Philosophical Essay on Probabilities,* he used the example of the French lottery to illustrate this false belief. Those playing the lottery tended to favor numbers that had not been lottery winners recently. The thinking was that such numbers were long overdue for showing up on the winning lottery ticket since they had not been selected for quite some time. This belief was obviously mistaken. As Laplace wrote, "The past ought to have no influence on the future."[9] The odds of a number being chosen is clearly not affected by the past history of whether that number has been selected or not, and yet this belief influenced lottery behavior in nineteenth-century French society (and in twenty-first-century American society for that matter).

Today one can still find this fallacy influencing those who play games of chance. For example, consider the bets placed in roulette on whether the ball will land on red or black. If there has been a consecutive series of red coming up, many more people will begin to place their bets on black. Again, the mistaken belief is that black is now overdue.

Research has confirmed this tendency. James Sundali and Rachel Croson analyzed actual gambling behavior in Reno, Nevada casinos. They found that for those who were making 50/50 bets in roulette, gamblers who had watched one spin of the wheel evenly divided their bets between red and black. However, as the wheel landed on red (or black) in consecutive spins, the betting changed significantly. After five consecutive reds, 65 percent of the bets were placed on black, and after six consecutive reds, 85 percent of the bets were on black.[10] Clearly the current spin of the roulette wheel is not influenced by what happened on the previous five spins, and yet gamblers were placing their bets as if it was.[11]

This fallacy can be found in other aspects of life. For example, parents who have had several children of the same gender may feel that they are now more likely to have a child of the other gender since that gender is overdue. Or in a study of Major League Baseball (MLB) umpires, if an umpire had called several borderline pitches in the exact same location a ball, they were more likely to call the next pitch in the same location a strike. As the authors write, "MLB umpires call the same pitches in the exact same location differently depending solely on the sequence of previous calls."[12] Again, the reason being that the gambler's fallacy induces "decision makers to erroneously alternate decisions because they mistakenly believe that streaks of affirmative or negative decision are unlikely to occur by chance."[13]

Gamblers and others are also susceptible to the hot streak or hot hand fallacy. When things are going well at the gambling table, we can fool ourselves into believing that luck is on our side. But of course, your current spell of good luck is no more dependent on the past than the idea that it is time for the roulette ball to land on black rather than red. The random factor does not abide by such a conjurer.[14]

Related to the gambler's fallacy is the mistaken belief that the distribution in small numbers will reflect the distribution in large numbers. Take the case of flipping a coin. The odds in any one flip are 50 percent heads, 50 percent tails. If we flip a coin 10,000 times, close to 50 percent of the total flips will be heads and close to 50 percent tails. However, if we flip a coin 10 times, the result could easily be seven heads and three tails. It is mistaken to think that the odds pertaining to a small number of cases will reflect the odds for a large number of cases.

This is illustrated in a story often told about statistics professors. On the first day of class, the professor assigns half the students in the room to select what they think a sequence of 50 coin flips should look like. The other half of students are given a computer program that can generate 50 random coin flips. Each group is then instructed to put their sequences on the board in front of the classroom. The professor has stepped out for 15 minutes while the students are working on their task. The professor then walks back into the classroom, and is able to immediately tell which of the sequences was generated by the computer and which by the students. How was this done?

The sequence that was generated by the computer and was truly random had longer strings of consecutive heads and tails, perhaps five or six in a row. In addition, the final tally of heads and tails was unevenly divided. On the other hand, the sequence generated by the students simulating what they thought was a random sequence did not have any of these long strings of heads or tails, and their overall number of heads and tails was similar. What was occurring was that the students were applying the large number probabilities to their smaller sample size of 50. The computer, on the other hand, was simply generating coin flips randomly, with the result being that within a small sample size there could very well be many more heads than tails, and that there could also be long strings of heads or tails. As an example, people will often assume that a sequence of coin flips with heads and tails such as "HTHTH" is more likely to happen than the sequence "HHHHT," yet their probability is the same.[15]

The moral of this story is to be very careful not to apply what we know to be the case in a large sample to a small sample. The small sample can and often does contain surprises. An awareness of this mistake can avoid some serious misperceptions and wrongly deduced decisions.

A third way in which we may be fooled by the random factor is in trying to find a pattern or meaning within randomness when there is none. The acceptance of the random factor can often be frustrating because almost instinctively we desire to find an explanation for things that occur. Amos Tversky was a seminal scholar in the field of cognitive psychology, and spent much of his time researching individual perceptions and decision making. He noted, "Very often the search for explanation in human affairs is a rejection of randomness."[16]

This search for meaning when there is none is related to the next section dealing with life not always being fair. We seek a sense of order and logic as we go about our lives. But the random factor does not follow these rules. Understanding this can actually be quite useful. It releases us from endlessly searching for causes and reasons that were never there. It allows us to live life as it is, rather than as how we might imagine it to be.

Life Is Not Always Fair

From childhood onward we may be told that life is not always fair when things do not go our way. But what exactly is fair, and how does randomness undermine this principle?

In prior work I have written about the meaning of justice and fairness within an American context.[17] One key component in how they have been interpreted is the principle of balance. For example, when someone works hard and plays by the rules, we often hope that they will receive their "just rewards." Or when a crime is committed, justice is seen as being served if the criminal is sentenced to a punishment that fits the nature and severity of the crime.

On the other hand, if an individual commits a serious crime and is neither apprehended nor punished, the feeling is that an injustice has occurred. Thus, in cases where individuals experience outcomes and consequences that are congruent with their prior actions and behaviors, the world is seen as just. Conversely, in situations where individuals experience outcomes and consequences that are incongruent with their prior actions and behaviors, the world is viewed as unjust.

This concept of balance can be visually seen in the symbol of justice found from local courtrooms to the U.S. Capitol—that of Themis or Lady Justice. Here one finds a woman, often blindfolded, holding a measuring scale in one hand and a sword in the other. In this image, justice is being portrayed as impartial and not beholden to special interests (hence the blindfold). The fact that she is holding the scales has a double meaning. They first imply that evidence should be weighed carefully in deciding how justice will be delivered. But they also connote that justice is served by balance. That is, prior actions and future consequences should be in balance and congruent with one another. Furthermore, the sword gripped in her right hand represents the strength and authority of justice, and acts as a balance to the judgment derived from the scales held in her left hand.

Closely related to the importance of balance within an American interpretation of justice is the emphasis upon deservedness. The basic concept is that within a just society, what you deserve in life should reflect your prior efforts, actions, and talents.

The gauge of deservedness has often been applied to the poor. This criterion has been used over the centuries, particularly since the English Poor Laws of 1601, to divide the poor into the categories of deserving and undeserving. The deserving poor are individuals deemed worthy of our compassion and assistance because they find themselves in poverty through little fault of their own. Consequently, an injustice has occurred. Such persons would include those who have suffered from an unavoidable illness or accident, children, widows, and so on.

On the other hand, individuals falling into the undeserving poor category are seen as meriting neither our compassion nor our assistance. Such poverty is perceived as being brought on as a result of a lack of initiative, laziness, bad decisions, or some other failing, and therefore impoverishment is a just and deserving consequence of prior behavior. The concept of deservedness has been applied to many other behaviors in American life including health outcomes, financial success, and academic accomplishment.

Certainly there are many times in life when such a sense of justice is affirmed. A student studying long and hard for an upcoming test aces the exam; a nurturing parent raises a thoughtful and caring child; a bigot eventually faces their own bigotry. These are times when there appears to be cause and effect, and that this association reflects the concept of justice as balance.

However, the random factor throws a wrench into this view of justice. In life as it is played out, bad things can happen to good people, and good things can happen to bad people. Chance and luck give little preference to the notions of balance and deservedness. In this regard, the random factor is blind to any sense of justice. The philosopher Nicholas Rescher states this well,

> The trenchant question of old (posed by unfortunate and fortunate alike) is: Why me; what have I done to deserve this? The irony of course is that the appropriate and correct answer is: Nothing! It is simply a matter of chance—of fortuitous luck.[18]

Understanding the role of chance in upsetting the proverbial apple cart of a just world injects a dose of reality into everyday life. Certainly we can attempt to rectify some of the negative consequences of the random factor (as discussed in the prior chapter), but we should not deceive ourselves into believing that the world is always fair. The role of our unpredictable companion ensures that it most assuredly is not.

Many years ago, Rabbi Harold Kushner wrote the best-selling *When Bad Things Happen to Good People*. In it he attempted to reconcile how God would allow bad things to happen to good people. His message was that these are basically random events. When they occur, one can turn to God for comfort and strength, but that "it's our role as humans to accept the randomness of the universe, not to blame God or ourselves for tragedies but to believe in God's omnipotent goodness as a nourishing force."[19]

Consequently, there may be times in life when there is little point to casting about for blame. The random factor simply does not abide by such a conjurer. Rather, it is the fickleness of a gust of wind that is the more apt analogy. In some respects this understanding may be liberating. Rather than searching for blame or a causal reason, randomness can relieve us from such a burden. It allows us to see the world as it is, rather than how we might have imagined it to be.

Perseverance

Given the fickleness and prevalence of the random factor, there is a strong argument to be made for the importance of perseverance in pursuing one's goals. Many decisions affecting us involve some element of randomness and luck. These decisions may have little to do with one's abilities or credentials, but rather with the whims of chance. As Michael Sauder observes, "We did not get the job we applied for because our application was misplaced by the hiring committee, but we assume we reached too far and attribute the outcome to our lack of worthiness."[20] In discussing the careers of those in the arts, Stephen Marche writes,

> All creative careers demand persistence because all creative careers require luck. Persistence is the siege you lay on fortune . . . In 2015, at a sxsw session, casting directors from Fox, Paramount, and Disney estimated that the talent of any actor counted for about 7 percent of the reason they were cast in any given role. Age and ethnicity and "box office value in China" all mattered more. Success as an actor is only incidentally related to talent or effort. Painters and sculptors and designers and dancers and musicians all create under the same capriciousness of fortune.[21]

The point that "persistence is the siege you lay on fortune" is an excellent one. One cannot control randomness and chance. But one can increase the odds that chance will shine in their favor by increasing the number of opportunities for a particular result to play out. The aphorism of "keeping many irons in the fire" is apropos.

In addition, by having more irons in the fire, one can also increase the importance of talent and skill carrying more weight. Think back to our discussion of the role of luck in sports. The more times that a team or individual has the opportunity to score, the less the role of chance and the greater the role of skill in influencing the final outcome.

Or take the case of a student applying to highly competitive universities. If one applies to only one such university, given that the chances are low for acceptance, the odds are high that the result will be a rejection. However, if one applies to several different universities, the odds become somewhat more favorable for an acceptance. Chance and luck are still in play, but given that the applicant has strong qualifications, these will have more influence over the likelihood of acceptance across a wider range of choices. By increasing the number of schools in play, one can begin to slightly diminish the role of chance.

I can personally attest to the fact that perseverance is critical in trying to rein in the capaciousness of chance. These examples all revolve around the world of publishing. When submitting a research paper to an academic journal for possible publication, it is almost always peer reviewed. This means that the editor of the journal will ask two to three scholars in the field to review the paper, and make their recommendations as to whether or not the journal should publish the paper. And here is where it is often the luck of the draw. Who those reviewers are, what they might be looking for in a paper, what their particular biases and theoretical perspectives may be—all can vary widely. The paper might have the misfortune of drawing reviewers who are unfavorably predisposed to the paper's findings and approach and will reject the paper for publication, while other reviewers may be extremely positive about the paper. Some reviewers may not have as much knowledge in the field as they should have. Or the reviewers may have had a bad day and are in a foul mood to accept a paper for publication. These and more can influence the chances of acceptance. While the quality and originality of the research is obviously important to the success of a paper, many other elements may be as important. The journal editor will generally defer to the judgment of the reviewers, making the expression "the luck of the draw" particularly appropriate.

I have had the exact same paper dismissed as irrelevant by one set of reviewers and praised for its importance to the field by another set of reviewers. In addition, an author may find that among the two or three reviewers that a paper has been sent out to, there is a strong disagreement among them as to the merits of article, or a disagreement about what aspects of the paper should be revised or strengthened.

This is why perseverance is important. Because of the role of chance in negatively impacting the acceptance of a paper, it behooves the author to submit their paper to additional journals given a rejection. By persevering, the odds of eventual acceptance are greatly increased.

A second example of the importance of perseverance is with regard to book publishing. There are legions of stories about highly regarded authors who have had their works rejected by numerous publishers until finally an editor agrees to accept the manuscript. Ernest Hemingway, Jack London, Marcel Proust, Beatrix Potter, Thomas Wolfe, and hundreds more had dozens of rejections before finally landing a publisher willing to go forward. The first of the *Harry Potter* books by J. K. Rowling was rejected 12 times before Bloomsbury finally accepted it. Stephen Marche writes, "It took Agatha Christie five years to find her way into print . . . *Twilight* was rejected fourteen times, *The Diary of Anne Frank* fifteen times, *A Wrinkle in Time* twenty-six, *Gone with the Wind* thirty-eight."[22]

These are obviously authors and books of both high literary and commercial value. And yet they were rejected over and over. Had they not persevered, the world would not have known about these masterpieces. How many other authors of high literary merit have we never heard of because they were rejected one too many times and simply gave up? The role of luck can be brutal in situations like these. Like reviewers for an academic paper, editors at publishing houses are very much subject to the whims of chance in considering a manuscript. Perhaps they were pressed for time on that day and simply gazed at the first page of the manuscript before making a hasty decision. Perhaps they were upset with something else when they looked at the manuscript. Perhaps the timing was not right for the publishing house to do a book on a particular subject matter. Perhaps they had one too many books under contract. These and dozens of other random events may have worked against acceptance. By increasing the pool of possible publishers, an author can increase their chances that a positive decision will eventually be made.

A final publishing example reflecting the role of chance pertains to major book awards. We might think of these as similar to the process described in chapter 4 regarding getting into Harvard. There generally must be a certain threshold of quality for a book to be seriously considered for such an award, but beyond that threshold, the random factor becomes the key player. Hundreds of books may be in consideration of an award, all with substantial literary quality. Furthermore, the subject matter of these books will vary widely. How is one to choose?

The merits of a book may strike a first reviewer much different than a second reviewer. In this case, the words subjectivity and random might as well be interchangeable. It is very much the luck of the draw in terms of which book wins the Pulitzer Prize and which books only made it to the final cut. And yet the near miss can hit hard as the author takes it as a reflection of their work, rather than perhaps the bad lunch that the reviewer had the afternoon they were considering the book.

In all of these cases, a strong argument can be made that given the omnipresence of the random factor, it is important to persevere in pursuing one's life goals. By doing so, one can begin to rein in the capriciousness of chance. Of course, perseverance has its limits. One cannot move forward in life without at some point deciding that perhaps a particular pursuit should be ended. But even in these cases, it is important to keep in mind that rather than simply blaming oneself, there may very well be other factors such as chance in play. Understanding the role of the random factor may make the disappointment a bit easier to swallow.

Using Probability to Help Navigate Uncertainty

Just as perseverance is a strategy for reining in some of the uncertainties of the random factor, relying on probabilistic thinking is another technique through which to utilize chance to one's benefit.

In chapter 3 we discussed statistical probability as a technique for guiding decision-making. The field of decision theory has arisen over the years as a way of using probabilities to help guide decisions in the face of uncertainty.[23] This approach combines two elements in choosing which decisions should be made. First, what is the potential payoff of a particular decision? In other words, what might be the costs and benefits of a particular course of action? And second, what are the odds or probabilities that such an outcome will come to fruition? By combining these two factors one can arrive at a best course of action.

The earlier-mentioned Robert Rubin describes how these principles have guided his approach to decision-making. He notes that throughout his career he has relied on his yellow notepad to help decide upon a course of action. He will jot down on the pad the potential benefits of a particular decision along with the perceived odds of it occurring. By combining the benefits and probabilities of various outcomes, Rubin then decides upon a course of action that attempts to take into account the world of uncertainty and the random factor.

However, being able to accurately assess both the perceived benefits and probabilities of a particular decision is more often art than science. There are many occasions, if not most, when we can only approximate what we think might be the likelihood of an event occurring as well as its potential payoff.

Nevertheless, probabilistic thinking can be a helpful approach in attempting to rein in some of the uncertainly of the random factor. Take the simple example of an individual trying to decide what field of work they should go into. They have narrowed their choices down to two, the first being accounting and the second being an investment advisor. They begin by consulting labor market data to determine the probability of successfully landing a job in each field. On a scale of 1 to 10, finding an accounting job rates a 7, while acquiring an investment advisor position rates a 4. They then ask themselves, how satisfied would I be in each job? The accounting job is rated as a 3 while the investment advisor is considered a 6. These two factors are then multiplied together, giving the accounting option an overall score of 21, while the investment advisor option achieves a score of 24. Pursuing the investment advisor route narrowly beats out the accounting route. By combining the factor of probability with the factor of payoff, our hypothetical individual is given some guidance on which might be the better choice to make. Of course, as mentioned above, the accuracy of this final tally is highly dependent on a correct assessment of both the probabilities and the potential payoffs. Nevertheless, this example illustrates the manner in which probabilities can be helpful in guiding decision-making in the face of uncertainty.

Experienced gamblers routinely use this approach. Whether it be blackjack or computer poker, the gambler assesses their probability of winning in combination with the potential payoff of the pot when placing their bets. The random factor is always in play, but over the course of many games, the gambler may be able to tilt the odds in their favor through probabilistic thinking. For example, blackjack players who are able to count and keep track of the cards that have been used will have a better idea of their probability of winning future hands, and on the basis of that, will adjust their betting behavior to reflect those odds.

As we go about our day, countless decisions are guided by considering the probabilities and the positives or negatives of various outcomes. Should I bring my umbrella to work today? The forecast predicts a 75 percent chance of rain. Although it might not rain, the chances are fairly good that it will. The cost of bringing my umbrella if it does not rain is low—only the inconvenience of having to carry it. On the other hand, the benefit of having my umbrella if it does rain is significant—being able to avoid getting soaked. In this way I can combine probability with the cost and benefit of a particular action to arrive at a reasonable decision.

Hidden Opportunities

Euripides wrote in 414 BC, "There is in the worst of fortune the best of chances for a happy change." Expressed in a more modern context, "When one door closes, another door opens." An unexpected benefit of the random factor is that it presents opportunities that we might not have imagined without chance itself intervening. This is one of the great advantages that the random factor can impart to us.

As I was in the process of writing this book, I would occasionally mention to friends and colleagues that I was working on a book dealing with the topics of luck and chance. Often they would remark, "What a fascinating topic, but I make my own luck." When people use this phrase, they are frequently referencing the idea that when opportunities come their way as a result of chance, they take advantage of them.

Think back on some of the ways in which randomness has exerted itself in our prior chapters. For example, in chapter 2 we saw that Phyllis Schlafly's involvement in preventing the Equal Rights Amendment from passing into law was the result of a chance occurrence. An unexpected telephone call set her on an entirely different course than she had been traveling on.

Or take the case of Hedy Epstein, who we listened to in chapter 6. Hedy was able to escape from a probable death in a Nazi concentration camp through a lucky twist of fate. This escape opened up for her a lifetime of work focusing on social justice and human rights. The random factor revealed the possibilities of hidden opportunities.

Or consider our earlier discussion in chapter 3 pertaining to serendipity in scientific discoveries. Such discoveries were the result of chance occurrences interacting with well-trained and curious investigators. Such serendipitous moments can also be a part of everyday life. Christian Busch writes in *The Serendipity Mindset,*

> Serendipity can be a profound source of joy and wonder, of those magical moments that make life meaningful and interesting. It can be a key part of our journey, of living a fulfilled and successful life. In short, it can give us back an enthusiasm for life, it can turn the unexpected from a potential threat into a source of delight. If a good life is the accumulation of good days, serendipity can fill our days with joy and with meaning.[24]

Consider some of the unexpected ways in which the random factor has influenced the direction of your own life. We discussed in chapter 6 some of the milestones that can happen in our lives. The specifics of those events may have been strongly influenced by chance. The job we find ourselves in, our significant others, where we reside—all of these and more may have been influenced by luck and chance. When one door was closing another door may have been opening.

Recognizing these opportunities can be a valuable life lesson. When such chances come our way, do we consider the possibilities that may lie ahead? This might be one of the great gifts that the random factor imparts to us. It opens up avenues that a moment earlier could not have been imagined.

This represents an almost magical quality of the random factor. Like a magician pulling a rabbit out of the hat, the random factor presents us with opportunities that we had not known existed. The key to this magic is how open and receptive are we to considering these opportunities. It is the interaction of chance with agency that produces wholly unintended and positive outcomes. The lesson here is to be open to the possibilities that the random factor may present us with.

Yet too often we are unaware of or disregard these opportunities. The moral of this story is to try and remain vigilant to the unexpected. By keeping an open mind, we allow ourselves greater options in how our lives may unfold. In addition, these unexpected opportunities enable us to exert a degree of control in terms of shaping the outcomes of our lives. That is, when chance events do occur, what is our response and reaction to such an event? This is where individual agency comes into play.

There can also be much to learn from the unanticipated events that the random factor may steer our way. They enable us to learn new lessons and perhaps revisit old ones. These uninvited guests are sometimes the best teachers in providing us with a clearer roadmap to the future.

As discussed throughout this book, randomness is critical in understanding the particular twists and turns that our life course takes. But we also have an active role to play in influencing how such randomness may manifest itself. For example, are we able to take advantage of an opportunity that comes our way? Do we overcome an unavoidable adverse event that has happened to us? Can we learn and grow from a particular string of good or bad luck? Depending upon our social and economic resources, we may be more or less able to react to such events positively.

In this sense there is a dynamic exchange that occurs between randomness and agency. An intricate dance takes place between these two partners, with both partners exerting an influence on where and when the next steps will occur.

The Spice of Life

As the quote by Arthur Schlesinger at the beginning of this chapter indicates, chance and randomness give life its interest and intrigue. If everything were preordained, we would undoubtedly be bored to death. Imagine watching a sporting event knowing beforehand who the victor will be (which is why those who prerecord such events generally do not want to know the final result until after they have watched the replay). Or imagine playing the lottery knowing that you lost. What would be the point? As Sophocles said, it is better to live on " 'the razor's edge of luck' than to succumb to the hubris of demanding certain outcomes."[25]

Chance and luck give life its dynamic quality. It is the random element that provides much of the spice to life. The excitement of watching a game is in not knowing what will happen. Even when one team is heavily favored over another, there is still the chance for an upset. This is what lies behind the saying "That's why they play the game." In Frank Norris's novel *The Octopus* the protagonist declares, "Chance! To know it when it came, to recognize it as it passed fleet as a wind-flurry, grip at it, catch at it blind, reckless, staking all upon the hazard of the issue, that was genius."[26]

Consider this as you begin each day. There is always the possibility that chance may come knocking on your door unannounced. As you check your emails or text messages, as you go about your routine, something out of the blue may happen. As Norris writes, "to recognize it as it passed fleet as a wind-flurry" is genius. I have found that what gives life much of its spark and intrigue is this unknown quantity.

Closely related to this idea is that much of life revolves around the journey and what might or might not happen along the way, rather than the destination. It is the unknown of our precise direction that gives life its dynamic quality. We may have a rudimentary roadmap of where we are heading, but undoubtedly many unexpected twists and turns will be encountered along the way. Or in the lines penned by singer songwriter Tom Waits,

> Most vagabonds I knowed don't ever want to find the culprits,
> That remains the object of their long relentless quest.
> The obsession's in the chasing, and not the apprehending,
> The pursuit, you see, and never the arrest.

A fascinating individual I interviewed for my *Chasing the American Dream* project was Charles Lowenhaupt. Before becoming a lawyer and wealth advisor, Charles had spent a year teaching English to ninth and tenth graders at a Priory School that was part of a Benedictine monastery on the East Coast. He talked about some of the lessons he learned from that experience through his interactions with the Benedictine monks.

> There are wonderful stories from those guys, and I use them all the time in our business. One of the propositions I really encourage on young people, is it isn't getting someplace, it's going someplace that gives you the fun and satisfaction. And if you define failure too

completely, you don't try to go anyplace. For every success, there are ten failures. And if you're not ready to fail ten times, you'll never succeed.

So Father Francis Meyer told this story about how as a young man, he was an architect. His dream was to get offered a job at, I've forgotten the big architectural firm in New York. This is 80 years ago. And he was teaching at MIT. And one day he got a call from the firm saying, "We're offering you a job." And his first reaction was "How exciting! I've achieved my life's goal." And his second reaction was "But what do I do now?"

And as he told it, his choices were suicide or monastery, and he really didn't like blood. So he drank a whole lot, he put himself on a ship, he went to the monastery and became a monk.

Now that's a great story because it proves a fact that if you have one goal in life, and you achieve it, you're finished. That your goals have to be more about the journey than the destination. That's a pretty good lesson that I use.

The random factor imbues life with a depth and richness that would be absent without it. You might think you know what will happen tomorrow, but are you sure? The fact that there is an element of chance makes the game worth playing and certainly much more interesting. It is not knowing what may or may not happen along the journey that gives life its intrigue.

Recall from chapter 4 the actor Tom Spencer. Tom had committed his life to acting yet had never quite reached the big time. Nevertheless, his was a life full of professional rewards and unanticipated twists and turns. At the end of our interview I asked Tom what was one of the most unusual things that he had experienced during his long career in the theater. He started to laugh and said, "Very few actors can top this story. I actually had an audience member led away from one of my performances in handcuffs." "How in the world did that happen?" I asked. Tom sat back and told the following story:

It was the second show of a Saturday night, which happened very late. Obviously everybody there had been really drinking. We always hated those performances. God only knows what would happen, and they were yelling.

So we were doing a play called *The Trail of the Wandering Winds* [laughing]. And this other actor and I, they put these fake beards on us, and we looked like ZZ Top [laughing]. I played this terrible hillbilly. The young actress was like my niece or something. I had this jug of corn liquor. And I'm like drinking this stuff, and I'm kind of like looking, and I say, "Ah, you sure do look good, little Lula Mae, yeah, you're looking better all the time." And I'm drinking this.

So all of a sudden I start stalking her around the table, and she's got one of these Shirley Temple-type wigs, big curls hanging down. She was a very pretty girl. And so I'm following her around the table. And when I got to the point where I had my back to the audience, all of a sudden I heard someone yell.

There were people talking, but all of a sudden over the noise of the crowd, I heard someone go, "Screw her, Festus!" And it was loud! So I continued on, and all of a sudden I saw her, the young girl just like backing up. And so I heard it again. The guy yells again, "Screw her, Festus!" I thought oh, man. So I turn around to look out, and I see this huge gorilla of a guy.

He's walking down, and there was an orchestra that separated the stage and there were stairs that went up on either side. He came all the way down to the orchestra pit, and he said, "Well you gonna screw her or not?" I looked at him, and I said, "Pretty much not!" He said, "Then I will!!!"

Oh my god!

He started up (the stairs). So Sam Peterson [the stage manager] got out this yellow scarf, and he came running down. He looked like Errol Flynn in *The Dawn Patrol*. He had this scarf trailing out the back and he had these three little waiters he recruited coming down. And he pushed him, and they tackled this guy. He threw one guy off into the orchestra pit. Fortunately, just at that time, the cops arrived. Somebody had had the foresight to call the cops. So they came down, they pounded him, and hauled him away [laughing].

Did you then continue [laughing]?

I think by that point there was no need to. It was pandemonium [laughing]. A friend of mine said, "You know, maybe you should try a legitimate stage" [laughing all around].

Here again we have the hand of chance giving life its element of intrigue. Tom's story and many others are what gives life its unpredictability and force. Rather than something to fear, the random factor can impart an energy that would be lacking without it.

In this chapter we have touched upon some of the personal lessons, insights, and benefits to be learned from our unpredictable companion. They include a sense of humility and empathy, feelings of gratitude, a healthy skepticism regarding meritocracy, being careful not to be fooled by luck, a heightened understanding that life is not always fair, the importance of perseverance, the ability to use probability to one's advantage, hidden opportunities, and the dynamism that makes life interesting and worth living.

This is not to deny that there is also very much a downside to chance and luck. Certainly we have seen across these chapters many instances of bad breaks and bad luck. As the blues legend Albert King sang in "Born under a Bad Sign": "Been down since I began to crawl. If it wasn't for bad luck, I wouldn't have no luck at all." The random factor can bring stress, uncertainty, and catastrophe with it.

Yet I am reminded of the age-old wisdom that there is no life without death, and there is no death without life. The two are intertwined, just as the random factor is intertwined with the motion of our lives. The result is that we would surely be diminished without our unpredictable partner helping to guide and lead us across the dance floor of life.

10 *Our Unpredictable Companion*

In the air about him he seemed to feel an influence, a sudden new element, the presence of a new force. It was Luck, the great power, the great goddess, and all at once it had stooped from out the invisible, and just over his head passed swiftly in a rush of glittering wings.

—FRANK NORRIS, 1903

From the first sentence of chapter 1 we began our exploration of the random factor by considering the path upon which we have traveled. I asked you to consider some of the means that have enabled you to arrive at where you are today. Many things undoubtedly came to mind. But the one element that we often forget about is the random factor. Across these pages we have explored some of the ways in which chance and luck can ultimately shape our lives and the world around us.

As noted in the introductory chapter, novelist Thornton Wilder's main protagonist in his Pulitzer Prize-winning *The Bridge of San Luis Rey* was a Franciscan monk named Brother Juniper. By happenstance, Brother Juniper witnesses the collapse of a Peruvian bridge in which five people are in the wrong place at the wrong time the moment the bridge gives way, hurtling them to their deaths. He wonders to himself, What sense can be made of this tragedy? Was there something in the background of these five individuals that could provide a clue to this senseless event? Brother Juniper spends the next six years of his life trying to uncover the logic behind this tragic twist of fate. His investigation is guided by a puzzle: "Either we live by accident and die by accident, or we live by plan and die by plan." After six years, his quest to resolve this question turns up empty-handed.

In my office I have a letter that Thornton Wilder wrote just after the book was published. The letter is dated May 15, 1928, and addressed to a reader who had asked several questions about the book. Wilder at the time was still a French teacher and dormitory master at the Lawrenceville School in New Jersey, which continues to this day as a preparatory high school. He begins by noting that his busy duties as a teacher prevent him from going into greater detail, but he writes that he regards the conclusion of the book as "unresolved" and then ends by quoting the Russian playwright Anton Chekhov, "The business of literature is to ask questions fairly, not to answer them."[1]

The fair question that Wilder asks, "Do we live by accident and die by accident, or do we live by plan and die by plan?," is one of universal importance. Our journey throughout *The Random Factor* has hopefully provided a tentative answer to this critical question. And the answer is that it is both—we live by both accident and plan. Chance, luck, and randomness are present throughout our lives and the world around us. They are constant but unpredictable companions as we make our way through life. But life is not solely about the random factor. Rather, randomness is an active participant that intersects with the many other elements that push our lives forward.

We have explored these patterns across the chapters. The historical timeline that we inherit is driven along by specific forces and processes, but it is also shaped and bent by chance. In chapter 2 we discussed several key turning points in history that might have played out much differently had the random factor not exerted itself. Likewise, our own life trajectories are pushed along by strong currents such as class, race, and gender, but within those currents are the ripples of randomness. This was particularly the case when we considered the specifics of our life, such as the job we find ourselves in, who we form relationships with, or where we reside. Each of these has been strongly shaped by the element of chance.

A second theme touched upon throughout these pages has been the particular importance of timing with respect to fortuitous or not fortuitous events. An early lucky break can lead to a much different life trajectory than one that occurs later on. So too with an unlucky event. As Ed Smith notes in chapter 5, an early critical chance event in one's life is like a boulder that diverts the course of a stream, changing it forever. The process of cumulative advantage or disadvantage is very much in play in these situations. Likewise, historical chance events may be dependent upon timing for them to be impactful.

The importance of the economic context in which the random factor takes place is another emergent theme. Randomness happens to everyone, but the types of random events may vary sharply depending upon one's economic class. In addition, the manner in which we are able to respond to these random events varies by social and economic class. The result is that the random factor can often accentuate the inequalities in society. The social policies outlined in chapter 8 are one way of using the concept of chance to create a more equitable society.

A fourth theme is the unawareness that many of us have while in the presence of the random factor. As economist Robert Frank writes, "In the normal course of events, few of us give much thought to how seemingly minor random events often profoundly alter our lives."[2] Unlike the epigraph at the start of this chapter, we often do not notice luck with her glittering wings passing over us. Only in hindsight do we recognize the role that she may have played in dramatically altering our lives. By having a greater awareness of the random factor as it occurs, we can position ourselves to take fuller advantage of the opportunities that may present themselves.

Finally, the random factor invites us to be partners in this tango across the dance floor. True, we cannot know many of the things that will be coming our way, but once they appear, we have the opportunity to respond, react, learn, and perhaps take advantage of the unforeseen. Rather than a passive bystander, we can become an active participant.

Perhaps this is the most important lesson to be learned from the random factor. It enables us to see ourselves and the world around us in a new light. It teaches us that there is a mysterious and ever-present energy to the world. We can recognize and take advantage of this energy as well as marvel in its wonder. The uncertainty of what lies around the corner is what gives life much of its spark.

Imagine a world in which there was no surprise or chance. A world in which everything was simply a fait accompli. A world in which A always lead to B which always lead to C. I for one would find such a world quite empty. The random factor opens a door to a world of possibilities. Many of these possibilities are paths we could not have imagined. Like a fog that has been lifted, the random factor enables us to see and consider unforeseen options.

With respect to the social science community of which I am a part, the recognition and acknowledgment of the random factor is long overdue. As argued throughout this book, it allows us to understand a forgotten dimension of ourselves and the world around us. Chance and luck are vital components that help fill out our stories. The random factor may be just as important in affecting life outcomes as the standard array of socioeconomic variables used in the social sciences to model the life course. As sociologist Howard Becker points out,

Everyone knows that most of the things that happen to them happen "by accident," and this is particularly true of the things that are most

important to us, like our choice of a career or a mate. Yet social science theory looks for determinate causal relationships, which do not give an adequate account of this thing that "everyone knows." If we take the idea of "it happened by chance" seriously, we need a quite different kind of research and theory than we are accustomed to.[3]

Within the social science disciplines, if one is able to explain 35 percent of the variance pertaining to an event, that is considered quite good. In other words, even in the best social science models, well over half of what is occurring is left unexplained. This unexplained variance is often described as "noise."

I would argue that much of this "noise" is in fact the random factor exerting itself. By its very definition, randomness is extremely difficult to measure and model in a quantitative equation. The fact that even in the best-case scenario we are only able to explain or predict 35 percent of an event's occurrence should serve as a wake-up call to the reality that something else is operating behind the scenes. Part of that something else is the random factor.

One of the ways in which we can begin to unpack the influence of chance is through the process of in-depth interviewing. Throughout this book we have seen various ways in which the random factor has exerted itself. This is often revealed through individuals sharing their experiences and stories. Those experiences can reveal the hand of chance at work. The recognition of the random factor addresses a glaring omission within the social sciences in general and within sociology in particular. By allowing the random factor to enter the stage, we are in a much better position to more fully understand life as it is lived.

It may also be possible in the future to begin to quantitatively measure the magnitude of the random factor in certain situations. Several of the studies we have looked at employed simulation techniques to determine the role of chance in affecting an outcome.

Future work may be able to shed even further light upon detecting the presence of randomness in particular aspects of life.

On a final note, there is one last gift that the random factor bestows upon us. And that is the gift of hope. Embedded within the concept of chance lies the promise of possibility. Over the years I have interviewed hundreds of people from many walks of life. In the course of these discussions, I have listened to their stories, their troubles, and their dreams. From these dialogues I have learned a most valuable lesson. And that is, hope is what sustains us throughout our lives.

Whether such hopes are large or small, they are essential in providing the impetus to carry on and move forward. A life without hope is a life knee-deep in quicksand. Central to all of our hopes and dreams is the possibility that one day they will come true. And here is where the random factor delivers its greatest gift. No matter our position, no matter our situation, there is always the chance that at least some of our hopes and dreams will be fulfilled. The odds may be low, but they are not zero. As one respondent told psychologist David Krantz in his study of those who play the lottery, "What the hell, for a couple of bucks, I can dream about all the things I can't have. I'd like to win but I also enjoy hoping."[4] Or as historian John Gillies writes, "Most people have preferred to be ruled by Fortuna, for seeing life as a lottery provided that glimmer of hope otherwise denied by experience."[5]

Chance and luck as our unpredictable companions hold out the possibility that beyond and over the ridge we will meet up with our goals. The phrase "there is always a chance" epitomizes this sentiment. The fact that there is always a chance translates to "there is always hope." Where there is chance, there is hope. In this sense the random factor allows for dreams and aspirations to take flight. And if some of those dreams and aspirations are not reached, then our random companion will have nevertheless made our journey an eventful one.

In his presidential inaugural address on a bitterly cold January day in 1965, Lyndon Johnson concluded his remarks by stating,

For this is what America is all about. It is the uncrossed desert and the unclimbed ridge. It is the star that is not reached and the harvest that is sleeping in the unplowed ground.

The random factor challenges us to envision crossing that desert and climbing that ridge. It opens up avenues that may not have been apparent a moment earlier. It imparts a sense of possibility. It enables us to consider the unimaginable. After all, there is always a chance.

Acknowledgments

In a book dealing with the role of chance in our lives and the world around us, it is only appropriate for the author to thank his lucky stars. There have been many twists and turns in my life to arrive at where I am now, and many people to thank along the way. The thank you's could certainly take up a chapter by themselves.

As pointed out throughout these pages, in thinking back upon such twists and turns, I have discovered that often the little random things in life are ultimately the most profound. Small acts of kindness; a stranger's interest in one's work; a compliment or encouraging word from a colleague. These and so many more are what give meaning and motivation to one's career and scholarship. But let me mention one particularly important group in my journey.

Teachers play a critical role in influencing our lives. As a teacher myself, I am quite aware of the potential influence we exert upon the lives of our students. Yet this influence may only become apparent years later when a former student knocks unexpectedly on our office door or sends an email or text message out of the blue thanking us for igniting an interest in a particular subject matter.

So in this spirit I would like to thank all of my former teachers and professors who shared their insights and wisdom about the world we live in. Sir Isaac Newton wrote in a 1675 letter to a colleague, "If I have seen further [than others], it is by standing on the shoulder of giants." We owe a huge debt of gratitude to those who have blazed a trail before us, and have helped to light the way for those to come.

With respect to this particular book, I have been most fortunate to benefit from the expertise and insights of many colleagues and friends. They have either read earlier chapters and drafts of the manuscript, or provided much needed advice pertaining to specific areas of research. They include Joel Best, Mimi Chapman, Karen Coburn, Jeannette Cooperman, Gerald Early, Steve Fazzari, Robert Frank, Sarah Gehlert, Edward Lawlor, Jonathan Losos, Charles Lowenhaupt, Joseph Marcus, Andrew Martin, Margaret Olsen, Shanta Pandey, David Queller, Barry Rosenberg, Matthew Rousu, Michael Sauder, Barbara Schaal, Alan Templeton, and Jacob Witt. In addition, I would like to pass along my thanks to Michael Bierman, who has provided graphical design advice and insights over the years on many of my projects.

There is one person whom I would like to especially thank. Over the years, Edward Lawlor has been a wellspring of inspiration for my research and scholarship. As a dean, a colleague, and a friend, Eddie has provided the encouragement and wisdom that is so important in enabling one to see clearly and stay the path. He provided extensive feedback regarding this book with many excellent ideas and suggestions. It goes without saying that my wheel of fortune has turned upward as a result of Eddie's unwavering support across the past 20 years.

The team at the University of California Press has been superb to collaborate with. It was appropriately by chance that *The Random Factor* wound up on their desk. I had reached out to my former editor at Oxford University Press, Maura Roessner, who is now an editor at University of California Press. Maura suggested that I get in touch with Naomi Schneider. I had known of Naomi for many years as being one of the best editors in the business. The perception of excellence turned out to be the reality. Working with Naomi on this project has been an absolute delight. In addition, Aline Dolinh was incredibly helpful in organizing and pulling together the various pieces of the manuscript, Paul Tyler provided excellent copyediting assistance, Emily LeGrand constructed the index, Kevin Barrett Kane designed the captivating cover, and Katryce Lassle was a key player in the book's promotional materials.

In addition, I would like to thank my publicist, Leah Poulos, at PressShop. Leah and her crew did an excellent job in getting the word out about an earlier book of mine, and undoubtedly will work their magic with this book as well.

And of course, when thanking one's lucky stars, one must end with the luckiest break of all. Finding my lifelong partner, Anne, was truly hitting the proverbial jackpot. This has only been surpassed by giving birth to our two wonderful children, Libby and Kian. May the luckiest of stars shine upon you, and may you always have the wind at your back.

Notes

Chapter 1

1. Mark Robert Rank, Thomas A. Hirschl, and Kirk A. Foster, *Chasing the American Dream: Understanding What Shapes Our Fortunes* (New York: Oxford University Press, 2014).

2. Lawrence M. Eppard, Mark Robert Rank, and Heather E. Bullock, *Rugged Individualism and the Misunderstanding of American Inequality* (Bethlehem, PA: Lehigh University Press, 2020).

3. Thornton Wilder, *The Bridge of San Luis Rey* (New York: HarperCollins, 2014), 5.

4. Wilder, *Bridge of San Luis Rey*, 7.

5. Garrett M. Graff, *The Only Plane in the Sky: An Oral History of 9/11* (New York: Avid Reader Press, 2019).

6. Or take the case of Tim Lang, who witnessed both the terrorist attacks on the World Trade Center on February 26, 1993, and 9/11. The 1993 attack was the result of a half-ton bomb placed in a van and detonated in the garage of the towers. The *New York Times* reports that Lang

> hadn't wanted to go into the city that day, but his partner insisted he was needed at a 12:30 meeting. A reluctant Mr. Lang left his New Jersey condo and drove his Toyota 4Runner through the cold, late-morning gray.
>
> As he headed down a ramp into the World Trade Center's underground garage, a zooming Ford Taurus cut ahead of him. After a brief wait, the two vehicles entered the garage, the Ford making a right and the Toyota turning left.

Seconds later the bomb exploded. The person who turned right was killed. Lang, who turned left, was injured but escaped. The decision to go right or left was the difference between life and death, and it was a completely random decision. See *New York Times,* "He Survived the Trade Center Bombing: 'I Always Knew They'd Be Back,'" February 26, 2023.

7. Garrett M. Graff, "On 9/11, Luck Meant Everything," *The Atlantic,* September 10, 2019.

8. Steven D. Hales, *The Myth of Luck: Philosophy, Fate, and Fortune* (London: Bloomsbury Academic, 2020), 19.

9. David M. Robinson, "The Wheel of Fortune," *Classical Philology* 41 (1946): 212–13.

10. Christoph H. Luthy and Carla Rita Palmerino, "Conceptual and Historical Reflections on Chance (and Related Concepts)," in *The Challenge of Chance: A Multidisciplinary Approach from Science and the Humanities,* ed. Klaas Landsman and Ellen van Wolde (New York: Springer, 2016), 15.

11. Boethius, however, does opine on good fortune versus bad fortune. In *The Consolation of Philosophy* he writes,

> Bad fortune, I think, is more use to a man than good fortune. Good fortune always seems to bring happiness, but deceives you with her smiles, whereas bad fortune is always truthful because by changing she shows her true fickleness. Good fortune deceives, but bad fortune enlightens. With her display of specious riches good fortune enslaves the minds of those who enjoy her, while bad fortune gives men release through the recognition of how fragile a thing of happiness is.

From Stephen Marche, *On Writing and Failure* (Windsor, Ontario: Field Notes, 2023), 48.

12. Niccolo Machiavelli, *The Prince: Revised* (Ingersoll, Ontario: Devoted, 2019), 72.

13. Machiavelli, *Prince: Revised,* 72.

14. Machiavelli, *Prince: Revised,* 73.

15. Jackson Lears, *Something for Nothing: Luck in America* (New York: Viking, 2003), 33.

16. Voltaire, *The Philosophical Dictionary* (New York: E. R. Dumont, 1901), sv.

17. See also George Musser, "Is the Cosmos Random? (Einstein's Assertion That God Does Not Play Dice with the Universe Has Been Misinterpreted)," *Scientific American* 313 (2015): 88–93.

18. Musser, "Is the Cosmos Random?," 93.

19. Ernest Nagel, "Determinism in History," *Philosophy and Phenomenological Research* 20 (1960): 291–317.

20. Luthy and Palmerino, "Conceptual and Historical Reflections," 42.

21. Michael Sauder, "A Sociology of Luck," *Sociological Theory* 38 (2020): 194.

22. Sauder, "Sociology of Luck," 195–96.

23. In addition, statisticians and econometricians have devoted considerable time to modeling and better understanding the "random error" in human behavior.

24. Nicholas Rescher, *Luck: The Brilliant Randomness of Everyday Live* (Pittsburgh: University of Pittsburgh Press, 1995), 87–88.

25. Sauder, "Sociology of Luck," 211–12.

26. Rescher, *Luck*, 28.

27. Albert Bandura, "The Psychology of Chance Encounters and Life Paths," *American Psychologist* 37 (1982): 747.

28. Michael J. Mauboussin, *The Success Equation: Untangling Skill and Luck in Business, Sports, and Investing* (Boston: Harvard Business Review Press, 2012), 15–16.

29. Kristopher Jansma, "My Not-So-Bad Birth Defect," *New York Times*, June 10, 2018, sec. SR, p. 10.

Chapter 2

1. Volker Ullrich, *Hitler: Ascent 1889–1939* (New York: Alfred A. Knopf, 2016), 34.

2. Ullrich, *Hitler*, 28.

3. Ullrich, *Hitler*, 27.

4. William L. Shirer, *Berlin Diary: The Journal of a Foreign Correspondent, 1934–1941* (Baltimore: Johns Hopkins University Press, 2002), 246–47.

5. Martin J. Sherwin, *Gambling with Armageddon: Nuclear Roulette from Hiroshima to the Cuban Missile Crisis* (New York: Alfred A. Knopf, 2020), 3.

6. Kai Bird and Martin J. Sherwin, *American Prometheus: The Triumph and Tragedy of J. Robert Oppenheimer* (New York: Alfred A. Knopf, 2005).

7. Sherwin, *Gambling with Armageddon*, 20.

8. Sherwin, *Gambling with Armageddon*, 27.

9. Sherwin, *Gambling with Armageddon*, 448.

10. Jeff Nussbaum, *Undelivered: The Never-Heard Speeches That Would Have Rewritten History* (New York: Flatiron Books, 2022), 179.

11. David Weigel and Jose A. DelReal, *Washington Post*, March 11, 2016.

12. Walter Johnson, *The Broken Heart of America: St. Louis and the Violent History of the United States* (New York: Basic Books, 2020).

13. Robert Samuels and Toluse Olorunnipa, *His Name Is George Floyd: One Man's Life and the Struggle for Racial Justice* (New York: Viking, 2022).

14. Philip E. Tetlock and Dan Gardner, *Superforecasting: The Art and Science of Prediction* (New York: Crown, 2015), 7.

15. Rosa Parks and James Haskins, *Rosa Parks: My Story* (New York: Dial Books, 1992), 116.

16. Donnie Williams and Wayne Greenhaw, *The Thunder of Angels: The Montgomery Bus Boycott and the People Who Broke the Back of Jim Crow* (Chicago: Chicago Review Press, 2005), 48.

17. Jefferson Cowie, *Freedom's Dominion: A Saga of White Resistance to Federal Power* (New York: Basic Books, 2022).

18. It should be noted that there was also a nonrandom element to this historical event. Nine months prior to the Rosa Parks arrest, a 15-year-old girl named Claudette Colvin had also refused to give up her seat on a Montgomery bus and was arrested. The NAACP had been looking for a case to rally the community around in order to begin the bus boycott. However, because Colvin was unmarried and pregnant at the time, the civil rights campaigners felt that hers was not the right one to launch a boycott. That would have to wait until Rosa Parks, who was seen as a more respectable and sympathetic case. In this respect, there was a very deliberate decision made to wait until the right circumstance came about. However, Colvin was one of five plaintiffs in the *Browder v. Gayle* court case that eventually came before the Supreme Court, in which it ruled that the Montgomery bus segregation was unconstitutional, and on December 20, 1956, ordered Montgomery and the state of Alabama to end the segregation permanently. It was but a twist of fate that Rosa Parks became a household name, while Claudette Colvin was largely forgotten until recently.

19. Many additional examples could be given to illustrate the role of random sparks helping to ignite social movements. Mothers Against Drunk Driving (MADD), the anti-nuclear movement, Occupy Wall Street, and others have taken off due to a seemingly random event. For example, the tragic death of a 13-year-old girl led her mother, Candace Lightner, to establish the nonprofit organization MADD. Cari Lightner and a friend were walking on May 3, 1980, to a church carnival when a four-time DUI drunk driver plowed into Cari from behind, throwing her 125 feet, and leaving her dead on the pavement. This horrible accident was the beginning of the MADD movement, which has fought over the past four decades to prevent such tragic and unnecessary deaths from occurring.

20. Shirer, *Berlin Diary*, 585.

21. Shirer, *Berlin Diary*, 586.

22. Oscar Handlin, *Chance or Destiny: Turning Points in American History* (Westport, CT: Greenwood Press, 1977), 212.

23. David McCullough, *Brave Companions: Portraits in History* (New York: Simon & Schuster, 1992), xiv.

24. Nussbaum, *Undelivered*, 105.

Chapter 3

1. Michelle Z. Donahue, "Dino-Killing Asteroid Hit Just the Right Spot to Trigger Extinction," *National Geographic,* November 11, 2017.

2. Donahue, "Dino-Killing Asteroid."

3. In addition, earth science professor Toby Tyrrell empirically demonstrates that chance played a key role in causing the earth's climate to remain habitable throughout 3 or 4 billion years, again allowing life as we know it to form; see Tyrell, "Chance Played a Role in Determining Whether Earth Stayed Habitable," *Communications Earth & Environment* 1 (2020).

4. Hanne Strager, *A Modest Genius: The Story of Darwin's Life and How His Ideas Changed Everything* (CreateSpace Independent Publishing Platform, 2016), 11.

5. As epidemiologist George Smith writes, "If it were not for apparently chance events he would not have been present on the voyage of the Beagle, and we would probably be celebrating Alfred Russell Wallace as the founder of the theory of natural selection. Indeed, the narratives of people's lives often emphasize serendipity and misfortune at crucial turning points that apparently had a major influence on their trajectories." George Davey Smith, "Epidemiology, Epigenetics and the 'Gloomy Prospect': Embracing Randomness in Population Health Research and Practice," *International Journal of Epidemiology* 40 (2011): 541.

6. Strager, *Modest Genius*, 101.

7. Sean B. Carroll, *A Series of Fortunate Events: Chance and the Making of the Planet, Life, and You* (Princeton, NJ: Princeton University Press, 2020), 118.

8. Ed Smith, *Luck: What It Means and Why It Matters* (London: Bloomsbury, 2012), 222.

9. Curtis Johnson, *Darwin's Dice: The Idea of Chance in the Thoughts of Charles Darwin* (New York: Oxford University Press, 2015), 111.

10. Jonathan B. Losos, *Improbable Destinies: Fate, Chance, and the Future of Evolution* (New York: Riverhead Books, 2017), 95.

11. Losos, *Improbable Destinies*, 334.

12. Losos, *Improbable Destinies*, 335.

13. St. Louis Tornado History, Wikipedia, 2023.

14. Susan Elizabeth Hough, *Predicting the Unpredictable: The Tumultuous Science of Earthquake Prediction* (Princeton, NJ: Princeton University Press, 2016), 224.

15. Hough, *Predicting the Unpredictable*, 225.

16. Edward N. Lorenz, "Predictability: Does the Flap of a Butterfly's Wings in Brazil Set Off a Tornado in Texas?," paper presented at the American Association for the Advancement of Science, Washington DC, December 29, 1972.

17. Gerald Jay Sussman and Jack Wisdom, "Chaotic Evolution of the Solar System," *Science* 257 (1992): 56–62.

18. Intergovernmental Panel on Climate Change, *Climate Change 2022: Impacts, Adaptation and Vulnerability*, Working Group II Contribution to the Sixth Assessment Report of the Intergovernmental Panel on Climate Change.

19. Intergovernmental Panel on Climate Change, *Climate Change 2022*.

20. Dominic Lusinchi, "'President' Landon and the 1936 *Literary Digest* Poll," *Social Science History* 36 (2012): 23–54.

21. Lusinchi, "'President' Landon," 38.

22. For a definitive history of the rise of statistical probability in the seventeenth and eighteenth centuries, see Ian Hacking, *The Emergence of Probability: A Philosophical Study of Early Ideas about Probability, Induction and Statistical Inference* (New York: Cambridge University Press, 2006). Hacking places the beginnings of serious probabilistic thinking at around 1660.

23. Hales, *Myth of Luck*, 23.

24. Peter Bernstein, *Against the Gods: The Remarkable Story of Risk* (New York: John Wiley & Sons, 1996), 1.

25. Bernstein, *Against the Gods*, 57.

26. Lears, *Something for Nothing*, 21.

27. Mark R. Rank, *Confronting Poverty: Tools for Understanding Economic Hardship and Risk*, https://confrontingpoverty.org/.

28. Robert E. Rubin, "I Don't Have the Secret to Making Hard Decisions, but I Do Have a Yellow Note Pad," *New York Times*, May 14, 2023, sec. SR, p. 5.

29. Such an approach has a long history behind it. John Wilkins, the Bishop of Chester, wrote in 1675: "In all the ordinary affairs of life men are used to guide their actions by this rule, namely to incline to that which is most probable and likely when they cannot attain any clear unquestionable certainty." Or Joseph Butler, writing in his 1736 book, *Analogy of Religion*, notes that "probability is the very guide in life." Hacking, *Emergence of Probability*, 82.

30. Robert K. Merton and Elinor Barber, *The Travels and Adventures of Serendipity* (Princeton, NJ: Princeton University Press, 2004).

31. Christian Busch, *The Serendipity Mindset: The Arts and Science of Creating Good Luck* (London: Penguin Books, 2020), p. 26.

32. Merton and Barber, *Travels and Adventures*, 282. The famous quote "chance favors the prepared mind" is from Louis Pasteur.

33. For further examples of serendipity, see M. De Rond, "The Structure of Serendipity," Cambridge Judge Business School, Working Paper Series, WP 07/2005, University of Cambridge, July 2005.

34. John Ziman, *Real Science: What It Is and What It Means* (New York: Cambridge University Press, 2000), 217.

35. Ziman, *Real Science*, 217.

Chapter 4

1. At the start of the 2005 film *Match Point*, the viewer is shown a tennis ball going back and forth over the net. The narrator's voice is then heard saying,

> The man who said, "I'd rather be lucky than good," saw deeply into life. People are afraid to face how great a part of life is dependent on luck. It's scary to think so much is out of one's control. There are moments in a match when the ball hits the top of the net, and for a split second it can either go forward or fall back. With a little luck, it goes forward and you win. Or maybe it doesn't, and you lose.

At that point the ball hits the top of the net and bounces straight up, suspended in the frame. The film then explores how our constant companion of luck plays out in the lives of the film's characters. Similar to this is the Yiddish expression, "Better an ounce of luck than a pound of gold."

2. Mauboussin, *Success Equation*.

3. Mauboussin, *Success Equation*, 81.

4. Matthew Futterman, "Why the World's Best Skiers Don't Always Win at the Olympics," *New York Times*, February 7, 2022, sec. D, p. 8.

5. The term was coined by Tommy Armour, a golf champion in the 1920s and 1930s, to explain why he left tournament play.

6. Burton G. Malkiel, *A Random Walk Down Wall Street: The Time-Tested Strategy for Successful Investing* (New York: W.W. Norton, 2020), 26.

7. Malkiel, *Random Walk*, 155.

8. Georgette Jasen, "Journal's Dartboard Retires after 14 Years of Stock Picks," *Wall Street Journal,* April 18, 2002.

9. Will Steward, "Lusha the Chimpanzee Outperforms 94% of Russia Bankers with Her Investment Portfolio," *Daily Mail,* January 12, 2010.

10. Bernstein, *Against the Gods,* 297.

11. Malkiel, *Random Walk,* 147.

12. Malkiel, *Random Walk,* 176.

13. One of the most spectacular collapses in stock speculation was the hedge fund Long Term Capital Management. Despite being guided by sophisticated computer algorithms and the theory of Nobel Prize winner Myrone Scholes, and despite impressive gains during its beginning years, it eventually lost 4.6 billion dollars, was bailed out by the Federal Reserve Bank of New York, and liquidated in 1998.

14. Maria Konnikova, *The Biggest Bluff: How I Learned to Pay Attention, Master Myself, and Win* (New York: Penguin Press, 2020), 21.

15. Oliver Roeder, *Seven Games: A Human History* (New York: W.W. Norton, 2022), 9.

16. Sandrine Hermand-Grisel, "History of Surrealism in Photography," *All About Photo,* posted August 20, 2021.

17. More recent examples of incorporating chance into performance were the 1986 and 2011 concert tours of legendary singer-songwriter Elvis Costello. Called the "Spectacular Spinning Songbook" in 1986 and the "Return of the Spectacular Spinning Songbook" in 2011, a huge game-show spinning wheel was located on the stage that included the titles of 40 songs by Costello. Different audience members were invited up to the stage to spin the wheel, which would then determine the next number that Costello would perform. In this manner, much of the set list and order of performances for each night were determined completely by chance.

18. Andrew Anthony, "Interview: Bryan Cranston," *The Guardian,* October 27, 2012.

19. Yet even a musician as talented as Hamiet could momentarily be paralyzed by someone with supreme natural gifts. That someone was Aretha Franklin. As we ended our interview, Hamiet shared this experience of first accompanying Aretha with her full orchestra:

> Aretha started singing. I was on the third tune before I realized I wasn't even playing. We did the introductions. She came out and nothing could come out of my mouth. It was on the third or fourth tune before I realized I was not playing. And I said, 'Oh shit.' I went that night and apologized profusely to

the conductor. He kind of looked at me and smiled and said, "Man, don't worry about it. I've done it. She does that to me. Sometimes I'm up there and the band just keeps going." I said, "Oh, so you have to get use to being around her?" He said, "Yeah, that's exactly right."

20. John F. Callahan, *The Collected Essays of Ralph Ellison* (New York: Modern Library, 2003), 488.

21. Tom was certainly as committed to his profession as was Hamiet. As he put it,

> I've developed a theory over the years. This is like the heart of the whole thing. Every time I take a role, every time I go on stage whether I'm acting, or whether I'm directing, my goal is I want the audience to come out of the theater saying, "That was the best god damn thing I have ever seen. And now I know why human beings have done live theater for 5,000 years. And I know something, or I sense something about the human condition, now, that I didn't quite know two and a half hours before this. And even if I can't quite put it into words, my life is enriched by it."
>
> And I'm the first one to admit, I may never have achieved that goal, but that doesn't make it any less worthy a goal. So that's it. That's what sustains me in this strange obsession that I have developed with acting.

22. Mihaly Csikszentmihalyi, *Creativity: Flow and the Psychology of Discovery and Invention* (New York: HarperCollins, 1996), 46.

23. Leonard Mlodinow, *The Drunkard's Walk: How Randomness Rules Our Lives* (New York: Vintage Books, 2009), 217.

24. Vivi E. Lu and Dekyi T. Tsotsong, "Harvard College Accepts Record-Low 3.43% of Applicants to Class of 2025," *Harvard Crimson*, April 7, 2021.

25. Peter Arcidiancono, Josh Kinsler, and Tyler Ransom, "Legacy and Athlete Preferences at Harvard," *National Bureau of Economic Research*, Working Paper 26316, September 2019.

26. Michael Kinsley, "Why White, Preppy Men Need an Affirmative-Action Reality Check," *Vanity Fair*, August 13, 2015.

27. Michael J. Sandel, *The Tyranny of Merit: What's Become of the Common Good?* (New York: Farrar, Straus and Giroux, 2020), 185.

28. Sandel, *Tyranny of Merit*, 186.

29. Janice Kaplan and Barnaby Marsh, *How Luck Happens: Using the Science of Luck to Transform Work, Love, and Life* (New York: Dutton, 2018), 172.

30. Sherwin, *Gambling with Armageddon*, 3.

31. Nassim Nicholas Taleb, *The Black Swan: The Impact of the Highly Improbable* (New York: Random House, 2010), xxiii.

32. Taleb, *Black Swan*, 298.

33. Rescher, *Luck*, 128.

Chapter 5

1. Raoul Martinez, *Creating Freedom: The Lottery of Birth, the Illusion of Consent, and the Fight for Our Future* (New York: Pantheon Books, 2016), 3.

2. Alan R. Templeton, *Population Genetics and Microevolutionary Theory* (New York: John Wiley & Sons, 2021).

3. Stephen Pinker, *The Blank Slate: The Modern Denial of Human Nature* (New York: Penguin Books, 2016), 450.

4. Steven Pinker, "Why Nature and Nurture Won't Go Away," *Daedalus* 133 (2004): 16.

5. One of the first of these experiments was with roundworms. Caleb Finch and Thomas Kirkwood looked at a group of genetically identical roundworms raised on identical diets. They found that longevity varied considerably among the worms. See Caleb E. Finch and Tom Kirkwood, *Chance, Development, and Aging* (New York: Oxford University Press, 2000). In another study published in *Science*, Gerd Kempermann and colleagues looked at genetically identical mice, and found that cognitive development in the mice varied widely as a result of chance events occurring at the genetic level. See Gerd Kempermann, "Emergence of Individuality in Genetically Identical Mice," *Science* 340 (2013): 756–59. Gary Marcus, in summarizing these results, writes, "Different creatures, even from the same species, can grow up differently, and develop significantly different brains—even if their genomes are identical, and even if their environments are, too." See Gary Marcus, "Mice, Men, and Fate," *New Yorker*, May 13, 2013.

6. Smith, "Epidemiology, Epigenetics," 547.

7. Smith, "Epidemiology, Epigenetics," 537.

8. Leslie A. Pray, "DNA Replication and Causes of Mutation," *Nature Education* 1 (2008): 214.

9. Smith, "Epidemiology, Epigenetics," 550.

10. George M. Martin, "Nature, Nurture, and Chance: Their Roles in Interspecific and Intraspecific Modulations of Aging," *Annual Review of Gerontology and Geriatrics* 34 (2014): 278.

11. Stephen Rice, David Trafimow, and Rian Mehta, "The Case for Adding Randomness to the Nature-Nurture Debate," *Issues in Social Science* 3 (2015): 128.

12. Stepah Jurajda and Daniel Munich, "Admission to Selective Schools, Alphabetically," *Economics of Education Review* 29 (2010): 1100–109.

13. Jurajda and Munich, "Admission," 1101.

14. C. Mirjam Van Praag and Bernard M. S. Van Praag, "The Benefits of Being Economics Professor A (rather than Z)," *Economica* 75 (2008): 782–96.

15. Van Praag and Van Praag, "Benefits," 788.

16. Van Praag and Van Praag, "Benefits," 792.

17. Liran Einav and Leeat Yariv, "What's in a Surname? The Effects of Surname Initials on Academic Success," *Journal of Economic Perspectives* 20 (2006): 175–88. For an overall review of the literature, see Matthias Weber, "The Effects of Listing Authors in Alphabetical Order: A Review of the Empirical Evidence," *Research Evaluation* 27 (2018): 238–45.

18. Simon M. Laham, Peter Koval, and Adam Alter, "The Name-Pronunciation Effect: Why People Like Mr. Smith More than Mr. Colquhoun," *Journal of Experimental Social Psychology* 48 (2012): 752.

19. Marianne Bertrand and Sendhil Mullainathan, "Are Emily and Greg More Employable than Lakisha and Jamal? A Field Experiment on Labor Market Discrimination," *American Economic Review* 94 (2004): 991–1013.

20. For a review of this literature, see Kevin Lang and Ariella Kahn-Lang Spitzer, "Race Discrimination: An Economic Perspective," *Journal of Economic Perspectives* 34 (2020): 68–89.

21. Malcolm Gladwell, *Outliers: The Story of Success* (New York: Little, Brown, 2008), 23.

22. For greater detail on this effect, see Robert O. Deaner, Aaron Lowen, and Stephen Cobley, "Born at the Wrong Time: Selection Bias in the NHL Draft," *PLOS ONE* 8 (2013): e57753.

23. Gladwell, *Outliers*, 28.

24. One study indicates that children with later birth dates in the school year are less likely to hold leadership positions in high school. See Elizabeth Dhuey and Stephen Lipscomb, "What Makes a Leader? Relative Age and High School Leadership," *Economics of Education Review* 27 (2008): 173–83. Another study found evidence that the number of CEOs born in the months of June and July was almost one third less than one would expect on the basis of chance. Individuals born in these months would have been the very youngest in their class during their K–12 years of schooling. See Quianqian Du, Huasheng Gaob, and Maurice

D. Levi, "The Relative-Age Effect and Career Success: Evidence from Corporate CEOs," *Economics Letters* 117 (2012): 660–62.

25. Kasey D. Buckles and Daniel M. Hungerman, "Season of Birth and Later Outcomes: Old Questions, New Answers," *Review of Economics and Statistics* 95 (2013): 714–15. See also H. Jurges and K. Schneider, "Why Young Boys Stumble: Early Tracking, Age and Gender Bias in the German School System," *German Economic Review* 12 (2011): 371–94; A. M. Muehlenweg and P. A. Phuani, "The Evolution of the School-Entry Effects in a School Tracking System," *Journal of Human Resources* 45 (2010): 407–38.

26. See Douglas H. Frank, "As Luck Would Have It: The Effect of the Vietnam Draft Lottery on Long-Term Career Outcomes," *Industrial Relations* 51 (2012): 247–74, for how men with a lottery number placing them at a higher likelihood of induction were underrepresented among top U. S. executives in the 1990s.

27. Pamela J. Smock and Christine R. Schwartz, "The Demography of Families: A Review of Patterns and Change," *Journal of Marriage and Families* 82 (2020): 9–34.

28. Roland Neil and Robert J. Sampson, "The Birth Lottery of History: Arrest over the Life Course of Multiple Cohorts Coming of Age, 1995–2018," *American Journal of Sociology* 126 (2021): 1167.

29. Richard A. Easterlin, *Birth and Fortune: The Impact of Numbers on Personal Welfare* (Chicago: University of Chicago Press, 1987).

30. Sharon Sassler and Daniel T. Lichter, "Cohabitation and Marriage: Complexity and Diversity in Union-Formation Patterns," *Journal of Marriage and the Family* 82 (2020): 35–61.

31. Gladwell, *Outliers*.

32. Neil and Sampson, "Birth Lottery."

33. Neil and Sampson, "Birth Lottery," 1170.

34. Angelina R. Sutin, Yannick Stephan, Martina Luckette, Damaris Ashwanden, Hi Hyun Lee, Amanda A. Sesker, and Antonio Terracciano, "Differential Personality Change Earlier and Later in the Coronavirus Pandemic in a Longitudinal Sample of Adults in the United States," *PLOS ONE*, September 28, 2022.

35. Ahmet Riza Sahlin, Aysegul Erdogan, Pelin Mutlu Agaoglu, Yeliz Dineri, Ahmet Ysuf Cakirci, Mahmut Egemen Senel, Ramazan Azim Okyay, and Ali Muhittin Tasdogan, "2019 Novel Coronavirus (COVID-19) Outbreak: A Review of the Current Literature," *Eurasian Journal of Medicine and Oncology* 4 (2020): 1–7; Yi-chi Wu, Ching-Sung Chen, and Yu-Jiun Chan, "The Outbreak of COVID-19: An Overview," *Journal of Chinese Medical Association* 83 (2020): 217–20.

36. Sutin et al., "Differential Personality Change," 10.

37. Sutin et al., "Differential Personality Change," 12.

38. Smith, *Luck*, 198–99.

Chapter 6

1. Pinker, *Blank Slate*, 396.

2. Bandura, "Psychology of Chance Encounters," 747.

3. Ben Waber, Jennifer Magnolfi, and Greg Lindsay, "Workspaces That Move People," *Harvard Business Review,* October 2014.

4. Keith Sawyer, *Group Genius: The Creative Power of Collaboration* (New York: Basic Books, 2007).

5. Jon Gertner, *The Idea Factory: Bell Labs and the Great Age of American Innovation* (New York: Penguin Books, 2012).

6. Waber et al., "Workspaces That Move People."

7. Natalie Engels, "Fostering Casual Collisions—and Creativity—in a Virtual World," Gensler, April 7, 2020.

8. Keith Pennington and Myles Shaver, "A Compelling Reason for Returning to the Office? Serendipity," *Minneapolis Star Tribune,* August 23, 2023.

9. Debra L. Blackwell and Daniel T. Lichter, "Homogamy among Dating Cohabiting and Married Couples," *Sociological Quarterly* 45 (2004): 719–37.

10. Personal communication, Robert Pollack, February 14, 2023.

11. Bandura, "Psychology of Chance Encounters," 748.

12. Anne Roe and Rhonda Baruch, "Occupational Changes in the Adult Years," *Personal Administration* 30 (1967): 121–28.

13. Jim E.H. Bright, Robert G.L. Pryor, and Lucy Harpham, "The Role of Chance Events in Career Decision Making," *Journal of Vocational Behavior* 66 (2005): 561.

14. Bright et al., "Role of Chance Events," 573.

15. Mark Granovetter, *Getting a Job: A Study of Contacts and Careers* (Chicago: University of Chicago Press, 1974), ix.

16. Granovetter, *Getting a Job*, 22.

17. Steve McDonald, "Right Place, Right Time: Serendipity and Informal Job Matching," *Socio-Economic Review* 8 (2010): 325.

18. Til von Wachter and Stefan Bender, "In the Right Place at the Wrong Time: The Role of Firms and Luck in Young Workers' Careers," *American Economic Review* 96 (2006): 1679–705; Joanna Bornat, Leroi Henry, and Parvati Raghuram, "The Making of Careers, the Making of a Discipline: Luck and Chance

in Migrant Careers in Geriatric Medicine," *Journal of Vocational Behavior* 78 (2011): 342–50.

19. James C. March and James G. March, "Almost Random Careers: The Wisconsin School Superintendency, 1940–1972," *Administrative Science Quarterly* 22 (1977): 408.

20. Mark Robert Rank, https://confrontingpoverty.org/the-musical-chairs-of-poverty/.

21. Christopher Jencks, *Inequality: A Reassessment of the Effect of Family and Schooling in America* (New York: Basic Books, 1972), 227.

22. Joseph G. Altonji, Disa M. Hynsuo, and Ivan Vidangos, "Individual Earnings and Family Income: Dynamics and Distribution," National Bureau of Economic Research, Working Paper 30095, May 2022; John Geweke and Michael Keane, "An Empirical Analysis of Earnings Dynamics among Men in the PSID: 1968–1989," *Journal of Econometrics* 96 (2000): 293–356; Samuel Bowles, Herbert Gintis, and Melissa Osborne Groves, *Unequal Chances: Family Background and Economic Success* (New York: Russell Sage Foundation, 2005).

23. There is a clear difference between Americans and Europeans in their perceptions of the role of luck in determining income. For example, economists Alberto Alesina and Edward Glaeser report that 30 percent of Americans believe that luck determines income whereas 54 percent of those within the European Union say so. See Alberto Alesina and Edward L. Glaeser, *Fighting Poverty in the US and Europe: A World of Difference* (New York: Oxford University Press, 2004.

24. Alessandro Pluchino, Alessio Emanuell Biondo, and Andrea Rapisarda, "Talent Versus Luck: The Role of Randomness in Success and Failure," *Advances in Complex Systems* 21 (2018): 1850014-2.

25. Pluchino et al., "Talent Versus Luck," 1850014-27. In addition, see Jerker Denrell and Chengwei Liu, "Top Performers Are Not the Most Impressive When Extreme Performance Indicates Unreliability," *Proceedings of the National Academy of Sciences* 109 (2012): 9331-36.

26. Robert Frank, "Before Tea, Thank Your Lucky Stars," *New York Times*, April 26, 2009.

27. Robert Frank, *Success and Luck: Good Fortune and the Myth of Meritocracy* (Princeton, NJ: Princeton University Press, 2016), 55.

28. Mark Robert Rank, *Confronting Poverty: Economic Hardship in the United States* (Los Angeles: Sage, 2021).

29. Mark Robert Rank, *The Poverty Paradox: Understanding Economic Hardship amid American Prosperity* (New York: Oxford University Press, 2023).

30. Mark Robert Rank, *Living on the Edge: The Realities of Welfare in America* (New York: Columbia University Press, 1994), 90–91.

31. Stephen Menendian, Arthur Galles, and Samir, "The Roots of Structural Racism: Twenty-First Century Racial Residential Segregation in the United States," Council for the Homeless, 2021.

32. Raj Chetty, Nathaniel Hendren, and Lawrence F. Katz, "The Effects of Exposure to Better Neighborhoods on Children: New Evidence from the Moving to Opportunity Experiment," *American Economic Review* 106 (2016): 855–902.

33. Nicole M. Fortin, Andrew J. Hill, and Jeff Huang, "Superstition in the Housing Market," *Economic Inquiry* 52 (2014): 974–93.

34. Matthew Shum, Wei Sun, and Guangliang Ye, "Superstition and 'Lucky' Apartments: Evidence from Transaction-Level Data," *Journal of Comparative Economics* 42 (2014): 109–17.

35. Kristallnacht is often considered the beginning of the Holocaust. Up until this event, the persecution of Jews in Germany had taken place primarily through antisemitic politics of discrimination. Kristallnacht introduced mass physical violence as a further means of persecution.

36. The Dachau concentration camp outside of Munich was originally opened on March 22, 1933, less than two months after Hitler had taken power in Germany. It was the first concentration camp established by the Nazis, and served as a model for others to come. Between 1933 and 1938, prisoners at Dachau were primarily German nationals who were arrested for political reasons. After 1938, the camp held a variety of prisoners from various occupied countries of the Third Reich.

37. Edward D. Kleinbard, *What's Luck Got to Do with It? How Smarter Government Can Rescue the American Dream* (New York: Oxford University Press, 2021), xi.

38. A popular example of this comes from the 1998 movie *Sliding Doors*. The story plot follows what happens in the life of a young woman named Helen under two different scenarios. In the first version, Helen rushes down the stairway in a London subway station attempting to catch the train home, only to arrive a fraction of a second late as the subway doors close. In the second scenario, she rushes down the stairway in the same London station at the exact same time, but by a fraction of a second is able to make it onto the train. The movie then follows how Helen's life is substantially altered as a result of the simple act of catching or not catching that particular train on that particular day at that particular moment. The differences are both subtle and profound.

Chapter 7

1. A striking example of a near miss (sadly, only for one) was the airplane crash that killed rock and rollers Buddy Holly, Ritchie Valens, and J. P. Richardson (the Big Bopper) outside of Clear Lake, Iowa, on February 3, 1959. They along with Dion and the Belmonts and Frankie Sardo were on a concert tour of the upper Midwest dubbed the "Winter Dance Party." The weather was brutal, the tour bus broke down repeatedly, and the distance between venues was extreme. The tour included 24 Midwestern cities in 24 days spread out over hundreds of miles. By the time they reached their eleventh stop in Clear Lake, Iowa, Holly decided to charter a plane to get to the next concert in Morehead City, Minnesota, which is directly across the Red River from Fargo, North Dakota. The plane could carry three passengers plus the pilot.

According to Dion Dimucci, during the early part of the show at the Surf Ballroom on Monday, February 2, while Frankie Sardo was on stage, Holly called Dion, Valens, and Richardson into the dressing room. According to Dion, Holly said, "I've chartered a plane, and we're the guys making the money so we should be the ones flying ahead; the only problem is there are only two available seats." Dion, Richardson, and Valens agreed to flip a coin to decide who of the three would get the two seats. Whoever flipped heads would get to go on the plane. Richardson was up first and flipped heads, ensuring he would claim the first seat on the plane. Next up, Dion also won the flip, getting heads, but after learning the price of the plane fare, chose to give up his seat to Valens, who had become sick at this point of the tour. After this impromptu meeting in the dressing room, Richardson, Dion, Valens, and Holly each gave their performances in front of 1,500 fans. After the concert, Holly, Valens, and Richardson drove a few miles to the Mason City Municipal Airport, where the plane was waiting to take them to Minnesota. The plane took off at 12:55 a.m., and five minutes later crashed, killing all four on board.

Meanwhile, Dion had boarded the bus along with the rest of the tour members, which drove overnight, arriving in Morehead City the next morning. When they arrived at the hotel, he learned that the plane Holly had chartered had crashed, killing all four. He immediately realized that it was only luck that was the difference between life and death and how close he had come to dying. In fact, he had won the coin flip, and therefore was entitled to have the last seat on the airplane, but at the last minute decided to give up his seat to Richie Valens.

An alternative scenario of the fateful coin flip for the last seat on the plane was recalled by Bob Hale, a local DJ at the time and the emcee for the evening. After

Valens closed out his four-song set with "La Bamba," there was a short intermission before the second half of the show. During the intermission, Valens asked Holly's guitarist, Tommy Allsup, for his spot on the plane, but Allsup refused. Finally, Valens suggested to Allsup, "I'll tell you what. Let's flip for it." Allsup agreed, but neither had a coin in his pocket. Hale then offered, "I have a quarter, Ritchie. You call it." Valens called heads, the coin was flipped, and it landed on heads. Hale declared, "Okay, Ritchie. You're flying." Valens was reported to have said, "That's the first time I've ever won anything in my life."

I recently visited the Surf Ballroom and stood in the dressing room where the coin flip took place. Like the image on the cover of this book, I could imagine the coin being suspended in midair with the fate of at least two individuals held in the balance. But there is one last ironic twist to this story. The night of the Clear Lake concert was originally an open date on the tour schedule. There was no concert planned for Monday, February 2. It was only added to the schedule a few days before. Had it not been a late addition to the tour, Buddy Holly, Richie Valens, and J. P. Richardson might very well be alive to this day.

2. Smith, *Luck*, 199.

3. Mark R. Rank, "Reducing Cumulative Inequality," in *Toward a Livable Life: A 21st Century Agenda for Social Work*, ed. Mark Robert Rank (New York: Oxford University Press, 2020), 94–113.

4. Robert K. Merton, "The Matthew Effect in Science: The Reward and Communication Systems of Science Are Considered," *Science* 159 (1968): 56–63; Robert K. Merton, "The Matthew Effect in Science, II: Cumulative Advantage and the Symbolism of Intellectual Property," *Isis* 79 (1988): 606–23.

5. Merton, "Matthew Effect in Science, II," 606.

6. Thomas A. DiPrete and Gregory M. Eirich, "Cumulative Advantage as a Mechanism for Inequality: A Review of Theoretical and Empirical Developments," *Annual Review of Sociology* 32 (2006): 271–97.

7. Mark Robert Rank, *The Poverty Paradox: Understanding Economic Hardship Amid American Prosperity* (New York: Oxford University Press, 2023).

8. Stanford Open Policing Project, https://openpolicing.stanford.edu/, 2023.

9. Janie L. Jeffers, "Justice Is Not Blind: Disproportionate Incarceration Rate of People of Color," in *Race and Social Policy*, ed. Sandra Edmonds Crewe (London: Routledge, 2023); Adero S. Jernigan, "Driving While Black: Racial Profiling in America," *Law and Psychology Review* 24 (2000): 127–38.

10. Tony Messenger, *Profit and Punishment: How America Criminalizes the Poor in the Name of Justice* (New York: St. Martin's Press, 2021).

11. Messinger, *Profit and Punishment*.

12. Messinger, *Profit and Punishment*, xvi.

13. Sharon Begley, "Most Cancer Cases Arise from 'Bad Luck,'" *Scientific American*, March 24, 2017.

14. Julia Evangelou Strait, "Most Cases of Never-Smokers' Lung Cancer Treatable with Mutation-Targeting Drugs," news release, Washington University School of Medicine, September 30, 2021; Ramaswamy Govindan, "Genomic Profiling of Lung Adencarcinoma in Never-Smokers," *Journal of Clinical Oncology* 39 (2021): 3747–57.

15. Luthy and Palmerino, "Conceptual and Historical Reflections," in Landsman and van Wolde, *Challenge of Chance*, 15.

16. Busch, *Serendipity Mindset*.

Chapter 8

1. Kleinbard, *What's Luck Got to Do with It?*

2. John Rawls, *A Theory of Justice* (Cambridge, MA: Harvard University Press, 1971).

3. Rawls, *Theory of Justice*, 12.

4. Rawls, *Theory of Justice*, 61.

5. Rawls, *Theory of Justice*, 14–15.

6. John Rawls, *Political Liberalism* (New York: Columbia University Press, 1996).

7. John Rawls, *Justice as Fairness: A Restatement* (Cambridge, MA: Harvard University Press, 2001).

8. Rank et al., *Chasing the American Dream*.

9. Cass R. Sunstein, *The Second Bill of Rights: FDR's Unfinished Revolution and Why We Need It More than Ever* (New York: Basic Books, 2004).

10. Derek Bok, *The State of the Nation: Government and the Quest for a Better Society* (Cambridge, MA: Harvard University Press, 1996), 311.

11. Leonard Beeghley, *The Structure of Social Stratification in the United States* (Boston: Allyn and Bacon, 2000), 143.

12. Martin N. Marger, *Social Inequality: Patterns and Process* (New York: McGraw Hill, 2014), 226.

13. Martin Gilens, *Why Americans Hate Welfare: Race, Media, and the Politics of Antipoverty Policy* (Chicago: University of Chicago Press, 1999).

14. Everett Carl Ladd, *The American Ideology: An Exploration of the Origins, Meaning, and Role of American Political Ideas* (Storrs, CT: Roper Center for Public Opinion Research, 1994).

15. James R. Kluegel and Eliot R. Smith, *Beliefs about Inequality: Americans' View of What Is and What Ought to Be* (Hawthorne, NY: Aldine de Gruyter, 1986).

16. Robert Putnam, *Our Kids: The American Dream in Crisis* (New York: Simon & Schuster, 2015), 206, 34.

17. Judith A. Chafel, "Societal Images of Poverty: Child and Adult Beliefs," *Youth and Society* 28 (1997): 445–46.

18. For example, see Amartya Sen, *Development as Freedom* (New York: Anchor Books, 2000).

19. Rank, *Toward a Livable Life*.

20. Kleinbard, *What's Luck Got to Do with It?*, xiii.

21. Kleinbard, *What's Luck Got to Do with It?*, 136.

22. And in fact I have also created a poverty risk calculator that allows one to enter their demographic characteristics and, on the basis of those factors, estimate their risk of poverty in the next 5, 10, or 15 years. The website can be accessed at www.confrontingpoverty.org.

23. Rank, *Poverty Paradox*.

24. Rank, *Poverty Paradox*.

25. Rank, *Confronting Poverty*.

26. We currently have a form of a guaranteed income as well as negative income tax in the Earned Income Tax Credit program. This program is designed to provide a supplement to low-income wage earners. However, it is only open to those currently employed and earning a wage. The EITC is not available to those who are unemployed or out of work. Furthermore, it is largely focused on households with children. Single men and women receive much less from the EITC.

27. Milton Freidman, *Capitalism and Freedom* (Chicago: University of Chicago Press, 1962).

28. Kleinbard, *What's Luck Got to Do with It?*, 173.

29. Robert Haveman, *Starting Even: An Equal Opportunity Program to Combat the Nation's New Poverty* (New York: Simon and Schuster, 1988), 30.

30. Lyndon B. Johnson, "The President's Inaugural Address, January 20, 1965," *Public Papers of the Presidents of the United States: Lyndon B. Johnson,* vol. I, entry 27, pp. 71–74 (Washington, DC: U.S. Government Printing Office, 1965).

31. National Center for Education Statistics, "Back to School Statistics," 2020.

32. Linda Darling-Hammond and Laura Post, "Inequality in Teaching and Schooling: Supporting High-Quality Teaching and Leadership in Low-Income Schools," in *A Nation at Risk: Preserving Public Education as an Engine for Social Mobility,* ed. Richard D. Kalenberg (New York: Century Foundation Press, 2000), 127.

33. Jonathan Kozol, *Savage Inequalities: Children in America's Schools* (New York: Crown, 1991).

34. U.S. Department of Education, Equity and Excellence Commission, *For Each and Every Child: A Strategy for Education Equity and Excellence* (Washington, DC: Education Publications Center, 2013), 12.

35. Emily Hunnum and Yu Xie, "Education," in *The Oxford Handbook of the Social Sciences of Poverty*, ed. David Brady and Linda M. Burton (New York: Oxford University Press, 2016), 462–85.

36. Jennifer Hochschild and Nathan Scovronick, *The American Dream and the Public Schools* (New York: Oxford University Press, 2003), 12–13.

37. Erica Frankenberg, Jongyeon Ee, Jennifer B. Ayscue, and Gary Orfield, "Harming Our Common Future: America's Segregated Schools 65 Years after *Brown*," The Civil Rights Project, May 10, 2019, p. 9.

38. Frankenberg et al., "Harming Our Common Future," 9.

39. Ann Owens, "Unequal Opportunity: School and Neighborhood Segregation in the USA," *Race and Social Problems* 12 (2020): 29–41.

40. Hochschild and Scovronick, *American Dream*, 5.

41. Hochschild and Scovronick, *American Dream*, 23.

42. Thomas M. Shapiro, *The Hidden Cost of Being African American: How Wealth Perpetuates Inequality* (New York: Oxford University Press, 2004).

43. Michelle Jackson and Brian Holzman, "A Century of Educational Inequality in the United States," *Proceedings of the National Academy of Sciences* 117.32 (2020): 19108–15.

44. Daniel P. McMurrer and Isabel V. Sawhill, *Getting Ahead: Economic and Social Mobility in America* (Washington, DC: Urban Institute Press, 1998), 69.

45. Greg J. Duncan and Richard J. Murnane, *Whither Opportunity? Rising Inequality, Schools, and Children's Life Chances* (New York: Russell Sage Foundation, 2011), 15.

46. Kleinbard, *What's Luck Got to Do with It?*, xiii.

Chapter 9

1. Seymour Martin Lipset, *American Exceptionalism: A Double-Edged Sword* (New York: W. W. Norton, 1996).

2. Sandel, *Tyranny of Merit*, 227.

3. For example, in his speech before the Republican Convention in Cleveland in July 2016, Trump remarked that "nobody knows the system better than me,

which is why I alone can fix it," referring to his presumed ability to remake the political system.

4. Robert Emmons, *Thanks!: How Practicing Gratitude Can Make You Happier* (New York: HarperOne, 2008).

5. Sandel, *Tyranny of Merit*, 25.

6. Kleinbard, *What's Luck Got to Do with It?*, 26.

7. Lears, *Something for Nothing*, 22.

8. Robert E. Rubin, *The Yellow Pad: Making Better Decisions in an Uncertain World* (New York: Penguin Press, 2023), 55, 57.

9. Ben Cohen, *The Hot Hand: The Mystery and Science of Streaks* (New York: Custom House, 2020), 139.

10. James Sundali and Rachel Croson, "Biases in Casino Betting: The Hot Hand and the Gambler's Fallacy," *Judgment and Decision Making* 1 (2006): 1–12.

11. A famous example of this fallacy that cost gamblers considerable money took place at the Monte Carlo Casino on August 18, 1913. On that date, the roulette table saw 26 straight spins of the ball falling on black. During this streak, gamblers were placing increasingly larger bets that the ball would fall on red. Only on the 27th spin did the ball fall on red. Those placing their bets before the 27th spin lost millions of francs as a result of their faith in the gambler's fallacy.

12. Daniel L. Chen, Tobias J. Moskowitz, and Kelly Shue, "Decision Making under the Gambler's Fallacy: Evidence from Asylum Judges, Loan Officer, and Baseball Umpires," *Quarterly Journal of Economics* 131 (2016): 1184.

13. Chen et al., "Decision Making," 1232.

14. The hot hand fallacy has been applied extensively to the sport of basketball. For anyone who has ever played or watched a basketball game, there is a phenomenon known as the hot hand. This is when a shooter seems as if they cannot miss in terms of putting the ball in the basket. Nevertheless, an influential 1985 paper by Thomas Gilovich, Robert Vallone, and Amos Tversky analyzed data that appeared to show there was no such thing as the hot hand in basketball. Other research also found little support for the hot hand in basketball, and this became the accepted belief for over 30 years. However, a recent study by Joshua Miller and Adam Sanjurjo showed that the mathematics behind those studies was flawed, and that the data did indeed confirm that there was such a thing as the hot hand. A shooter who was on a hot streak was more likely to sink their next basket than when they were not. While the hot hand may apply to behaviors that we exert some control over, it most certainly does not apply to pure games of chance. See Joshua B. Miller and Adam Sanjurjo, "A Bridge from Monty Hall to the Hot Hand: The Principle of Restricted Choice," *Journal of Economic Perspectives* 33 (2019): 144–62.

15. Chen et al., "Decision Making."

16. Cohen, *Hot Hand*, 91.

17. Mark R. Rank, "Why Poverty and Inequality Undermine Justice in America," in *Routledge International Handbook of Social Justice,* ed. Michael Reisch, 436–47 (New York: Routledge Press, 2014).

18. Rescher, *Luck*, 21.

19. Jane Eisner, "The Deep, Difficult Comfort of 'When Bad Things Happen to Good People,'" *Washington Post,* May 9, 2023; Harold S. Kushner, *When Bad Things Happen to Good People* (New York: Anchor Books, 1981).

20. Sauder, "Sociology of Luck," 196.

21. Marche, *On Writing and Failure*, 19.

22. Marche, *On Writing and Failure*, 22–23.

23. The beginnings of decision theory are often traced back to the mathematician Pascal's well-known wager posed in the seventeenth century. His wager deals with should you or should you not believe in God. Pascal writes, "God is, or he is not. Which way should we incline? Reason cannot answer." As a result, according to Pascal, one should consider the consequences of whether to believe or not. Let us take the case of someone who decides to believe. What happens when they die? If God does not exist, then it makes no difference whether they believed or not. In other words, there are no repercussions. However, if God does exist, then their reward is eternal salvation. Now let us look at the individual choosing not to believe. Again, if God does not exist, then when they die there are no repercussions for their lack of belief. However, if God does exist, then the consequence of their not believing is eternal damnation. Clearly salvation is infinitely preferable to damnation, and as a result, believing in God is the smart choice in terms of the wager posed by Pascal. See Hacking, *Emergence of Probability*, for a more detailed discussion.

24. Busch, *Serendipity Mindset*, 288.

25. Lears, *Something for Nothing*, 15.

26. Frank Norris, *The Octopus* (New York: Doubleday, 1901), 185.

Chapter 10

1. Thornton Wilder was a particularly important influence upon the historian David McCullough. As an undergraduate English major at Yale, McCullough noted that Wilder, who lived close to New Haven, was a familiar face on campus. McCullough recalled about Wilder: "When asked how he settled on the subjects of his plays and novels, he said he would imagine a story he would love to see per-

formed on stage or to read in a book; if, after checking around, he found no one had written what he was looking for, he would write it himself, so he could see it performed or read it." David McCullough, *The Johnstown Flood, 50th Anniversary Edition* (New York: Simon & Schuster, 2018), 16. My writing of this book has been somewhat in the same spirit. This is the book that I would like to read on the subject, and my hope is that you will find it so as well.

2. Frank, *Success and Luck*, 143.

3. Howard S. Becker, "'FOI POR ACASO': Conceptualizing Coincidence," *Sociological Quarterly* 35 (1994): 183.

4. David L. Krantz, "Taming Chance: Social Science and Everyday Narratives," *Psychological Inquiry* 9 (1998): 89.

5. John R. Gillis, "'A Triumph of Hope over Experience': Chance and Choice in the History of Marriage," *International Review of Social History* 44 (1999): 52.

Bibliography

Alesina, Alberto, and Edward L. Glaeser. *Fighting Poverty in the US and Europe: A World of Difference*. New York: Oxford University Press, 2004.

Altonji, Joseph G., Disa M. Hynsuo, and Ivan Vidangos. "Individual Earnings and Family Income: Dynamics and Distribution." National Bureau of Economic Research, Working Paper 30095, May 2022.

Arcidiancono, Peter, Josh Kinsler, and Tyler Ransom. "Legacy and Athlete Preferences at Harvard." National Bureau of Economic Research, Working Paper 26316, September 2019.

Bandura, Albert. "The Psychology of Chance Encounters and Life Paths." *American Psychologist* 37 (1982): 747–55.

Becker, Howard S. "'FOI POR ACASO': Conceptualizing Coincidence." *Sociological Quarterly* 35 (1994): 183–94.

Beeghley, Leonard. *The Structure of Social Stratification in the United States*. Boston: Allyn and Bacon, 2000.

Begley, Sharon. "Most Cancer Cases Arise from 'Bad Luck.'" *Scientific American*, March 24, 2017.

Bernstein, Peter. *Against the Gods: The Remarkable Story of Risk*. New York: John Wiley & Sons, 1996.

Bertrand, Marianne, and Sendhil Mullainathan. "Are Emily and Greg More Employable than Lakisha and Jamal? A Field Experiment on Labor Market Discrimination." *American Economic Review* 94 (2004): 991–1013.

Bird, Kai, and Martin J. Sherwin. *American Prometheus: The Triumph and Tragedy of J. Robert Oppenheimer*. New York: Alfred A. Knopf, 2005.

Blackwell, Debra L., and Daniel T. Lichter. "Homogamy among Dating Cohabiting and Married Couples." *Sociological Quarterly* 45 (2004): 719–37.

Bok, Derek. *The State of the Nation: Government and the Quest for a Better Society.* Cambridge, MA: Harvard University Press, 1996.

Bornat, Joanna, Leroi Henry, and Parvati Raghuram. "The Making of Careers, the Making of a Discipline: Luck and Chance in Migrant Careers in Geriatric Medicine." *Journal of Vocational Behavior* 78 (2011): 342–50.

Bowles, Samuel, Herbert Gintis, and Melissa Osborne Groves. *Unequal Chances: Family Background and Economic Success.* New York: Russell Sage Foundation, 2005.

Bright, Jim E. H., Robert G. L. Pryor, and Lucy Harpham. "The Role of Chance Events in Career Decision Making." *Journal of Vocational Behavior* 66 (2005): 561–76.

Buckles, Kasey D., and Daniel M. Hungerman. "Season of Birth and Later Outcomes: Old Questions, New Answers." *Review of Economics and Statistics* 95 (2013): 711–24.

Busch, Christian. *The Serendipity Mindset: The Arts and Science of Creating Good Luck.* London: Penguin Books, 2020.

Callahan, John F. *The Collected Essays of Ralph Ellison.* New York: Modern Library, 2003.

Carroll, Sean B. *A Series of Fortunate Events: Chance and the Making of the Planet, Life, and You.* Princeton, NJ: Princeton University Press, 2020.

Chafel, Judith A. "Societal Images of Poverty: Child and Adult Beliefs." *Youth and Society* 28 (1997): 445–46.

Chen, Daniel L., Tobias J. Moskowitz, and Kelly Shue. "Decision Making under the Gambler's Fallacy: Evidence from Asylum Judges, Loan Officer, and Baseball Umpires." *Quarterly Journal of Economics* 131 (2016): 1181–241.

Chetty, Raj, Nathaniel Hendren, and Lawrence F. Katz. "The Effects of Exposure to Better Neighborhoods on Children: New Evidence from the Moving to Opportunity Experiment." *American Economic Review* 106 (2016): 855–902.

Cohen, Ben. *The Hot Hand: The Mystery and Science of Streaks.* New York: Custom House, 2020.

Cowie, Jefferson. *Freedom's Dominion: A Saga of White Resistance to Federal Power.* New York: Basic Books, 2022.

Csikszentmihalyi, Mihaly. *Creativity: Flow and the Psychology of Discovery and Invention.* New York: HarperCollins, 1996.

Darling-Hammond, Linda, and Laura Post. "Inequality in Teaching and Schooling: Supporting High-Quality Teaching and Leadership in Low-Income Schools." In *A Nation at Risk: Preserving Public Education as an Engine for Social Mobility,* edited by Richard D. Kalenberg, 127–67. New York: Century Foundation Press, 2000.

Deaner, Robert O., Aaron Lowen, and Stephen Cobley. "Born at the Wrong Time: Selection Bias in the NHL Draft." *PLOS ONE* 8 (2013): e57753.

Denrell, Jerker, and Chengwei Liu. "Top Performers Are Not the Most Impressive When Extreme Performance Indicates Unreliability." *Proceedings of the National Academy of Sciences* 109 (2012): 9331–36.

De Rond, M. "The Structure of Serendipity." Cambridge Judge Business School, Working Paper Series, WP 07/2005, University of Cambridge, July 2005.

Dhuey, Elizabeth, and Stephen Lipscomb. "What Makes a Leader? Relative Age and High School Leadership." *Economics of Education Review* 27 (2008): 173–83.

DiPrete, Thomas A., and Gregory M. Eirich. "Cumulative Advantage as a Mechanism for Inequality: A Review of Theoretical and Empirical Developments." *Annual Review of Sociology* 32 (2006): 271–97.

Donahue, Michelle Z. "Dino-Killing Asteroid Hit Just the Right Spot to Trigger Extinction." *National Geographic,* November 11, 2017.

Du, Quianqian, Huasheng Gaob, and Maurice D. Levi. "The Relative-Age Effect and Career Success: Evidence from Corporate CEOs." *Economics Letters* 117 (2012): 660–62.

Duncan, Greg J., and Richard J. Murnane. *Whither Opportunity? Rising Inequality, Schools, and Children's Life Chances.* New York: Russell Sage Foundation, 2011.

Easterlin, Richard A. *Birth and Fortune: The Impact of Numbers on Personal Welfare.* Chicago: University of Chicago Press, 1987.

Einav, Liran, and Leeat Yariv. "What's in a Surname? The Effects of Surname Initials on Academic Success." *Journal of Economic Perspectives* 20 (2006): 175–88.

Emmons, Robert. *Thanks!: How Practicing Gratitude Can Make You Happier.* New York: HarperOne, 2008.

Engels, Natalie. "Fostering Casual Collisions—and Creativity—in a Virtual World." Gensler, April 7, 2020.

Eppard, Lawrence M., Mark Robert Rank, and Heather E. Bullock. *Rugged Individualism and the Misunderstanding of American Inequality.* Bethlehem, PA: Lehigh University Press, 2020.

Finch, Caleb E., and Tom Kirkwood. *Chance, Development, and Aging.* New York: Oxford University Press, 2000.

Fortin, Nicole M., Andrew J. Hill, and Jeff Huang. "Superstition in the Housing Market." *Economic Inquiry* 52 (2014): 974–93.

Frank, Douglas H. "As Luck Would Have It: The Effect of the Vietnam Draft Lottery on Long-Term Career Outcomes." *Industrial Relations* 51 (2012): 247–74.

Frank, Robert. *Success and Luck: Good Fortune and the Myth of Meritocracy.* Princeton, NJ: Princeton University Press, 2016.

Frankenberg, Erica, Jongyeon Ee, Jennifer B. Ayscue, and Gary Orfield. "Harming Our Common Future: America's Segregated Schools 65 Years after *Brown.*" The Civil Rights Project, May 10, 2019.

Friedman, Milton. *Capitalism and Freedom.* Chicago: University of Chicago Press, 1962.

Gertner, Jon. *The Idea Factory: Bell Labs and the Great Age of American Innovation.* New York: Penguin Books, 2012.

Geweke, John, and Michael Keane. "An Empirical Analysis of Earnings Dynamics among Men in the PSID: 1968–1989." *Journal of Econometrics* 96 (2000): 293–356.

Gilens, Martin. *Why Americans Hate Welfare: Race, Media, and the Politics of Antipoverty Policy.* Chicago: University of Chicago Press, 1999.

Gillis, John R. " 'A Triumph of Hope over Experience': Chance and Choice in the History of Marriage." *International Review of Social History* 44 (1999): 47–54.

Gladwell, Malcolm. *Outliers: The Story of Success.* New York: Little, Brown, 2008.

Govindan, Ramaswamy. "Genomic Profiling of Lung Adencarcinoma in Never-Smokers." *Journal of Clinical Oncology* 39 (2021): 3747–57.

Graff, Garrett M. "On 9/11, Luck Meant Everything." *The Atlantic,* September 10, 2019.

Graff, Garrett M. *The Only Plane in the Sky: An Oral History of 9/11.* New York: Avid Reader Press, 2019.

Granovetter, Mark. *Getting a Job: A Study of Contacts and Careers.* Chicago: University of Chicago Press, 1974.

Hacking, Ian. *The Emergence of Probability: A Philosophical Study of Early Ideas about Probability, Induction and Statistical Inference.* New York: Cambridge University Press, 2006.

Hales, Steven D. *The Myth of Luck: Philosophy, Fate, and Fortune.* London: Bloomsbury Academic, 2020.

Handlin, Oscar. *Chance or Destiny: Turning Points in American History.* Westport, CT: Greenwood Press, 1977.

Haveman, Robert. *Starting Even: An Equal Opportunity Program to Combat the Nation's New Poverty.* New York: Simon and Schuster, 1988.

Hermand-Grisel, Sandrine. "History of Surrealism in Photography." *All About Photo,* posted August 20, 2021.

Hochschild, Jennifer, and Nathan Scovronick. *The American Dream and the Public Schools*. New York: Oxford University Press, 2003.

Hough, Susan Elizabeth. *Predicting the Unpredictable: The Tumultuous Science of Earthquake Prediction*. Princeton, NJ: Princeton University Press, 2016.

Hunnum, Emily, and Yu Xie. "Education." In *The Oxford Handbook of the Social Sciences of Poverty*, edited by David Brady and Linda M. Burton, 462–85. New York: Oxford University Press, 2016.

Intergovernmental Panel on Climate Change. *Climate Change 2022: Impacts, Adaptation and Vulnerability*. Working Group II Contribution to the Sixth Assessment Report of the Intergovernmental Panel on Climate Change, 2022.

Jackson, Michelle, and Brian Holzman. "A Century of Educational Inequality in the United States." *Proceedings of the National Academy of Sciences* 117.32 (2020): 19108–15.

Jeffers, Janie L. "Justice Is Not Blind: Disproportionate Incarceration Rate of People of Color." In *Race and Social Policy*, edited by Sandra Edmonds Crewe. London: Routledge, 2023.

Jencks, Christopher. *Inequality: A Reassessment of the Effect of Family and Schooling in America*. New York: Basic Books, 1972.

Jernigan, Adero S. "Driving While Black: Racial Profiling in America." *Law and Psychology Review* 24 (2000): 127–38.

Johnson, Curtis. *Darwin's Dice: The Idea of Chance in the Thoughts of Charles Darwin*. New York: Oxford University Press, 2015.

Johnson, Lyndon B. "The President's Inaugural Address, January 20, 1965." *Public Papers of the Presidents of the United States: Lyndon B. Johnson*, vol. I, entry 27, pp. 71–74. Washington, DC: U.S. Government Printing Office, 1965.

Johnson, Walter. *The Broken Heart of America: St. Louis and the Violent History of the United States*. New York: Basic Books, 2020.

Jurajda, Stepah, and Daniel Munich. "Admission to Selective Schools, Alphabetically." *Economics of Education Review* 29 (2010): 1100–109.

Jürges, Hendrik, and Kerstin Schneider. "Why Young Boys Stumble: Early Tracking, Age and Gender Bias in the German School System." *German Economic Review* 12 (2011): 371–94.

Kaplan, Janice, and Barnaby Marsh. *How Luck Happens: Using the Science of Luck to Transform Work, Love, and Life*. New York: Dutton, 2018.

Kempermann, Gerd. "Emergence of Individuality in Genetically Identical Mice." *Science* 340 (2013): 756–59.

Kinsley, Michael. "Why White, Preppy Men Need an Affirmative-Action Reality Check." *Vanity Fair*, August 13, 2015.

Kleinbard, Edward D. *What's Luck Got to Do with It? How Smarter Government Can Rescue the American Dream.* New York: Oxford University Press, 2021.

Kluegel, James R., and Eliot R. Smith. *Beliefs about Inequality: Americans' View of What Is and What Ought to Be.* Hawthorne, NY: Aldine de Gruyter, 1986.

Konnikova, Maria. *The Biggest Bluff: How I Learned to Pay Attention, Master Myself, and Win.* New York: Penguin Press, 2020.

Kozol, Jonathan. *Savage Inequalities: Children in America's Schools.* New York: Crown, 1991.

Krantz, David L. "Taming Chance: Social Science and Everyday Narratives." *Psychological Inquiry* 9 (1998): 87–94.

Kushner, Harold S. *When Bad Things Happen to Good People.* New York: Anchor Books, 1981.

Ladd, Everett Carl. *The American Ideology: An Exploration of the Origins, Meaning, and Role of American Political Ideas.* Storrs, CT: Roper Center for Public Opinion Research, 1994.

Laham, Simon M., Peter Koval, and Adam Alter. "The Name-Pronunciation Effect: Why People Like Mr. Smith More than Mr. Colquhoun." *Journal of Experimental Social Psychology* 48 (2012): 752–56.

Lang, Kevin, and Ariella Kahn-Lang Spitzer. "Race Discrimination: An Economic Perspective." *Journal of Economic Perspectives* 34 (2020): 68–89.

Lears, Jackson. *Something for Nothing: Luck in America.* New York: Viking, 2003.

Lipset, Seymour Martin. *American Exceptionalism: A Double-Edged Sword.* New York: W. W. Norton, 1996.

Lorenz, Edward N. "Predictability: Does the Flap of a Butterfly's Wings in Brazil Set Off a Tornado in Texas?" Paper presented at the American Association for the Advancement of Science, Washington DC, December 29, 1972.

Losos, Jonathan B. *Improbable Destinies: Fate, Chance, and the Future of Evolution.* New York: Riverhead Books, 2017.

Lu, Vivi E., and Dekyi T. Tsotsong. "Harvard College Accepts Record-Low 3.43% of Applicants to Class of 2025." *Harvard Crimson*, April 7, 2021.

Lusinchi, Dominic. "'President' Landon and the 1936 *Literary Digest* Poll." *Social Science History* 36 (2012): 23–54.

Luthy, Christoph H., and Carla Rita Palmerino. "Conceptual and Historical Reflections on Chance (and Related Concepts)." In *The Challenge of Chance: A Multidisciplinary Approach from Science and the Humanities,* edited by Klaas Landsman and Ellen van Wolde, 9–47. New York: Springer, 2016.

Machiavelli, Niccolo. *The Prince: Revised.* Ingersoll, Ontario: Devoted, 2019.

Malkiel, Burton G. *A Random Walk Down Wall Street: The Time-Tested Strategy for Successful Investing.* New York: W. W. Norton, 2020.

March, James C., and James G. March. "Almost Random Careers: The Wisconsin School Superintendency, 1940–1972." *Administrative Science Quarterly* 22 (1977): 377–409.

Marche, Stephen. *On Writing and Failure.* Windsor, Ontario: Field Notes, 2023.

Marger, Martin N. *Social Inequality: Patterns and Process.* New York: McGraw Hill, 2014.

Martin, George M. "Nature, Nurture, and Chance: Their Roles in Interspecific and Intraspecific Modulations of Aging." *Annual Review of Gerontology and Geriatrics* 34 (2014): 267–84.

Martinez, Raoul. *Creating Freedom: The Lottery of Birth, the Illusion of Consent, and the Fight for Our Future.* New York: Pantheon Books, 2016.

Mauboussin, Michael J. *The Success Equation: Untangling Skill and Luck in Business, Sports, and Investing.* Boston: Harvard Business Review Press, 2012.

McCullough, David. *Brave Companions: Portraits in History.* New York: Simon & Schuster, 1992.

McCullough, David. *The Johnstown Flood, 50th Anniversary Edition.* New York: Simon & Schuster, 2018.

McDonald, Steve. "Right Place, Right Time: Serendipity and Informal Job Matching." *Socio-Economic Review* 8 (2010): 307–31.

McMurrer, Daniel P., and Isabel V. Sawhill. *Getting Ahead: Economic and Social Mobility in America.* Washington, DC: Urban Institute Press, 1998.

Menendian, Stephen, Arthur Galles, and Samir Gambhirl. *The Roots of Structural Racism: Twenty-First Century Racial Residential Segregation in the United States.* Council for the Homeless, 2021.

Merton, Robert K. "The Matthew Effect in Science: The Reward and Communication Systems of Science Are Considered." *Science* 159 (1968): 56–63.

Merton, Robert K. "The Matthew Effect in Science, II: Cumulative Advantage and the Symbolism of Intellectual Property." *Isis* 79 (1988): 606–23.

Merton, Robert K., and Elinor Barber. *The Travels and Adventures of Serendipity.* Princeton, NJ: Princeton University Press, 2004.

Messenger, Tony. *Profit and Punishment: How America Criminalizes the Poor in the Name of Justice.* New York: St. Martin's Press, 2021.

Miller, Joshua B., and Adam Sanjurjo. "A Bridge from Monty Hall to the Hot Hand: The Principle of Restricted Choice." *Journal of Economic Perspectives* 33 (2019): 144–62.

Mlodinow, Leonard. *The Drunkard's Walk: How Randomness Rules Our Lives.* New York: Vintage Books, 2009.

Muehlenweg, A.M., and P.A. Phuani. "The Evolution of the School-Entry Effects in a School Tracking System." *Journal of Human Resources* 45 (2010): 407–38.

Musser, George. "Is the Cosmos Random? (Einstein's Assertion That God Does Not Play Dice with the Universe Has Been Misinterpreted)." *Scientific American* 313 (2015): 88–93.

Nagel, Ernest. "Determinism in History." *Philosophy and Phenomenological Research* 20 (1960): 291–317.

National Center for Education Statistics. "Back to School Statistics." 2020.

Neil, Roland, and Robert J. Sampson. "The Birth Lottery of History: Arrest over the Life Course of Multiple Cohorts Coming of Age, 1995–2018." *American Journal of Sociology* 126 (2021): 1127–78.

Norris, Frank. *The Octopus.* New York: Doubleday, 1901.

Nussbaum, Jeff. *Undelivered: The Never-Heard Speeches That Would Have Rewritten History.* New York: Flatiron Books, 2022.

Owens, Ann. "Unequal Opportunity: School and Neighborhood Segregation in the USA." *Race and Social Problems* 12 (2020): 29–41.

Parks, Rosa, and James Haskins. *Rosa Parks: My Story.* New York: Dial Books, 1992.

Pinker, Stephen. *The Blank Slate: The Modern Denial of Human Nature.* New York: Penguin Books, 2016.

Pinker, Steven. "Why Nature and Nurture Won't Go Away." *Daedalus* 133 (2004): 5–17.

Pluchino, Alessandro, Alessio Emanuell Biondo, and Andrea Rapisarda. "Talent Versus Luck: The Role of Randomness in Success and Failure." *Advances in Complex Systems* 21 (2018): 1850014-2.

Pray, Leslie A. "DNA Replication and Causes of Mutation." *Nature Education* 1 (2008): 214.

Putnam, Robert. *Our Kids: The American Dream in Crisis.* New York: Simon and Schuster, 2015.

Rank, Mark Robert. *Confronting Poverty: Economic Hardship in the United States.* Los Angeles: Sage, 2021.

Rank, Mark R. *Confronting Poverty: Tools for Understanding Economic Hardship and Risk.* https://confrontingpoverty.org/, 2023.

Rank, Mark Robert. *Living on the Edge: The Realities of Welfare in America.* New York: Columbia University Press, 1994.

Rank, Mark Robert. *The Poverty Paradox: Understanding Economic Hardship amid American Prosperity.* New York: Oxford University Press, 2023.

Rank, Mark R. "Reducing Cumulative Inequality." In *Toward a Livable Life: A 21st Century Agenda for Social Work,* edited by Mark Robert Rank, 94–113. New York: Oxford University Press, 2020.

Rank, Mark Robert. *Toward a Livable Life: A 21st Century Agenda for Social Work.* New York: Oxford University Press, 2020.

Rank, Mark R. "Why Poverty and Inequality Undermine Justice in America." In *Routledge International Handbook of Social Justice,* edited by Michael Reisch, 436–47. New York: Routledge Press, 2014.

Rank, Mark Robert, Thomas A. Hirschl, and Kirk A. Foster. *Chasing the American Dream: Understanding What Shapes Our Fortunes.* New York: Oxford University Press, 2014.

Rawls, John. *Justice as Fairness: A Restatement.* Cambridge, MA: Harvard University Press, 2001.

Rawls, John. *Political Liberalism.* New York: Columbia University Press, 1996.

Rawls, John. *A Theory of Justice.* Cambridge, MA: Harvard University Press, 1971.

Rescher, Nicholas. *Luck: The Brilliant Randomness of Everyday Life.* Pittsburgh: University of Pittsburgh Press, 1995.

Rice, Stephen, David Trafimow, and Rian Mehta. "The Case for Adding Randomness to the Nature-Nurture Debate." *Issues in Social Science* 3 (2015): 121–31.

Robinson, David M. "The Wheel of Fortune." *Classical Philology* 41 (1946): 207–16.

Roe, Anne, and Rhonda Baruch. "Occupational Changes in the Adult Years." *Personal Administration* 30 (1967): 121–28.

Roeder, Oliver. *Seven Games: A Human History.* New York: W. W. Norton, 2022.

Rubin, Robert E. *The Yellow Pad: Making Better Decisions in an Uncertain World.* New York: Penguin Press, 2023.

Sahlin, Ahmet Riza, Aysegul Erdogan, Pelin Mutlu Agaoglu, Yeliz Dineri, Ahmet Ysuf Cakirci, Mahmut Egemen Senel, Ramazan Azim Okyay, and Ali Muhittin Tasdogan. "2019 Novel Coronavirus (COVID-19) Outbreak: A Review of the Current Literature." *Eurasian Journal of Medicine and Oncology* 4 (2020): 1–7.

Samuels, Robert, and Toluse Olorunnipa. *His Name Is George Floyd: One Man's Life and the Struggle for Racial Justice.* New York: Viking, 2022.

Sandel, Michael J. *The Tyranny of Merit: What's Become of the Common Good?* New York: Farrar, Straus and Giroux, 2020.

Sassler, Sharon, and Daniel T. Lichter. "Cohabitation and Marriage: Complexity and Diversity in Union-Formation Patterns." *Journal of Marriage and the Family* 82 (2020): 35–61.

Sauder, Michael. "A Sociology of Luck." *Sociological Theory* 38 (2020): 193–216.

Sawyer, Keith. *Group Genius: The Creative Power of Collaboration.* New York: Basic Books, 2007.

Sen, Amartya. *Development as Freedom.* New York: Anchor Books, 2000.

Shapiro, Thomas M. *The Hidden Cost of Being African American: How Wealth Perpetuates Inequality.* New York: Oxford University Press, 2004.

Sherwin, Martin J. *Gambling with Armageddon: Nuclear Roulette from Hiroshima to the Cuban Missile Crisis.* New York: Alfred A. Knopf, 2020.

Shirer, William L. *Berlin Diary: The Journal of a Foreign Correspondent, 1934–1941.* Baltimore: Johns Hopkins University Press, 2002.

Shum, Matthew, Wei Sun, and Guangliang Ye. "Superstition and 'Lucky' Apartments: Evidence from Transaction-Level Data." *Journal of Comparative Economics* 42 (2014): 109–17.

Smith, Ed. *Luck: What It Means and Why It Matters.* London: Bloomsbury, 2012.

Smith, George Davey. "Epidemiology, Epigenetics and the 'Gloomy Prospect': Embracing Randomness in Population Health Research and Practice." *International Journal of Epidemiology* 40 (2011): 537–62.

Smock, Pamela J., and Christine R. Schwartz. "The Demography of Families: A Review of Patterns and Change." *Journal of Marriage and Families* 82 (2020): 9–34.

Stanford Open Policing Project. https://openpolicing.stanford.edu/, 2023.

Strager, Hanne. *A Modest Genius: The Story of Darwin's Life and How His Ideas Changed Everything.* CreateSpace Independent Publishing Platform, 2016.

Strait, Julia Evangelou. "Most Cases of Never-Smokers' Lung Cancer Treatable with Mutation-Targeting Drugs." News release, Washington University School of Medicine, September 30, 2021.

Sundali, James, and Rachel Croson. "Biases in Casino Betting: The Hot Hand and the Gambler's Fallacy." *Judgment and Decision Making* 1 (2006): 1–12.

Sunstein, Cass R. *The Second Bill of Rights: FDR's Unfinished Revolution and Why We Need It More than Ever.* New York: Basic Books, 2004.

Sussman, Gerald Jay, and Jack Wisdom. "Chaotic Evolution of the Solar System." *Science* 257 (1992): 56–62.

Sutin, Angelina R., Yannick Stephan, Martina Luckette, Damaris Ashwanden, Hi Hyun Lee, Amanda A. Sesker, and Antonio Terracciano. "Differential Personality Change Earlier and Later In the Coronavirus Pandemic in a Longitudinal Sample of Adults in the United States." *PLOS ONE*, September 28, 2022.

Taleb, Nassim Nicholas. *The Black Swan: The Impact of the Highly Improbable.* New York: Random House, 2010.

Templeton, Alan R. *Population Genetics and Microevolutionary Theory.* New York: John Wiley & Sons, 2021.

Tetlock, Philip E., and Dan Gardner. *Superforecasting: The Art and Science of Prediction.* New York: Crown, 2015.

Tyrell, Toby. "Chance Played a Role in Determining Whether Earth Stayed Habitable." *Communications Earth & Environment* 1 (2020): 61.

Ullrich, Volker. *Hitler: Ascent 1889–1939.* New York: Alfred A. Knopf, 2016.

U.S. Department of Education, Equity and Excellence Commission. *For Each and Every Child: A Strategy for Education Equity and Excellence.* Washington, DC: Education Publications Center, 2013.

Van Praag, C. Mirjam, and Bernard M.S. Van Praag. "The Benefits of Being Economics Professor A (rather than Z)." *Economica* 75 (2008): 782–96.

Voltaire. *The Philosophical Dictionary.* New York: E.R. Dumont, 1901.

von Wachter, Til, and Stefan Bender. "In the Right Place at the Wrong Time: The Role of Firms and Luck in Young Workers' Careers." *American Economic Review* 96 (2006): 1679–705.

Waber, Ben, Jennifer Magnolfi, and Greg Lindsay. "Workspaces That Move People." *Harvard Business Review Magazine,* October 2014.

Weber, Matthias. "The Effects of Listing Authors in Alphabetical Order: A Review of the Empirical Evidence." *Research Evaluation* 27 (2018): 238–45.

Wilder, Thornton. *The Bridge of San Luis Rey.* New York: HarperCollins, 2014 [1927].

Williams, Donnie, and Wayne Greenhaw. *The Thunder of Angels: The Montgomery Bus Boycott and the People Who Broke the Back of Jim Crow.* Chicago: Chicago Review Press, 2005.

Wu, Yi-chi, Ching-Sung Chen, and Yu-Jiun Chan. "The Outbreak of COVID-19: An Overview." *Journal of Chinese Medical Association* 83 (2020): 217–20.

Ziman, John. *Real Science: What It Is and What It Means.* New York: Cambridge University Press, 2000.

Index

Center for Near Earth Object Studies at NASA's Jet Propulsion Laboratory, 45

Chafel, Judith, 185–186

chance and luck: in academic paths, 130–131; accidents, 92–94; in art, 81–83; awareness of, 14; big breaks, 83–88; Csikszentmihalyi on, 87–88; deservedness and, 219; difficulty in measuring and modeling, 11; in DNA discovery, 66; dynamic interactions of, 12; evening out of, 167–172; fear of, 152; as fundamental element of life, 12, 123–124; games, 79–81; in historic literature, 5–8; in income, 135–136; insurance protecting against, 187; meritocracy and, 212–213; nature vs nurture, 101–106; persistence of, 121; presenting opportunities, 226–227; random walks and, 75–78; role of in history, 40–43; role of in natural selection, 46–50; in sports, 68–75, 70t, 221, 253n1; suggesting humility, 208; term definitions, 17–18; timing of, 153–156; understudied nature of, 3, 10–11, 238–239; in university admissions, 88–91

Chance or Destiny: Turning Points in American History (Handlin), 42

chaos theory, 52

Chasing the American Dream: Understanding What Shapes Our Fortunes (Rank), 2, 84, 123, 140, 163–164, 230

Chekhov, Anton, 236

Chicago, IL, 119

Chicxulub impactor, 44–45

childhood events, influenced by chance,104–105

Chodas, Paul, 45

Christie, Agatha, 222

civil rights movement, 35, 38–40, 180, 250n18

Clear Lake, IA, 262n1

climate change, 54–55, 251n3

Clinton administration, 63, 212

close calls, 93

coincidence definition, 19

coin flips, 61, 215–216, 262n1

collective responsibility, 213

Colvin, Claudette, 250n18

computers, 117–118

conservatives, 175, 188

Consolation of Philosophy (Boethius), 7, 248n11

contingency definition, 19

Copernicus, Nicolaus, 46

Costello, Elvis, 254n17

court costs, 162–163

Courtenay, Bryce, 1

Covid-19 pandemic, 120–121, 127–128

Cowles, Alfred, 76

Cranston, Bryan, 84

creativity, 81–83, 127–128

Crick, Francis, 66

crime, theories of, 119–120

Croson, Rachel, 214

Cruz, Nelson, 68–69

Csikszentmihalyi, Mihaly, 87–88

Cuban Missile Crisis, 26–30, 43

cumulative advantage/disadvantage, 13, 112, 156–160, 171, 199, 201–202

cumulative likelihood, of economic insecurity, 190–191

Current Population Survey, 56

Dachau concentration camp, 145, 261n36. *See also* Nazi Germany

Darling-Hammond, Linda, 197–198

Darwin, Charles, 9, 46–50, 251n5

D-Day Invasion, 43

decision-making, influenced by probability, 224–225

decision theory, 11, 268n23

Declaration of Independence, 180

de Fermant, Pierre, 60

demography, 115, 116, 134

de Montmort, Pierre Remond, 60

deservedness, 192–193, 218, 219

determinism, 9, 11

Dialogues (Plato), 7

Dickens, Charles, 163

Difference Principle, 184–186

Dimucci, Dion, 262n1

dinosaurs, 44–45

disease, 103–104, 164–166

DNA, 65–66, 103

Doll, Richard, 103–104

domino effects, 138

Donohue, Jerry, 66

draft, military, 113–114

driving while Black, 161–162

Drunkard's Walk, The (Mlodinow), 88

Duncan, Greg, 202

Earned Income Tax Credit program, 265n26

earthquakes, 51

Easterlin, Richard, 116–117

Ecclesiastes, 123, 208

economic bill of rights, 180

economic context of luck, 13, 40–41, 116–117, 164–166, 237

economic floor, 186–187, 204

economic insecurity, 189–192

economic professors, study of last names, 108–109

education, equal access to public, 196–201

Egypt, 37, 38. *See also* Arab Spring

Einav, Liran, 109

Einstein, Albert, 9, 46

Eisenhower, Dwight, 43

Eler, Georg, 25

Ellison, Ralph, 86

empathy and humility, 206–209

empirical probability, 61. *See also* probability

Engels, Natalie, 127

English Poor Laws of 1601, 218

Epstein, Hedy, 142–148, 227

equality of opportunity, 186–187, 194–203, 204, 211

Equal Rights Amendment, 31–34, 227

equity, 105, 137, 156–158, 165–166, 183–184

Ethiopia, 148–150

Euripides, 68, 226

Europeans, compared to Americans, 260n23

everyday life, luck in: accidents, 92–94; art, 81–83; big breaks, 83–88; games, 79–81; in random walks, 75–78; in sports, 68–75; university admissions, 88–91

evolution by natural selection, 9, 46–50

exquisite corpse, 81–83

Fahey, John, 84

Fail Safe (1964), 30

failure, 201, 212, 230–231

fairness, 168–169, 216–220. *See also* equity

fame, role of chance, 84–88

Family Assistance Plan, 193

fascism, 41

Federal Reserve Bank of New York, 254n13

Ferguson, MO, 35–36

Finch, Caleb, 256n5

FitzRoy, Robert, 46

Kozol, Jonathan, 199

Krantz, David, 240

Kristallnacht, 143–144, 261n35. *See also* Nazi Germany

Kushner, Harold, 219

Kuwait, 37. *See also* Arab Spring

labor market. *See* job market

Lady Justice, 217–218

Laham, Simon, 109

Landon, Alf, 58, 59. *See also Literary Digest* poll

Lang, Tim, 247n6

Laplace, Pierre-Simon, 214

Las Vegas, NV, 79–80

Latino students, 200

Lawrenceville School, 236

laws of motion and universal gravitation, 9, 46. *See also* Newton, Sir Issac

Lears, Jackson, 60, 212–213

Lebensraum, 41

level playing field, 196

liberals, 175–176

liberties, 176–177, 179, 204

Liberty Principle, 179–184

Libya, 37, 38. *See also* Arab Spring

life expectancy, 102

life paths: of Benedictine monks, 230–231; catastrophes in, 4–5; insurance as protection from bad luck, 188–189; randomness in shaping, 1–2, 3, 166; serendipity in, 227–228; starting points in, 178–179. *See also* ripples and currents; structural conditions

Literary Digest poll, 57–59

Living on the Edge (Rank), 138

location, home, 139–142

Long Term Capital Management, 254n13

Lorenz, Edward, 52, 53

Losos, Jonathan, 49–50

lotteries, 214

Lowenhaupt, Charles, 230–231

luck and chance. *See* chance and luck

lucky numbers, 141

lung cancer, 165. *See also* cancer

Lusha the circus monkey, 76

Lusinchi, Dominic, 58–59

Luthy, Christoph, 10

Machiavelli, Niccolo, 7–8

Major League Baseball (MLB), 215. *See also* baseball

Malkiel, Burton, 75, 76–77

Manhattan Project, 64

Mann, Horace, 65, 196–197

March, James, 132

Marche, Stephen, 220, 222

marital homogamy, 128

Marmame, Richard, 202

Marmor, Theodore, 188

marriage market, 115

Marrero, Eli, 74

Martin, George, 106

Martin, Trayvon, 36. *See also* Black Lives Matter movement

Martinez, Raoul, 100, 104

Massachusetts Institute of Technology (MIT), 52, 54

Match Point (2005), 253n1

Matthew Effect, 156–160, 168. *See also* cumulative advantage/disadvantage

Mauboussin, Michael, 18, 70

McCullough, David, 42–43, 268n1

McDonald, Steve, 131–132

McMurrer, Daniel, 201–202

meaning, search for, 216–217, 235–236

measuring and modeling chance, 11, 239–240

Pauling, Linus, 66
pay-to-stay statutes, 162–163
peer review, luck involved, 221–222
pencils, 82–83
Pennington, Keith, 127
peppered moth, 48
perseverance, in relation to chance, 220–224
personal attributes, as affecting life outcomes, 166–167
personal computer age, 117–118
personality, 102, 120–121, 166–167
personal responsibility, 213
Peterson, Sam, 233
Philosophical Essay on Probabilities (Laplace), 214
Pinker, Steven, 101–102, 123–124
Pirnie, Alexander, 113
planetary orbits, 54
Plato, 7
Pliny, 6
Pluchino, Alessandro, 136–137
poker, 79–80. *See also* gambling
police, 161–162
Political Liberalism (Rawls), 177–178
political liberty, 176–177
polling, 57–59
Popular Electronics, 117–118
positive psychology, 209
Post, Laura, 197–198
poverty: deservedness and, 218; as economic insecurity measures, 189–190, 190t; health and, 165–166; Lyndon B. Johnson on, 196; pay-to-stay statutes and, 162–163; randomness amplifying, 13, 36–37, 105; right to vote and, 183–184; risk calculator, 63, 265n22; risk of, 137–138, 189–191; schooling and, 196–201; simulator, 134; universal safety net preventing, 186–187

precision drugs, 165–166
Predicting the Unpredictable (Hough), 51
Prince, The (Machiavelli), 7–8
probabilistic thinking, 63, 225–226
probability, 11, 61, 63–64, 214–216, 224–226
Profit and Punishment: How America Criminalizes the Poor in the Name of Justice (Messenger), 162–163
pronunciation of names, 109
protests, 35–40
public education, 196–201
public office, running for, 182–183
publishing, 221–222, 223
Putnam, Robert, 185

racial profiling, 161–162
racial segregation, 139, 162, 200
racism, 35–36, 109–110, 139, 161–162
random error, 249n23
randomization, 56–57
randomness: difficulty of for humans, 77; fooled by, 213–217; as fundamental element of life, 12; in human behavior, 106; insurance as protection against, 188–189; interplay with natural processes, 49; interplay with social processes, 40–43; measuring, 11; in music, 83, 85–86; in natural selection process, 47; in nature vs nurture debate, 101–106; in poverty risk, 189–191; in selecting a name, 106–110; in success, 136–137; term definition, 18–19
random sampling, 55–60
random walk theory, 75–78
Rassokha, Vice Admiral, 28. *See also* Cuban Missile Crisis

Founded in 1893,
UNIVERSITY OF CALIFORNIA PRESS
publishes bold, progressive books and journals
on topics in the arts, humanities, social sciences,
and natural sciences—with a focus on social
justice issues—that inspire thought and action
among readers worldwide.

The UC PRESS FOUNDATION
raises funds to uphold the press's vital role
as an independent, nonprofit publisher, and
receives philanthropic support from a wide
range of individuals and institutions—and from
committed readers like you. To learn more, visit
ucpress.edu/supportus.